PRINCE OF PIRATES

PRINCE OF PIRATES

The Temenggongs and the Development of Johor and Singapore 1784–1885

Carl A. Trocki

NUS PRESS
SINGAPORE

National University of Singapore
AS3-01-02, 3 Arts Link
Singapore 117569

Fax: (65) 6774-0652
E-mail: nusbooks@nus.edu.sg
Website: http://www.nus.edu.sg/nuspress

First Edition 1979
Second Edition 2007
Reprint 2012
Reprint 2013

ISBN 978-9971-69-376-3 (Paper)

National Library Board Singapore Cataloguing in Publication Data

Trocki, Carl A.
Prince of pirates : the temenggongs and the development of Johor and Singapore, 1784–1885 / Carl A. Trocki. – 2nd ed. – Singapore : NUS Press, 2007.
p. cm.
Includes bibliographical references and index.
ISBN-13 : 978-9971-69-376-3 (pbk.)

1. Johor – History. 2. Singapore – History. 3. Malaya – History. I. Title.

DS598.J7
959.5103 — dc22

SLS2007037568

Typeset by: Scientifik Graphics (Singapore) Pte Ltd
Printed by: Mainland Press Pte Ltd

To

Orrawin, Rebecca, and Carl

Contents

Illustrations

Figures

Maps

Tables

Plates

Acknowledgements

The research for this study was supported by a Fulbright-Hays Graduate Fellowship and also by a London-Cornell Grant. They made possible the field-work which I did in Malaysia and Singapore in 1970–71. A National Defense Foreign Study Fellowship (Title VI) provided funds to support me during a year while I was writing. I am also deeply grateful for the support of the Cornell University Southeast Asia Program without which none of this would have been possible.

In addition to the many scholars who have gone before me, I acknowledge my debt to many people, both at Cornell and in Singapore and Malaysia who contributed their time, skill, and energy to assist me in the completion of this study. In particular, I owe a debt of gratitude to Joseph W. Ink who introduced me to the study of history and the East India Company. Likewise, I am grateful to Oliver Wolters, Benedict Anderson, and Knight Biggerstaff who read and criticized versions of this manuscript.

Numerous colleagues have been kind enough to save me from committing many more glaring errors than presently exist. Among them are my brother, David Trocki, Leonard and Barbara Andaya and Diane Lewis. Lee Poh Ping and Jennifer Cushman generously allowed me to bounce ideas off them and contributed of their own expertise. Mrs. Orrasa Jirapinyo drew the maps which appear here, and Joyce Nakahara deserves special thanks for her assistance in proofreading. I am also deeply grateful to Sr. Mary Philip Trauth S.N.D. and to Miss Yvonne Settles.

Of the many people in Johor and Singapore who helped to make my work possible, I offer warm thanks to my good friends Enche Hussain Muhammad of the Johor State Secretariat and to Mr. Loh Peng Tong and Mr. M. Rajadurai. Enche Zainal Abidin bin Abdul Talib assisted me by transcribing hundreds of *jawi* documents. I also owe deep gratitude to Enche Basri of the Johor Archives and his staff for their generous assistance and understanding while I worked there. I am also grateful for the access which I was allowed to the materials in the University of Singapore Library and the National Library, Singapore. I also thank Mr. Peter Tng Sing Tuan and Miss Lim Pet Joo for their unflagging support, interest, and assistance.

Abbreviations

Bijd.	Bijdragen tot de Taal-, Land-, en Volkenkunde (The Hague)
JIA	Journal of the Indian Archipelago and East Asia
JMBRAS	Journal of the Malayan Branch of the Royal Asiatic Society
———	Journal of the Malaysian Branch of the Royal Asiatic Society
JSBRAS	Journal of the Straits Branch of the Royal Asiatic Society
JSS	Journal of the Siam Society
JSSS	Journal of the South Seas Society
MJTG	Malayan Journal of Tropical Geography
SDT	Straits Daily Times
SFP	Singapore Free Press
SJB	Surat Jual-Beli
SKMK-I	Surat Keterangan Membuka Kebun (Buku Daftar Surat Berkebun) A.H. 1260–1320
SKMK-II	Buku Daftar Surat^2 Keterangan Membuka Kebun Gambir dan Lada Hitam, A.H. 1298–1325
SPBS	Surat Pajak Bahagian Sungai
SSD	Singapore and Straits Directory
SSFR	Straits Settlements Factory Records
SSR	Straits Settlements Records
SSSU	Salinan Surat di-Simpan oleh Setia Usaha
SSTP	Surat^2 Titah Perentah

Currencies and Weights

Currencies

The standard currency used in Southeast Asia during this period was the Spanish Dollar. Thus the symbol $ always refers to Spanish Dollars. The British East India Company generally kept its accounts in Rupees (usually Sicca) and sometimes in Pounds Sterling.

$100	£26.50
$100	252.27 Dutch Guilders
$100	₨210.85 Sicca
$100	₨220.34 Surat
$100	₨224.81 Madras
£100	$366.97
£100	₨773.76 Sicca

Weights

Tahil (Tael)	1.33 oz (3.77 gm)
Kati (6 Tahil)	1.33 lb (60.33 gm)
Pikul (100 Kati)	133.33 lb (60.48 kg)
Bahar (3 Pikul)	400 lb (181.44 kg)
Koyan (40 Pikul)	5,333.33 lb (2419.18 kg)

Introduction to the Second Edition[1]

When asked by the editors of the NUS Press to republish *Prince of Pirates*, I had to ask myself why I thought this book was important enough to once more offer it to the academic reading public. On rereading it, I see that much of the work I have done since 1979 has been a development and elaboration of ideas, insights and arguments first put forward in this study of Johor. So, for my own work, it has often acted as a compass, telling me where I should be going and what was important in my own scholarly vision. Beyond my own personal interests I believe the book continues to be of value for the broader readership, because it pioneered a number of new directions in the field. At the same time, it remains a key resource for the study of the early history of Singapore and Johor.

The book is important for a number of other reasons as well. Not the least of these is that it was one of the first to challenge the colonialist paradigm which had previously dominated the writing of Malay/Singapore history. One thing I tried to do, besides relying heavily on indigenous sources, was to find the links connecting British Malaya to its roots in the pre-colonial Malay world and to establish its continuities with the general flow of Southeast Asian history. This meant linking eighteenth century Johor-Riau with nineteenth century Johor-Singapore. It also meant explaining and expanding the role played by Malays and Chinese in the growth of the colonial enterprise. In doing so, I believe that I have been able to offer a more complete picture of the history of this period. Finally, the book was one of the first to stress the significance of the opium trade and especially of the opium farms in the success of the imperialism in Southeast Asia.

Prince of Pirates is unique in that it remains (unfortunately) one of the few studies which have resulted from research in the Johor Archives and which has placed data from that archive into general circulation.[2] This archive struck me as particularly rich in data on the social and economic development of the state in the nineteenth and early twentieth centuries. It was one of my hopes, on first publishing this book, that others should continue to mine that resource, but this has not happened. I can understand that for non-Malaysians, archival research has always been difficult because of the reluctance of the Malaysian government to grant research permits to foreign scholars. It still puzzles me, however, that Malaysian scholars, who have better access to these collections, have continued to ignore this resource. For me, the findings in the Kangchu records of the Johor Archives were the real eye-opener in my own work. They have provided much needed evidence of the operation of Chinese pepper and gambier industry in the region during the eighteenth and nineteenth centuries. Understanding Chinese business and its organization are key issues for those studying pre-modern Southeast Asia. Much has been written about Chinese business, but there is really not very much hard data on which to base those speculations. Only rarely have scholars found such detailed and useful data on the organization of an entire industry.

The Kangchu records also demonstrate the ability of the Malay rulers of Johor to grasp the opportunities which were available to them. The early rulers of Johor found it useful to record the award of every *surat sungai* (lit. "river document", the name of the grant of authority over a river valley) to every Chinese Kongsi (or company) over the course of the nineteenth and early twentieth centuries. This extraordinary circumstance has proven of major significance. No one else ever did this. No European colonial government, Dutch or English, with their mountains of documentation of so much irrelevant information, ever took the trouble to record the details by which the Chinese organized economic activity within their territories. Of course, the initiative of the Johor rulers was not only a matter of record-keeping, rather the records show their interest in the active management of the state as well as a willingness to engage directly with the Chinese settlers who were moving into the state.

The pepper and gambier planters were already in Singapore when Raffles arrived there in 1819. Aside from one or two pieces of correspondence in the Straits Settlements Records, there are no British records of these settlements. Although the British claimed the entire island, they seem to have been singularly uninterested in these people who quickly shouldered their way through the growing town of Singapore and started clearing land in the interior to plant pepper and gambier. These settlers also sailed out of Singapore's port and moved up the rivers flowing out of the western, northern and eastern shores of Singapore Island. Place names, such as Yeo Chukang, Lim Chukang and Chua Chukang, show that there were Kangchus living in Singapore in the early nineteenth century. We must assume that they conducted their business very much like those who later went to Johor. No Englishman, however, ever asked them what they were doing until the mid-1840s. Nor did the British government demand some account of their activity. On the other hand, this Malay "government" (such as it was in the 1840s and 1850s), carefully interviewed every potential Kangchu, and found out the number of people in his Kongsi and into how many shares it was divided, and who held the shares. These documents recorded names, dates, numbers of shares in each grant, and specified which river and on which bank their settlements were to be made. The documents demonstrate the Johor ruler's determination to create a "government", and by the 1870s, he was recognized as the "ideal of the new model Malay ruler".

The Kongsi, or "company", was a uniquely Chinese institution. Today, this is the general Chinese term for every kind of business. The word seems to have come into use in the late seventeenth or early eighteenth century. There were Kongsis among the gold miners in Borneo and among the tin miners in Bangka in the eighteenth century. I believe that Kongsis characterized most settlements of Chinese labourers in Southeast Asia after about 1700. They may even have existed among the first Chinese settlements on Taiwan in the 1680s.[3] Thomas Horsfield, Wang Tai Peng, Mary Somers Heidhues and James C. Jackson have written about the Borneo Kongsis and about Bangka. None of them had enough information at the time they wrote to have seen that the Kongsi represented a common pattern of economic organization that existed throughout the region.[4] In general, it represented a shareholding partnership between a capitalist (or his representative), and a group of labourers who undertook a planting or mining venture. Alternatively, it may have also represented a partnership between the captain of a junk and his officers (Wang 1995). Others have also argued that the term was borrowed from Dutch word *compagnie*. Whatever the origins of the term, it was later adopted to refer to any kind of shareholding enterprise.

The "discovery" of the Kongsi institution and of its role in the early settlement of Chinese in Southeast Asia led me to think about the periodization of the migration and to see the establishment of colonies or settlements of Chinese labourers in the region as an important watershed that ushered in a new period of Chinese interaction with Southeast Asia. We might call the years between 1720 and 1880 "the age of the Kongsi". This was an issue I began to explore more fully in my second book, *Opium and Empire*.[5] The period was marked by the appearance of settlements of labourers who produced raw commodities to ship back to China. Southeast Asian labour alone no longer seemed able to produce large enough quantities to satisfy the demands of the Chinese market for tin, pepper, gambier and gold.

This understanding of the Kongsi brought me to see the role it played in the Chinese diaspora, or perhaps expansion would be a better word. Chinese labourers, merchants, and mariners were not chased out of China, nor were they dragged out against their will. They travelled abroad, like so many others, to seek their fortunes. This was an important and missing piece of the puzzle to understanding the nature of the Chinese migration in the nineteenth century. I also came to hold a very different view of what were called Chinese "secret societies" in nineteenth-century Southeast Asia. Even though the secret societies may have evolved out of these Kongsis, initially they were neither criminal nor secret. They were worse, so far as colonial and indigenous governments were concerned. They were autonomous institutions of self-government.

The phenomenon of Chinese labour migration, beginning as it did in the early eighteenth century, shattered the old cliché: "the colonialists brought the Chinese to Southeast Asia". Not only did Chinese come on their own, in Chinese ships, with the assistance of Chinese capital, and to serve the Chinese economy, they also came at the request of native rulers who were eager to profit from their work. These rulers, like the kings of Siam, the Yamtuan Mudas of Riau, the Sultans of Palembang and Pontianak and the Temenggongs of Johor, invited them to come and develop their countries. I would estimate conservatively that there were already at least 100,000 Chinese hard at work in the broad region covering Bangka, Pontianak, Riau, Trengganu, Kelantan, and Phuket by 1780. They were there before the British established colonies (with the exception of Bencoolen) and were there much to the worry and chagrin of the Dutch.[6]

Another major issue which came to light in the Kangchu papers of the Johor Archives was opium. Each and every *surat sungai* explicitly gave to the Kangchu the "farming rights". These were the monopolies on the sale of opium, liquor, pork, and the provision of prostitution and gambling. The importance of opium consumption among the planters and the role of opium farming (the monopoly) by the Kangchus were issues that caused me to think long and hard about the system of labour, labour control, and about Chinese capitalism itself. All of these questions have continued to occupy my later works on the Chinese migration and on the history of Singapore.

Opium and Empire was an attempt to reconstruct the history of the opium farm in Singapore, and was really a direct sequel to work I had done on Johor. It had become clear to me that not only were the opium and spirit farms[7] of Johor and Singapore linked, but the histories of the two settlements were far more intimately connected than earlier accounts have suggested. *Prince of Pirates* was my first venture into the study of opium farming systems, but already at that point it was obvious that they were the most important financial institutions in colonial Southeast Asia. They were not only the foundation of Chinese capitalism in the region, but also the major fiscal supports of the colonial states and of the indigenous Southeast Asian states such as Johor and Siam. Singapore, for instance, gained from 40 to 60 per cent of its annual revenue from opium sales to its population between 1828 and 1930. Siam grossed about 35 per cent, as did the Netherlands East Indies and French Indochina. States such as Burma and the Philippines gained considerably less.[8]

As a result of this, the opium farmers, the Chinese *taukehs* (or merchants) who controlled these monopolies, were among the wealthiest and most powerful men in the region, if not in all of Asia at the time. They were also the most respected and trusted allies of the colonial and indigenous governments they served. Beyond this, it became clear that the same men who controlled the revenue farms of both Johor and Singapore (and ultimately of Riau and Melaka as well as other places) also were the major investors in pepper and gambier production. The Singapore-based Pepper and Gambier Society, or Kongkek, controlled all pepper and gambier production in the area around Singapore. Its members also controlled the opium and spirit farms for the same region and they used their profits from opium to supplement their incomes from pepper and gambier. In conjunction with this, the opium farmers also came to control the secret societies, particularly the Ngee Heng (also known as the Ghee Hin in Singapore), and were thus in a position to dominate both the production and consumption of the entire workforce.

In time, I came to understand that this was the fundamental pattern that characterized virtually all commodity production ventures in Southeast Asia during the nineteenth century. Whether in tin mining, gold mining, pepper and gambier planting or even rice agriculture, coolies and peasants found themselves caught in chains of indebtedness forged by opium and thus often ended up selling their labour for the drug. The opium farmers and the other capitalists who invested in their productions received saleable commodities at rock bottom prices.

The links between the settlements of Riau, Johor and Singapore have once again become an important issue. When I started out, trying to write the history of Johor, few academics and fewer policy makers were concerned by such connections. In order to write about Johor, I discovered I had to rewrite much of the early history of Singapore, an account which occupies much of the first third of this book. Beyond that, however, before I could understand that part of the history of Singapore, it was necessary to reconstruct the links between Singapore and Riau, the eighteenth century port on the island of Bentan just 50 or so kilometres south of Singapore.

I argued then that the pattern of trade which was established at Riau in the mid-eighteenth century was exactly the pattern that was taken over by Singapore after its foundation in 1819. To a certain extent this forced me to reconsider the Raffles/Crawfurd discourse about Singapore's history. Unfortunately, their version has continued to be a part of the myth. There is no doubt that T. S. Raffles and John Crawfurd, the British free trade policy and the security of British arms did much to guarantee the success of early Singapore, and made the foundation of the port a unique turning point in Southeast Asian history. On the other hand, it is wrong to pretend that the Malay, Bugis, and Chinese contributions were not significant. The Chinese junk trade, the settlements of Chinese labourers, the British trade in opium, guns and cloth, and the Bugis trading network had already been woven together under the management of Malay and Bugis rajas more than half a century before Raffles set foot on Singapore Island.

These were the chiefs whom Raffles, Crawfurd and others called "pirates". I should point out that the title of this book, *Prince of Pirates*, was a calculated piece of irony on my part, and an attempt to debunk a part of the myth. It was not my intention to present the Temenggong, or any other Malay chief, as a thief or an outlaw. It is true that some Europeans considered Temenggong Ibrahim to be associated with piracy in the waters around Singapore in the 1830s. It is important to understand, however, the ambiguity of his position at the time. He was born at a time when Malay princes still sought power through control of the sea and the sea peoples. When his father died in 1825 he was still a young man, and needed to establish his authority as a man of power. However, the ability to conduct an orderly administration of territory through the use of written records in conjunction with skilled officials was also a part of his heritage. This aspect of his background made it possible for him and his descendants to succeed in an age when so many of their contemporaries were destroyed by the colonial advance. Obviously, this is more than one would expect from a "pirate".

The so-called "native trade" was the lifeblood of early Singapore and it remained so until the 1870s, and all the free trade in the world could not have created it out of thin air. That trade, and the many important Malay and Chinese trading networks already existed before 1819, and they simply moved to Singapore and made it their base after 1819. On the British side, in addition to free trade and security, however, I think that the easy availability of opium and other forms of British capital such as European and Indian cloth, trade goods, and cash, were crucial factors in the rapid rise of Singapore. These last two factors often get far less attention than they deserve.

Both Johor and Riau became economic colonies of Singapore during the nineteenth century and, in many ways, have continued to be satellites of the Singapore economy. While political divisions often made economic relations somewhat clandestine, they continued nonetheless, often because of those divisions. It is only within the last two decades that the conception of the "Growth Triangle" has refocused attention on the three areas.

Much work remains to be done on the history of the settlement and development of Johor during the nineteenth and twentieth centuries. While we have a fairly complete record of Chinese Kangchu settlements in Johor (at least prior to 1915) no such record exists concerning the growth of Malay/Malaysian settlement of the state. Did many more Malays accompany Abu Bakar from Singapore to Johor? Certainly this was one pattern. It is also of interest, however, that many did not. Many Malays stayed behind and continue to populate Singapore. Were they all followers of Sultan Hussain and his family? One may wish, at some point, to see these loose ends of the region's history tied up.

It would be useful for local historians and those interested in the state's heritage to re-examine the settlement of the state and to make an effort to retrieve the remaining traces of what data do exist. Even in the years since I first wrote about Johor, the landscape has been radically altered. There is hardly a trace of the Johor Baharu that I first came to know in the early 1970s, and the suburban development of the city has virtually wiped out most traces of the settlements made in the day of Sultan Abu Bakar. Likewise succeeding waves of agricultural development in Johor, first rubber and then oil palm, have eliminated most traces of the old *kangkars*, or pepper and gambier settlements.

There remain, however, many gaps in this study. I used only a few Chinese sources in this book and not as many Malay sources as I had hoped. A considerable part of the Johor/Singapore story, not available to me when I wrote, has been examined by Christopher Wake. Perhaps one day his dissertation will be more readily available to other scholars.[9] Additional work has since been done on late nineteenth and early twentieth century Johor by Christopher Gray (1978), and in Malay by Haji Buyong Adil.

Moreover, I used no Dutch sources and relied on those few studies which had been translated, or on those who had based their work on the much richer Dutch sources, particularly for the pre-nineteenth century period. More recent works such as those by Leonard Blussé, Rheinhold Vos, and Diane Lewis, have added greatly to our understanding of events in the eighteenth and nineteenth century Malay world.[10] These need to be read in conjunction with *Prince of Pirates* for their more detailed accounts of events in the areas which later became part of the Netherlands Indies and are now in Indonesia. The *Tufhat al-Nafis* (the Malay/Bugis history of Riau), was only available to me as an unedited Romanised version. This has been replaced by the excellent translation by Barbara Andaya and Virginia Matheson.[11]

Likewise much has been added to accounts of Malay history in the late eighteenth and early nineteenth centuries by Barbara Andaya. Her accounts of Palembang and Jambi, and Perak have done much to expand our understanding of relations between the Dutch and Malays in that period.[12] More useful for the study of events in the Straits is the recent work of Timothy Barnard on Siak and his examination of the Siak Chronicle and the Dutch records.[13]

It surprises me that during the last 30 years so little has been done on the history of late nineteenth and early twentieth century Johor or any other Malay state history. Shaharil Talib has written about Trengganu and Kelantan.[14] Other interesting work was published on Kedah by Sharom Ahmat and more recently Wu Xiao An's study of Kedah has broken new ground.[15] All three benefited from earlier work on revenue farming and its place in the economic history of Southeast Asia. The forthcoming dissertation by Wong Yeetuan will offer a broad discussion of Penang's revenue farming system and its important Chinese merchant families.

The study of revenue farming added an important chapter to the history of indigenous rulers and their Chinese allies in Southeast Asia. It includes contributions from a number of quarters, in particular the work of James Rush on Java[16] and Jennifer Cushman on the Khaw family of Penang and Ranong.[17] Additional work on opium and opium farming has been undertaken by the French scholars working on Indochina, especially the studies of Chantal Decours-Gatin[18] and Philippe Le Failler.[19] Much of this more recent work was brought together by John Butcher and Howard Dick in their collection of articles on revenue farming in Southeast Asia.[20]

I would like to re-emphasize the continuing need to deconstruct and to examine carefully the legacy of colonial history and its impact on our current understanding of the history of Southeast Asia and of Malaysia and Singapore in particular. To my continuing surprise, the colonialist paradigms have proven far more durable than many of us expected back in the 1970s. It was an age when major changes seemed to be in the air, but the changes did not work out as many predicted. Although much creditable work has been done on

Malaysian, Thai and Philippine history of the nineteenth and early twentieth centuries, little of note has appeared about Singapore. Lee Kuan Yew's version of nineteenth century Singapore differs little from the colonialist accounts of C. M. Turnbull, Nicholas Tarling and others of their school.[21]

We should continue to challenge attitudes which would de-emphasize the role of indigenous peoples in the growth and prosperity of Singapore. The Temenggongs were vital to the successful expansion of British power and the colonial economy in the Malay world. The actions and policies of those proponents of the colonial enlightenment and free trade, Raffles and Crawfurd, have been overstated. Rather, one would credit other individuals such as Sir George Samuel Bonham (Governor of Singapore, 1837–1843)[22] for stopping piracy and for cooperating with the Temenggongs as they embarked on their careers as rulers of Johor. From this time until 1867, when the Colonial Office took over the administration of the Straits Settlements, the Singapore and Johor governments worked closely together, although sometimes at cross purposes, and not always at the initiative of the Europeans. The Malay chiefs and other Asians resident in Singapore lacked little in the way of ambition, ability and skill as rulers and managers.

Finally, I would add a word on the traditional Malay political system, or perhaps systems would be better. Both J. M. Gullick[23] and Anthony C. Milner[24] have done much to enhance our understanding of the systems of government in the Malay world before and during the colonial era. Nevertheless, little of what they say applies to Johor, Riau or Siak in the eighteenth and nineteenth centuries. Neither offers a discussion of the political economy of these states, nor do they consider in any real sense the importance of the entrepot as the foundation of Malay power. Neither seriously considers the issue of maritime power or influence on the part of Malay rulers. These are significant shortcomings in their approaches to Malay political culture. Malay states were not merely self-absorbed riverine enclosures, such as they describe. Malay *negeri* (or states) could also make themselves the centre of expansive maritime networks with lines of communication reaching throughout the Southeast Asian seas and stretching from Africa to China and Japan, and from the Persian Gulf to northern Australia.

These comments on the role of eighteenth and nineteenth century chiefs of Riau and Johor as sea lords are offered as a supplement to discussions of premodern Malay political culture. These issues have been further clarified and far more extensively discussed by Timothy Barnard in his recent work on Siak.[25] Likewise, the excellent collection of articles edited by Jaya Kathirithamby-Wells and John Villiers shows that the port-polity complex has long been an important element of the political culture of maritime Southeast Asia.[26]

The greater part of the *Prince of Pirates*, however, is the story of the development of Johor in the nineteenth century. The sea lords became land lords. The Temenggongs and their state prospered with the settlement of thousands of Chinese pepper and gambier planters. The readily saleable cash crops provided the state with a stable income. The Chinese who purchased opium, alcohol, pork, prostitutes, and gambling provided the state with a similarly stable tax base. In that respect, it resembled most of the colonial states in Southeast Asia as well as Siam. They all prospered from Chinese labour and opium. It is for this reason that I have continued to argue that the empire and even capitalism itself in Asia were largely based on opium.

In closing, I should apologize for the academic density of the book. An NUS student who had been forced (as an undergraduate) to read *Prince of Pirates* once exclaimed to me that my book not only had footnotes, but also had leg-notes. I'm afraid it still does. Although the first edition was a heavily revised version of my dissertation, it still bore many of the hallmarks of the work of an anxious graduate student afraid of omitting any possibly significant detail. Despite that anxiety, there were still some errors. I have been happy to correct them in this very slightly revised version. Even if I had the opportunity to substantially rewrite this book, I feel that there is little I could really change that would improve it. Most of my speculations and observations about Malay and Singapore history have, I feel, withstood the test of time. As it is, the study explains a number of trends which characterize modern Malaysia and Singapore. The countries have indeed been transformed, but they have not escaped their history.

Carl A. Trocki
January 2006

NOTES

1. I would like to thank Dr. John Butcher for reading and commenting on an earlier version of this piece.
2. In addition to the narrative description of the Kangchu system in this book, Appendix B provides the comparative list of *surat sungai* in the Johor Archives, *Surat Keterangan Membuka Kebun I & II (SKMKI and SKMKII)* and the list of Kangchus from the *Singapore and Straits Directory*, 1878. This, together with a more focused discussion, were published in my 1975 article, C. A. Trocki, "The Johor Archives and the Kangchu System, 1884–1910". *JMBRAS*, 48, pt. 1 (1975), pp. 1–46. The only exception to this was the late Christopher Gray's thesis, C. S. Gray, "Johore, 1910–1941: Studies in the Colonial Process" (New Haven, Department of History, Yale University, 1978).

3. Personal communication from Dr. Lin Man-houng of the Academia Sinica who noted that many early Chinese settlements in Taiwan bore names such as "Wu-fen" or "Ba-fen", meaning "Five Shares" or "Eight Shares" respectively.
4. M. S. Heidhues, "Company Island: A Note on the History of Belitung", Indonesia, Vol. 51 (Apr., 1991), pp. 1–20; T. Horsfield, "Report on the Island of Bangka", *JIAEA* 1 and 2, 1848; J. C. Jackson, "Mining in 18th Century Bangka: The Pre-European Exploitation of a 'Tin Island'", *Pacific Viewpoint*, 10, No. 2 (1969), pp. 28–54; J. C. Jackson, *Chinese in the West Borneo Goldfields: A Study in Cultural Geography* (Hull, University of Hull, 1970); T. P. Wang, *The Origins of Chinese Kongsi* (Selangor Darul Ehsan, Malaysia, Pelanduk Publications, 1995); M. S. Heidhues, "The First Two Sultans of Pontianak", *Archipel* 56 (1998), pp. 273–94.
5. C. A. Trocki, *Opium and Empire: Chinese Society in Colonial Singapore 1800–1910* (Ithaca, New York, Cornell University Press, 1990).
6. I base this figure on the statements of James C. Jackson, who estimated that there were at that time about 40,000 Chinese miners in western Borneo (including Sambas, Montrado, Pontianak and on the Kapuas River) and 25,000 mining tin on the island of Bangka. Based on the figures given by Begbie, I calculated there may have been about 10,000 pepper and gambier planters on the island of Bentan in Riau. P. J. Begbie, *The Malayan Peninsula*. Kuala Lumpur, Oxford University Press, 1967; J. C. Jackson, "Mining in 18th Century Bangka"; J. C. Jackson, *Chinese in the West Borneo Goldfields*. This does not include settlements that we know existed in Trengganu and other places on the Malay Peninsula and around the Gulf of Siam.
7. The "spirit" farm was the monopoly for the manufacture and sale of Chinese rice whiskey, often known as *samsu* in contemporary records. It was often auctioned together with the opium farm, but was far less lucrative.
8. C. A. Trocki, *Opium, Empire and the Global Political Economy*.
9. C. H. Wake, "Raffles and the Rajas: The Founding of Singapore in Malayan and British Colonial History", *JMBRAS*, 48, pt. 1 (1975), pp. 47–73; C. H. Wake, "Nineteenth Century Johore: Ruler and Realm in Transition" (Canberra, Australian National University, 1966).
10. D. Lewis, "The Last Malay Raja Muda of Johor", *Journal of Southeast Asian Studies* XIII (2) (September 1982), pp. 221–35; L. Blussé, *Strange Company: Chinese Settlers, Mestizo Women and the Dutch in VOC Batavia* (Dordrecht, Holland; Providence, RI, Floris Publications, 1988); R. Vos, *Gentle Janus, Merchant Prince: The VOC and the Tightrope of Diplomacy in the Malay World, 1740–1800* (Leiden, KITLV Press, 1993); D. Lewis, *Jan Compagnie in the Straits of Malacca, 1641–1795* (Athens, Ohio, Ohio University Center for International Studies, 1995).
11. R. Ali Haji ibn Ahmad, *The Precious Gift (Tuhfat al-Nafis)* (Kuala Lumpur, Oxford University Press, 1982).
12. B. W. Andaya, *To Live as Brothers: Southeast Sumatra in the Seventeenth and Eighteenth Centuries* (Honolulu, University of Hawaii Press, 1993).

13. T. Barnard, *Multiple Centers of Authority: Society and Environment in Siak and Eastern Sumatra, 1674–1827* (Leiden, KITLV Press, 2003).
14. Shaharil Talib, *After Its Own Image: The Trengganu Experience, 1881–1941* (Singapore, Oxford & New York, Oxford University Press, 1984).
15. X. A. Wu, *Chinese Business in the Making of a Malay State, 1882–1941: Kedah and Penang* (London & New York, RoutledgeCurzon, 2003).
16. J. R. Rush, *Opium to Java: Revenue Farming and Chinese Enterprise in Colonial Indonesia, 1800–1910* (Ithaca, New York, Cornell University Press, 1990).
17. J. W. Cushman, *Family and State: The Formation of a Sino-Thai Tin-mining Dynasty, 1797–1932* (Singapore, Oxford University Press, 1991).
18. C. Descours-Gatin, *Quand L'Opium Financait La Colonisation en Indochine: L'elaboration de la régie génerale de l'opium (1860–1914)* (Paris, Editions L'Hartmann (Ouvrage publie avec le concours du Centre National des Lettres), 1992).
19. P. Le Failler, "Le Mouvement International Anti-Opium et L'Indochine, 1906–1940", *History* (Provence, Université de Provence, 1993), p. 418 and Appendix, p. 83.
20. J. G. Butcher, and H. Dick, *The Rise and Fall of Revenue Farming: Business Elites and the Emergence of the Modern State in Southeast Asia* (New York, N.Y., St. Martin's Press, 1993).
21. N. Tarling, *Piracy and Politics in the Malay World: A Study of British Imperialism in Nineteenth-Century South-East Asia* (Singapore, Donald Moore Gallery, 1963); C. M. Turnbull, *A History of Singapore 1819–1988* (Kuala Lumpur, Oxford University Press, 1989); K. Y. Lee, *The Singapore Story: Memoirs of Lee Kuan Yew* (Singapore, New York, Prentice Hall, 1998).
22. Bonham had come to the east when he was 15 and had spent a number of years at Bengkulu before coming to Singapore in about 1820 or 1821 with Raffles. He had long been Assistant Resident and Resident Councillor in Singapore prior to becoming the actual governor.
23. J. M. Gullick, *Indigenous Political Systems of Western Malaya* (London, The Athlone Press, University of London, 1958); J. M. Gullick, *Malay Society in the Late Nineteenth Century: The Beginnings of Change* (Singapore, Oxford & New York, Oxford University Press, 1989).
24. A. C. Milner, *Kerajaan: Malay Political Culture on the Eve of Colonial Rule* (Tuscon, University of Arizona Press, 1982); A. C. Milner, *The Invention of Politics in Colonial Malaya: Contesting Nationalism and the Expansion of the Public Sphere* (Cambridge, Cambridge University Press, 1995).
25. T. Barnard, *Multiple Centers of Authority: Society and Environment in Siak and Eastern Sumatra, 1674–1827* (Leiden, KITLV Press, 2003).
26. J. Kathirithamby-Wells, and J. Villiers, eds., *The Southeast Asian Port and Polity: Rise and Demise* (Singapore, Singapore University Press, 1990).

Introduction to the First Edition

No country's history is so well documented yet so poorly understood as that of a former colony. This is particularly true in the case of Malaya. What normally passes as its history usually begins with a discussion of the "country" trade between India and China. The Malayan Peninsula and the Dutch were in the way, and had to be dealt with, so the story goes. It thus treats the foundation of Penang in 1786 as the beginning, then quickly moves to the foundation of Singapore and follows the growth of that settlement, the increase of its trade, and the gradual penetration of British influence in the Malay states of the Peninsula.

Throughout, the aims, intentions, and accomplishments of the Europeans are treated as being of primary importance. The standard histories tell a great deal about what the Europeans were trying to do; however, the story of what actually happened to the colonized areas is often neglected. More important, indigenous peoples and institutions are treated in a negative fashion. Much of the history that has been written to date does not exhibit that necessary awareness of the continuity between the Malay past and their present situation.

The process of colonization always has a traumatic effect on the cultural integrity of any society. This is doubly true in the case of the society's historical traditions. In the case of Malaya, the very function of writing history was taken over by the colonizing group. As a result, the region's past was reworked from an entirely new viewpoint with much emphasis laid on justification for the colonial take-over. Despite the commendable job of restoration of ancient texts and monuments that colonizers in most Southeast Asian countries undertook, the general shape of their histories has been found lacking in numerous areas. The shortcomings of colonial historians are most apparent in their treatment of the process of colonization and in the question of relations between the colonial power and indigenous groups.

This study is an attempt to remedy the imbalance. It accomplishes this firstly by adhering closely to the history of one Malay dynasty — that of the Temenggongs of Johor. People, particularly families, were the agents of continuity in the traditional Malay world, and not places. Secondly, this work pays close attention to political and economic institutions, because these culturally conditioned patterns of bringing about order and system tend to be linked with the people. When change occurs in the historical environment, the people begin by trying to modify and adapt their existing institutions in order to survive.

A third measure taken to establish a "Malay" viewpoint has been to base this study, as much as possible, on indigenous historical materials. Traditional works, such as the *Tufhat al-Nafis* and other chronicles, as well as more recent data, especially the documents of the Johor archives, make it possible to understand the indigenous perception of events. However, since the available Malay materials in no way offer a complete narrative, they have been supplemented by substantial reliance on the standard English language sources. These include the Straits Settlements Records, Straits Settlements Factory Records, Colonial Office Records (CO/273), as well as contemporary newspapers, books, articles, and other standard works.

Of particular importance are the Johor Archival records which make possible a much more definitive description of the gambier economy and the economic relationship between Singapore and Johor than has hitherto been presented. This study is the first scholarly attempt to make extensive and systematic use of the documents in this collection which deal with the Kangchu system.

The study begins with an examination of the Malay/Bugis entrepot of Riau in order to establish the status of the Malay state system at the end of the eighteenth century. Following the fall of Riau in 1784, there was a period of general disorganization and warfare in the archipelago which persisted well after the foundation of Singapore in 1819.

The history of the dynasty of the Temenggongs of Johor provides certain threads of continuity through this period of chaos. The most important representatives of the line were the nineteenth-century Temenggongs: Abdul Rahman (r. 1806–25), Daing Ibrahim (r. 1841–62), and Abu Bakar (r. 1862–95).

This group of Malays was closest to the agencies of change. The impact of the British was felt first by those Temenggongs who occupied Singapore together with them. Not only were these chiefs the first to exhibit the effects of the British influence but they themselves also had a substantial influence on the manner in which the power of Singapore was exerted in the surrounding Malay states.

However, the dynastic continuity that the Temenggongs represent is, in itself, insufficient. It is important to examine not the history of a state called Johor, or a territory called Johor, but of the political and economic institutions that sustained the Malay empire "below the wind". Both Singapore and Johor shared, in some respects, the heritage of the Malay maritime empire. Thus, what is important here is the history of the relationship between Johor and Singapore and, finally, with the rest of the world.

Temenggong Abdul Rahman was a sea lord, like most of the major Malay chiefs of his era. Before the founding of Singapore, he lived at Riau and Bulang and appears to have functioned as an official of the Riau entrepot under its Bugis rulers. Riau was a part of the ancient Kingdom of Johor, the maritime state which had dominated the southern part of the Malay Peninsula and eastern Sumatra since 1512. Abdul Rahman's domain has been styled a *perentah* in one Malay source. It was not really a state (or *negeri*) but a part of a larger political unit which at that time was very fragmented. There were then about five or six such groupings. Abdul Rahman's *perentah* consisted of a ring of islands in the northwestern part of the Riau Archipelago and included Singapore and a portion of the Johor coastline. There were about ten island *suku* of sea peoples living here who owed allegiance to the Temenggong. They may have numbered close to 10,000 at most, and were probably less.

There was, in fact, no "state" in the area now called Johor. At this time, "Johor" referred only to a vague geographical area, much of it insular. There was nothing of great importance on the land in any case. The Temenggong's government was really the sea peoples.

The phenomenon of piracy is indicative of the peculiar nature of the ancient Johor kingdom. It was essentially a maritime state. The major political and economic concerns of its rulers were the sea peoples of the Riau-Lingga Archipelago and the international trade route which passed through the Straits of Malacca. The state centred on a trading entrepot. This was the essence of the classical Malay state. The Riau entrepot of 1784 was but the last in a succession of similar "urban" centres whose history stretches back to Srivijaya in the seventh century.

This state system was more or less dictated by what one might term "ecological" realities. Until recently, the region of the Malay world offered only a limited range of possibilities to human endeavour. Although the area had been inhabited since the dawn of time, in 1800 it remained one of the most sparsely populated areas on earth. In the main, there was the jungle and the sea. Given traditional technology, human life could sustain itself only in small niches scattered throughout this desert of forest and water. These habitats were the islands, the beaches, and the riverbanks.

Even when cleared of forest, the land could only support small groups of people living in relative isolation. Overland communications were difficult if not impossible. This hostile environment prevented the establishment of dense concentrations of agricultural peoples and thus militated against the growth of any kind of powerful political unit on the land. Geography did, however, offer one positive advantage to the skilled maritime peoples of the coasts and islands. International trade routes between China and the West were forced to pass through the sieve-like network of islands, shoals, and channels which make up the Riau-Lingga Archipelago. Likewise, the pattern of the seasonal monsoons made this "land below the wind" a natural stopping-place.

Following the development of long-range east-west trade came the creation of political units in this region. These entrepot states were able to concentrate fairly large populations in one place because of the trade which supplied wealth to the ruler and food for his subjects. It also brought contact with other, more developed cultures, which supplied many of the cultural patterns by which Malays came to organize their lives. First, the state was "Indianized", then it was Islamicized — but it remained maritime.

The maritime empire was based on a trading city, usually located at, or controlled from, the Riau-Lingga Archipelago. The empire was ruled by a Sultan who exercised power through a grouping of officials or chiefs. At the centre were the sea lords, the chiefs who exercised direct control over the *orang laut* and who controlled the international and local trade. This group in fact usually dominated the office of the sultanate as well. Normally, these chiefs all seem to have been territorially associated with the south Johor or island area, but this was not always the case — any chief who could gather a following of sea peoples about him could bid for a share of power at the centre.

The second level of chiefs held power on the periphery. They controlled riverine *negeri* and drew their wealth from the trade passing along their rivers. At times when the Riau/Johor entrepot was prosperous and influential, they tended to be dependent upon it. When the centre was weak, they exercised a good deal of autonomy and, in some cases, managed to establish relatively stable dynasties within their river systems, as was the case of Perak and Selangor.

The dividing-line between the two levels was never a sharp one. Chiefs could rise up out of the hinterland, as it were, and seek power at the centre. Alternatively, sea lords from the entrepot could fall back onto the land and displace or subordinate the "natives". This is what happened in the east coast states of the Peninsula during the eighteenth century. There was a good deal of movement between the two levels, depending largely on the relative strength of the entrepot at any given time. As a result, there were continual intermarriages, alliances, and warfare among the Malay aristocrats. Despite the tendency for scholars to treat the class of Malay rajas as a single group, to distinguish them from the commoners, the distinction between sea lords and "land" lords is an important one.

Viewed from the entrepot, the riverine principalities of the Peninsula and Sumatra were of secondary importance. These areas supplied raw materials for the international trade network and could become troublesome if allowed too much independence. Malay trading empires were rarely based on riverine states. Power in this context was always sea power. Thus traditional political systems emphasized the control of a majority of sea peoples and the management of the trade. If the ruler of the entrepot was successful in these two policy objectives, then control of the outlying land areas was a relatively easy matter, for the balance of political and economic power was concentrated at the centre.

The traditional Malay maritime state was always a fragile entity. Its lines of control were the sea routes and its authority was strung out from island to island and from one river mouth to another. It was held together, as Professor O. W. Wolters has argued, primarily by wealth and the generally high standard of living which was possible only in the capital. The empires were extremely vulnerable to changes that affected the international trade, no matter how distant. The fall of a dynasty in China or the Napoleonic wars in Europe could and did have serious repercussions in the Malay world. Any decline in trade revenues seriously endangered the state's food supply, since food for these entrepot cities had always to be imported from Siam and Java. In such periods of "decline", the sea peoples had to fend for themselves by becoming pirates, and chaos would reign anew.

The realities of that world, however, did not change very much when the British founded Singapore in 1819. The new empire created by Raffles was initially formed in the image of earlier maritime states. This, in fact, is probably one of the reasons it was so successful. While it would be simplistic to say that this was an instance of "putting new wine in old bottles", it does appear that the early history of the port roughly paralleled that of Malacca and

Srivijaya. All three states had explosive growth patterns and owed much to the characteristic mobility of the maritime peoples.

From the Malay viewpoint, the foundation of Singapore was seen as an attempt to reorganize an empire based on the traditional pattern. The Temenggong sought to make himself the head of a refurbished empire in partnership with the English. This did not coincide with British aims, and the ensuing conflict led to a rearrangement in 1824 in favour of the East India Company. The Temenggong was dispossessed and lost all legal authority in Singapore. He and his followers were forced to move to Teluk Belanga, to the west of the town, and to leave their original site on the Singapore River. This agreement, however, overlooked the political and economic realities of the situation, and by 1835, it became clear that a number of readjustments were needed. In particular, the English viewed the problem of "piracy" as most intractable. Thus a new accommodation was reached with Ibrahim, the successor of the Temenggong with whom Raffles and Crawfurd had signed their treaties. He became the colony's official pirate suppressor.

While the Temenggongs are habitually treated by historians as having been outside the European power structure of Singapore, the facts suggest otherwise. In their negotiations, their wars and overall policies, the Temenggongs acted in the interest of the entrepot complex. Admittedly, they generally set their own priorities in these matters but the important factor is that they identified their own interests with those of the port, and not with those of the peninsular states.

Like the British, the Temenggongs viewed the world from the entrepot. Both parties identified themselves more with the interests of the port than with those of the other Malay chiefs who remained on the fringes. It was to their advantage to extend the political and economic influence of the port over the surrounding region. What conflict there was between the British and the Temenggongs should be properly viewed as an internal affair of the capital.

From the beginning, the relationship was an unequal one. The British held the ultimate balance of power, and, when it came to a confrontation, the Malay rulers had no choice but to submit. The Temenggongs' history is thus one of compromise after compromise and, in the final analysis, continual retreat. The position which these Malay chiefs held in Singapore was never given official recognition. The British saw it as only a temporary expedient. The sea peoples under the Temenggong were co-opted and gradually rendered harmless. By mid-century, the advances of European maritime technology, major shifts in the population balance of the region, and changes in the manner in which trade was conducted all tended to diminish the importance of the maritime Malays and the *orang laut*.

The Temenggong's political survival depended on his making the shift away from the role of sea chief to something more in keeping with the demands of the time. Since 1819, the island of Singapore had been populated by thousands of Chinese planters who grew pepper and gambier. In about 1844, when these planters had begun to feel overcrowded in Singapore, Temenggong Ibrahim began allowing them to move into Johor. This laid the foundation for his own territorial state on the mainland and, at the same time, supplied him with an independent source of wealth.

The state of Johor was the agency by which the apparatus of the Temenggong's government, or *perentah*, was transferred from the port to a piece of land. This then became a *negeri*. The group of dependents — minor chiefs, family members and hangers-on at Teluk Belanga who had formerly been called the following of the Temenggong — was transformed. They became bureaucrats who now learned how to administer the revenues of a Chinese agricultural system. The sea peoples, on whom these chiefs had once relied, faded into oblivion or moved to the land. They were no longer a source of wealth or power. The Temenggong and his followers, however, did not starve. With the wealth generated by their new Chinese subjects, they became the wealthiest Malays in the world.

In the beginning, Johor was like no other Malay state. It was an empty piece of land, desolate and unpopulated. The government of the Temenggong was built up from scratch. There were no local peoples or regional chiefs in Johor to help or, more likely, to hinder him. His only competition was the shadow of the old sultanate, and this soon vanished. It was thus a less complicated matter to send the Chinese into the interior. The local chiefs were Teluk Belanga Malays and all were the Temenggong's men. Like the Chinese and the British, these Malays saw Johor as a frontier. Their job was to encourage settlement in this hinterland of Singapore and, beyond this, to police the coastline and collect the Temenggong's revenues.

Modern Malaysia, with its system of communal politics, controlled by a small elite of Chinese and Malay magnates, grew out of the political and economic arrangements established during the nineteenth century. The question of how these came about is thus one of contemporary significance. The picture presented here is that of Malays attempting to accommodate themselves to the British presence while at the same time integrating the Chinese into their political system. In the face of the great changes sweeping the Malay world in this period, indigenous peoples had little but their traditional institutions and priorities to guide them. While their means did not always achieve the desired ends, they did have a decisive effect on the ultimate outcome. It is a mistake to consider them as having been only passive or, at best, reactionary elements in the colonial situation.

On the other hand, it is also a mistake to ignore the accommodations which the English had to make in order to rule the Malay world. Despite their immense resources and overwhelming physical power, they could not have been successful without substantial concessions to local conditions and compromises with indigenous institutions. While some historians have tended to view these expedients as imperfections or aberrations in colonial policy, it can also be argued that they made possible whatever gains the British achieved. In the broader sense, an appreciation of this circumstance is particularly important in understanding the relationship between Malaysia and Singapore.

If we consider Singapore in its indigenous context, it is clear that it was not only the successor of Dutch Malacca but, more immediately, the successor of Malayo-Bugis Riau. Singapore supplanted Riau and to a great extent reconstituted a type of maritime empire. The status of the other Malay states of the Peninsula, particularly Johor, should also be considered in their relationship to the various Straits Settlements which dominated their economies. The states of the Peninsula were dependencies of Singapore and Penang, in the first instance, and not of Britain. Beyond this, it will become clear that it was the Chinese, rather than the English, who established and maintained this colonial dependence.

This then is an outline of the "indigenous" viewpoint which this work proposes. It is not, in any sense of the word, nationalist history, and it would be presumptuous for a non-Malaysian to attempt such a history. It does, however, attempt to compensate in some respect for those studies which ignore the problem of continuity and the need for measuring historical change against some clear standard. It seems impossible to make any clear statement regarding the English impact on the Malay world without considering the political and economic institutions of that world prior to the European arrival. Furthermore, a consistent and logical narrative demands that one demonstrates what actually happened to the pre-colonial institutions and describe how they and the indigenous peoples received the forces of change. That is the aim of this study.

1

Prelude to Singapore

1784–1819

The term "Johor" is used by historians to refer to two different states — an old one and a new one. Old Johor was the maritime Malay empire that succeeded Malacca. It began in 1512 when the defeated Sultan of Malacca established a capital on the Johor River,[1] and gradually disintegrated in the eighteenth century. Sir Richard Winstedt has written the first comprehensive account of this state in his *A History of Malaya*.[2] Modern Johor occupies the southern tip of the Malay Peninsula and is one of the eleven states of the Federation of Malaysia. It dates from the mid-nineteenth century.

There are historical, geographic, and dynastic connections between these two states, as Winstedt has shown in his "History of Johor".[3] In many respects, the present state of Johor is a successor of the earlier empire. While the relationship between old Johor and modern Johor is undeniable, other Malay states, including Pahang, Trengganu, Selangor, Perak, and the nineteenth-century Residency of Riau, have as much claim to the heritage of old Johor as does new Johor. The dividing-line between the two, as near as one can make out, was the foundation of Singapore by Sir Thomas Stamford Raffles in 1819.

Raffles received the island of Singapore for the East India Company from a chief who was known as Abdul Rahman, Temenggong Sri Maharaja of Johor. He was one of the officials of the former Johor court which was then located at Riau on the island of Bentan.[4] As his domain, he claimed Singapore, a number of islands in the northern part of the Riau Archipelago, and a portion of the tip of the Malay Peninsula. In the course of the nineteenth century,

Temenggong Abdul Rahman and his successors gave up their claims to the island of Singapore and to the islands in Riau. They eventually concentrated all their efforts towards building up a government to rule the state which we now call Johor. By 1885, the state had reached its present boundaries and the ruler stood at the zenith of his power. In that year, he received the title of Sultan of the State and Territory of Johor from Queen Victoria.

This study is concerned with the family of the Temenggongs who created this new Johor — as the name of its capital, Johor Baharu, implies. It begins by examining the family's origins and their standing in the former Johor empire, and proceeds to study the manner in which they built their new state and the reasons they chose the methods they employed. These questions, it seems, have relevance not only for Johor but for every Malay state, and perhaps for any state that came under the influence of a foreign power during the nineteenth century.

Following Winstedt, one can usefully trace the family back to the beginning of the eighteenth century when the old kingdom of Johor began its decline. In many ways the rise of the Temenggongs developed in counterpoint to the decay of old Johor.

During the eighteenth century, the seat of the Johor empire came to be located at Riau. Here the Temenggongs represented a minor branch of the family which ruled the Johor empire after 1699. The key eighteenth-century Temenggong was Temenggong Abdul Jamal, who was a grandson of the founder of the second Johor dynasty. (See Figure 1)[5]

The reason for beginning with Temenggong Abdul Jamal is that he appears to be the first of this line who held only the office of Temenggong. Following him, the office became hereditary among his direct descendants. Before him, the office of Temenggong, like that of the Bendahara, circulated among various

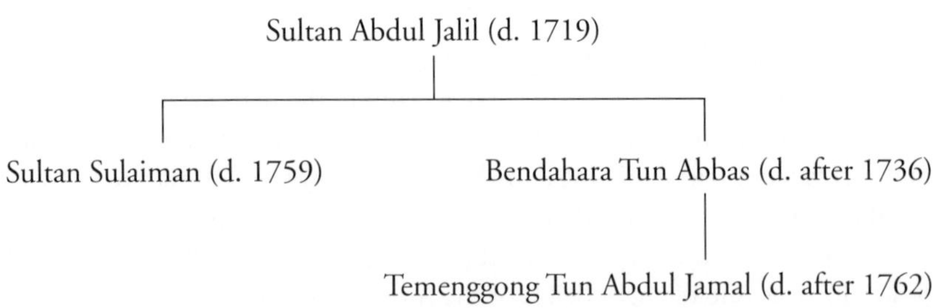

FIGURE 1
Genealogy of Temenggong Abdul Jamal

minor members of the Johor royal family.[6] We have no data on what these offices meant during the eighteenth century, nor do we know if they were always associated with the same territories. Winstedt has pointed out: "Sometimes there were Bendaharas of Trengganu as well as of Pahang and perhaps Temenggongs of Riau as well as of Johor."[7]

Given that there was some sort of territorial significance to the offices, there is no real answer to the question of what the territorial divisions actually meant in practice. After 1750, these distinctions become a little clearer. Riau remained the seat of the Johor empire and the site of the entrepot from which the state drew its wealth. It was ruled by the Yang Di-Pertuan Muda, a descendant of the Bugis chiefs who had moved into the state at the beginning of the century. The Sultan maintained a residence at Riau as well as at the island of Lingga to the south. The Bendahara, beginning with Temenggong Abdul Jamal's brother, Tun Abdul Majid, became increasingly identified with Pahang. It is from him that the present ruling house of Pahang traces its ancestry.

During the eighteenth century, the Temenggongs remained associated with Riau, or at least the immediate vicinity of the port. The island of Bulang appears to have been a family fief, and was perhaps the real headquarters of the Temenggongs during the second half of the century. Tun Abbas was buried there as was Temenggong Abdul Jamal and his own son Engku Muda.[8] Temenggong Abdul Rahman, although deeply involved in the politics of Riau before 1818, is also reported to have begun his career at Bulang.[9] The family did not shift its base to Johor until much later. However, the fact that the officer was never called the Temenggong of Bulang warns against putting too much stress on the territorial association here.[10] Rather, the evidence suggests that the office of Temenggong was closely associated with the main centre of the state at Riau, and it was only after 1818 that the family began to seek a different base.

We know very little about the function of the office of Temenggong at Riau in the mid-eighteenth century. During this period, the family was declining and there is only a sketchy version of its history. We learn of it only from the accounts of the partisans of rival families. For instance, the most reliable history of eighteenth-century Riau is the *Tufhat Al-Nafis*[11] which was written by a descendant of one of Riau's Yang Di-Pertuan Mudas. During the eighteenth century, these officials were engaged in a struggle for power with the Temenggongs. Another account, the *Hikayat Negeri Johor*,[12] has been identified as a Selangor-based history and thus connected with a lineage which was closely related to the Bugis of Riau. A third account, the *Hikayat Kerajaʼan*,[13] which was not available to the present writer, is said by Winstedt to represent the Temenggongs' side of the story.

It is best to begin with the classic definition of a Temenggong. For this, it is necessary to go back to fifteenth-century Malacca. Before 1512, the Bendahara and the Temenggong were the two major officers of the state. Newbold's translation of the "Code of Malacca" lists the Bendahara as second to the ruler and the Temenggong as third. A fourth officer was the Laksamana or admiral. The Bendahara was defined as "he who rules the peasantry, the army and those dependent on the state. His sway extends over all the islands, and it is he who is the king's law giver." The Temenggong was a kind of minister of Justice: "It is this functionary's duty to enquire diligently and to seek out persons who perpetrate crime, to prevent oppression, and to find and punish transgressors". In terms of precedence, the Code also notes: "Should the king mount his elephant, the Tumungong's place is at its head. The Lacsamana and the Sri Biji di Raja bear the king's sword in the rear."[14]

These descriptions of duties indicate that the state was visualized as being divided into three functional domains or spheres of influence. There were, in other terms, the peasantry or *ra'ayat*, the city, and the navy. The Bendahara, as a kind of Prime Minister, controlled the *ra'ayat* and the islands. In terms of people, this meant both the *orang laut* and the *orang benua*, or sea people and land people. Of this dual domain, the sea and the islands were undoubtedly the most important. In the sixteenth century, this was where the bulk of the population was located. Professor O. W. Wolters has remarked on the importance of the islands and believes that these sea peoples had been the major prop of the Malacca dynasty:

> Not merely were these off-shore islands situated at the crossroads of international sailing routes, enabling their inhabitants to intercept and molest travellers from India, China and the archipelago; the islanders, as we have seen, were also a sturdy maritime folk. The Malay chiefs who ruled in the islands had at their disposal the sea-gypsies ... It is not surprising that in the *Sejarah Melayu*, spheres of local power (*pegangan*) in this region are often measured by the number of three-masted cruisers at the disposal of the chiefs. Bentan is accredited with four hundred ships and has the largest complement mentioned in the text.[15]

On the land, there were forest dwellers and agricultural peoples. The former were useful in collecting forest produce. The agricultural peoples, mostly located near Malacca, had orchards and presumably produced a portion of the foodstuffs consumed by the city of Malacca.[16]

The city was the realm of the Temenggong. According to Winstedt's definition, he was the minister in charge of defence, police, and markets.[17] In his *A History of Malaya*, he describes the Temenggong Tun Mutahir of Malacca (later Bendahara) as a kind of municipal official who was in charge of the city police.[18] Perhaps we may also call him a kind of mayor.

Meilink-Roelofsz, in her discussion of Malacca, also indicates that the Temenggong was very much tied to the urban sector of the Sultan's domain:

> The *tumenggong*, whose authority only extended to the town of Malacca, had charge of the guard and jurisdiction over the town. All criminal cases came before him in the first instance and from there went onto the *bendahara*. The *tumenggong* was a very important personage as far as trade was concerned since he received all the import and export duties. According to Albuquerque the *tumenggong* also had jurisdiction over foreigners. In the Annals the *tumenggong* appears as sort of Minister of War and Justice. At court he was in charge of all ceremonies and official receptions, in which capacity the foreign merchants must have come to know him best because of their audiences at court, while they could also be summoned to appear before him if they infringed the laws of Malacca.[19]

He was under the Bendahara, but only in the sense that he was a direct deputy and often heir-apparent to the higher post of Bendahara. Temenggong Tun Mutahir (d. 1510) later became the Bendahara. While he was Bendahara, his son, Tun Hasan, held the office of Temenggong.[20] We have already mentioned similar examples of the close connection between the two offices during the eighteenth century as well, when three brothers and their sons held both offices in succession between about 1723 and 1762.

The third-ranking officer, the Laksamana, was in charge of a third functional domain, the navy. This appears to have covered a kind of extra-urban military force, which stood distinct from the larger mass of sea peoples. At certain periods of Malacca and Johor history, the Laksamana dominated the state in a swashbuckling way. Hang Tuah of Malacca was a good example of this type. The Laksamana Paduka Raja of the late sixteenth century was also quite powerful. Winstedt, quoting Dutch sources, notes that "the Dato Laksamana alias Paduka Raja and his sons administer the whole of Johore kingdom".[21] After this Laksamana's death in 1688, the rival faction under the Bendahara Tun Abdul Majid, Sri Maharaja, took power. It was this Bendahara who grew so bold as to found a new dynasty when the insane Sultan Mahmud was assassinated in 1699.

The period 1699–1722 was one of grave crisis for the Johor empire. These years have been the subject of an inquiry by Leonard Y. Andaya.[22] He describes the impact of the regicide of Sultan Mahmud II in 1699. After Bendahara Abdul Jalil declared himself Sultan, a pretender, Raja Kechil, rose up in Siak and won the allegiance of the navy of *orang laut* who had probably once served the Laksamana.[23] Abdul Jalil fled to Pahang and Raja Kechil assumed power on the Johor River. The Bendahara-Sultan, as Winstedt called him, was killed at Kuala Pahang in 1719.

In search of a new naval force to pit against the *orang laut* of Raja Kechil, the successor of Abdul Jalil, Sultan Sulaiman (d. 1759), recruited five Bugis[24] adventurers, all brothers. It was thus the Bugis and not the *orang laut* who supplied the naval forces necessary to defeat Raja Kechil. Andaya notes that these years saw the beginning of the decline of the *orang laut* within the Johor kingdom:

> The trauma of the regicide in 1699, which resulted in the confusion within the ranks of the Orang Laut and culminated in the betrayal of the new dynasty … was a significant turning point in the history of the Orang Laut people within the Malay world … the Orang Laut underwent such a significant metamorphosis in the eighteenth century that by the nineteenth century foreign observers were wont to characterize the Orang Laut groups they occasionally encountered as a shy, nomadic sea people of little consequence.[25]

Andaya reports that not all of the *orang laut* defected to Raja Kechil. The Temenggong and Bendahara controlled some forces of sea peoples during this period. But these alone were not sufficient to protect the new dynasty. There was thus a need for the stronger Bugis allies. The Bugis soon came to challenge the former position held by the *orang laut* and their chiefs, the Temenggong and the Bendahara.

By 1728, the new dynasty had regained a measure of control in the region and managed to occupy Riau and drive out Raja Kechil. But the intense struggle for power and recognition had brought significant changes in the new Johor state. Andaya has summarized the future of the state as follows:

> The old Kingdom of Johor under its new ruling house, the Bendahara family, survived on the strength of Bugis fighting men. The latter became an essential part of the power structure of Johor, but, like the Orang Laut, were never considered to be of the Malay community. The difference lay, however, in the greater aspirations and ambitions of the Buginese who would not be content to occupy the periphery of a Malay kingdom whose rulers owed their position to them [as had the *orang laut*]. The conflict of an outside group wanting to enter into the internal structure of a society and thereby encroaching on the privileges and positions of established members of that society is a theme in the history of Johor through the eighteenth century …[26]

The Malay-Bugis conflict at Riau can be seen, at least partially, in terms of a dynastic feud. The Bendahara family had originally taken over the Sultanate

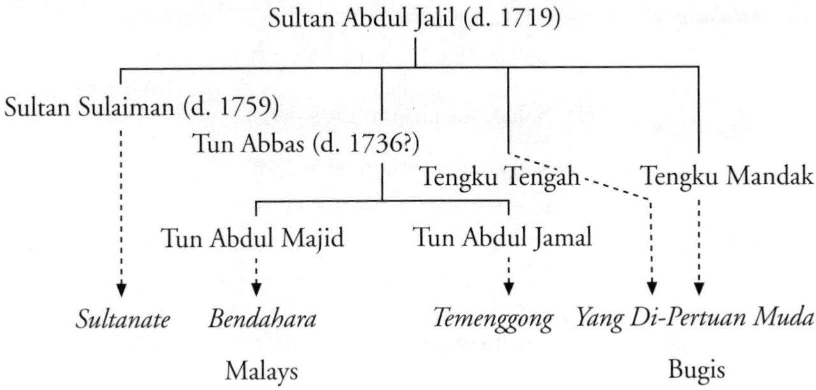

FIGURE 2
Johor Lineages and Offices

and most of the major offices of the Johor state. Later, two of the Bugis brothers married into the family. The main branches of the family and the various lineages were related to the major offices.[27] (See Figure 2)

From Abdul Jalil, we trace five lineages which lay at the heart of the Malay-Bugis conflict. As of about 1760, all of these lineages were competing among themselves for power in the Riau state. The three "Malay" lineages dominated the offices of Sultan, Bendahara, and Temenggong, while the two Bugis lines controlled the most powerful position, Yamtuan Muda, between them. The genealogies up to the beginning of the nineteenth century are as shown in Figure 3. The two Bugis Lineages which controlled the office of Yang Di-Pertuan Muda traced from marriages to two of Sultan Abdul Jalil's daughters.

The two Bugis lineages passed the office of Yamtuan Muda (Yang Di-Pertuan Muda) between them, from uncle to nephew, through the eighteenth century. All these lineages began to follow patrilineal succession in the nineteenth century.

In general, the two Bugis lineages proved the more cohesive faction, and from 1760 to 1784 they completely dominated the state. In 1784, they lost control of the Sultanate and were forced to flee from Riau after the Dutch defeated them. However, they regained power after 1805. Although there was conflict between the Bugis families, they generally presented a united front to the Malays during the eighteenth century.

The Malay faction was led by the Bendahara and the Temenggong.[28] In 1762 these two were defeated in a succession dispute with the Bugis, who

1. *Sultanate*

- Sultan Abdul Jalil (r. 1699–1719)
  - Sultan Sulaiman (r. 1728–59)
    - Sultan Abdul Jalil (r. 1759–60)
      - Sultan Ahmad (r. 1761)
      - Sultan Mahmud (r. 1762–1812)
        - Sultan Hussain of Singapore (r. 1819–35)
        - Sultan Abdul Rahman of Lingga (r. 1812–30)

2. *Bendaharas of Pahang*

- Sultan Abdul Jalil
  - Bendahara Tun Abbas (d. *c.* 1736)
    - Bendahara Tun Abdul Majid (r. 1757–1803)
      - B. Che Engku Sentul (d. 1803)
      - B. Tun Koris (r. 1803–6)
        - B. Tun Ali (r. 1806–47)

3. *Temenggongs of Johor*

- Sultan Abdul Jalil
  - Bendahara Tun Abbas
    - Temenggong Abdul Jamal = Raja Maimunah (d. *c.* 1765) [see below]
      - Daing Chelak
      - Daing Kechil
        - Temenggong Abdul Rahman (d. 1825)
          - Temenggong Ibrahim (r. 1825–62)
            - Temenggong Abu Bakar (r. 1862–95) [Maharaja after 1866 and Sultan in 1885]
      - Engku Muda (d. 1806) [*de facto* Temenggong]

FIGURE 3
Genealogies of Johor, 1700–1830

4. *The Yamtuan Mudas of Riau*

a. This was the lesser of the two lines:

Sultan Abdul Jalil

Tengku Tengah = Daing Parani (d. 1723)

- Daing Kemboja, 3rd Yamtuan Muda (d. 1777)
  - Raja Ali, 5th Yamtuan Muda (r. 1784–1806)
- Raja Maimunah [see above]

b. The other, more illustrious line was:

Sultan Abdul Jalil

Tengku Mandak = Daing Chelak, 2nd Yamtuan Muda (d. 1745)

- Raja Haji, 4th Yamtuan Muda (r. 1777–84)
  - Raja Ja'afar, 6th Yamtuan Muda (r. 1806–31)
- Raja Lumu, Sultan of Selangor
  - Sultans of Selangor

FIGURE 3
(Continued)

nominated their own candidate for Sultan (Sultan Mahmud III). As far as the *Tufhat Al-Nafis* is concerned, the Bendahara and the Temenggong then ceased to play any remarkable role in Riau politics until after 1784.[29] Temenggong Abdul Jamal was reputedly insane.[30] He seems to have been crafty enough, however, to attempt an alliance with the Bugis through his marriage to Raja Maimunah.[31] However, the marriage did the Temenggong little good in his relations with the Bugis. The *Tufhat* has left a description of the incident in which the Bugis ousted the Malays. It is of interest since it also gives us a brief view of Temenggong Abdul Jamal and his sons.

In 1762, the armed forces of the Malays and Bugis confronted each other at Riau. They were disputing the succession to the Sultanate after the deaths of Sultan Sulaiman and his two short-lived successors.

> The Malays and Bugis were sitting opposite each other. The Yang Di-Pertuan Muda Daing Kemboja and Raja Haji were sitting close to the Malay chiefs,

> and Daing Kemboja was staring at them. Then he saw Daing Kechil and Daing Chelak and Engku Muda, the three brothers, sitting next to the Temenggong, [their father], He commanded them: "Kechil! Chelak! Muda! Why are you not here at my side?" And the three brothers went over to the side of the Yang Di-Pertuan Muda because they were sons of Raja Maimunah, Daing Kemboja's sister.[32]

Then Daing Kemboja sat down on the Lion Throne (Singasahna) and took the infant Sultan Mahmud on his lap and installed him with the regalia.[33] Following the installation, the Malay chiefs rebelled but their move was aborted by the Bugis. The Malays were outmanoeuvred and all their weapons were confiscated and locked up in the fort at Pulau Bayan where they were guarded by Bugis warriors.[34]

Thus the Temenggong is shown to have been deserted by his own sons. He was defeated in his political ambitions and almost totally destroyed as a locus of power. The *Tufhat's* account can be compared with a Pahang story about Abdul Jamal.

In about 1757, Abdul Jamal is said to have become enraged when Sultan Sulaiman favoured one of the Bendahara's sons over his own. He went mad and killed the son of the Bendahara and then fled. On the way back to Riau, he captured a small boat and towed it with him as a prize. The Pahang version then notes that the Temenggong and his *two* sons were killed when the powder magazine of the craft exploded.[35]

Winstedt accepts the Pahang version, which would put the death of the Temenggong and all his sons at some date before 1762. This conclusion seems open to question. Winstedt himself admits that much of the dating and genealogical information in this text is clearly wrong, and this account directly contradicts the *Tufhat* which mentions a Temenggong and his three sons as being alive in 1762 at the coronation of Sultan Mahmud. Since the *Tufhat* clearly indicates that they were sons of Raja Maimunah and mentions them by name, it seems reasonable to discount the dates suggested by the Pahang story.

The *Tufhat* does report that Daing Chelak[36] was killed in an explosion or a fire on a boat that he had pirated, so there is undoubtedly some truth in the Pahang account, but it is difficult to say where it lies. The *Tufhat* is silent on the Temenggong's death; however, it may be that he and perhaps Daing Chelak died during the abortive Malay revolt in 1763–64. This would certainly go a long way towards explaining the failure of the Malays at Riau to reassert themselves during the next two decades.

Another interesting point in both accounts is the generally low estimate they have of Temenggong Abdul Jamal. He seems to have been considered an outcast by both sides. It is thus perhaps appropriate that he fathered a line of outcasts. Even his own sons deserted him in 1762 (or so the *Tufhat* would have us believe) and yet one of them, Engku Muda, eventually found himself in a similar situation. In order to show how this came about, it is necessary to examine events at Riau in the years that followed.

The state and the Sultanate now came under the control of the Bugis Yang Di-Pertuan Muda. If one assumes that the Temenggong and Daing Chelak died sometime in the later 1760s, that left only two sons surviving. These, Daing Kechil (also known as Tun Ibrahim) and Engku Muda (or Raja Muhammad), appear to have lived at Riau with their mother, Raja Maimunah. The mother was reportedly still alive in 1795, and Engku Muda died about 1806.[37] We know practically nothing about Daing Kechil, other than that he is mentioned as the father of Temenggong Abdul Rahman in most of the genealogies. It is not clear whether anyone became Temenggong after Abdul Jamal's death. One genealogy gives Ibrahim,[38] but the *Hikayat Negeri Johor* and the *Tufhat* are silent on the subject of the Temenggong between 1762 and 1784. It would appear that after Abdul Jamal died, the Bugis saw no reason to appoint a successor. This left Engku Muda and/or Daing Kechil disfranchised — they had no office and therefore no official status within the state.

Thus, one reason we cannot describe Temenggong Abdul Jamal's official duties at Riau is that he was out of power. There was no place for a Malay official in a state run by a Bugis Yang Di-Pertuan Muda. Former Temenggongs had always been subordinates of the major officer, whether he was a Bendahara or a Laksamana. Temenggongs only controlled the port. This was an important function and it was an office where one could grow very wealthy from revenue farms and taxes. After 1762, the Bugis Yamtuan Muda appears to have taken over the position formerly occupied by the Bendahara. For the Bugis, it must have been impossible to tolerate control of Bugis traders by a Malay official. Despite Temenggong Abdul Jamal's marriage to Raja Maimunah, he was not considered close enough to the Bugis to gain approval for his governance of the port. It is probable that he never exercised such powers under Daing Kemboja. However, this should not rule out the possibility that he *aspired* to such a function.

Bugis power was based on the large numbers of Bugis traders and warriors that the new officials had drawn to Riau. As the official directly in charge of foreigners, these Bugis traders should have been forced to deal with the Temenggong. However, since 1722 when the Bugis were taken into the Johor kingdom as major chiefs, all traders from the Celebes were under the authority of the Riau Bugis and not the Malays.[39] The management of the Celebes trade appears to have been directed through the offices of a native Bugis chief.[40] He does not seem to have had any particular title, but the genealogies show marriage alliances between the Yang Di-Pertuan Mudas and certain Bugis chiefs. A daughter of Daing Chelak (the second Yamtuan Muda) married one Arong Lengga. A daughter of Raja Haji married Engkau Karaeng Talibak, a major figure at Riau until 1818. These individuals may have supplanted the Temenggongs as direct rulers of foreigners at the port of Riau in the eighteenth century. At least, it is likely that they were in charge of the native Bugis traders who frequented the port. Thus the functions of the Temenggong as ruler of the port, governor of foreigners, collector of taxes, and chief of police had been taken over by the Bugis and their allies. This event was especially unfortunate for the Temenggong's family since it came at a time when Riau began to regain prominence as an international trading centre.

In taking control of Riau, the Bugis were able to capitalize on the tradition of the maritime state which had dominated the Straits since Srivijaya. Their entrepot became an unprecedented success, partly through their own efforts and partly through luck. The *Tufhat*, after giving a glowing account of Riau's prosperity in about 1780, notes that very few Malays shared in it.[41] For the average Malay this meant severe economic hardship. The Temenggong's family and followers, in particular, would have suffered badly. The Malay-Bugis feud was more than a dynastic conflict — it was social and economic warfare. The *orang laut* were replaced by thousands of Bugis traders and warriors who flocked to Riau and made it their base. The *Tufhat* indicates that by 1780 the Malay and Bugis populations of Riau were practically equal in size.[42] Not only were the Malays and *orang laut* unwanted — they were unnecessary.

The growth of Bugis Riau was largely an economic phenomenon. A complex of new trading patterns grew up around the port in the latter part of the eighteenth century. The basic features of these new patterns involved a gradual trend towards an increased demand for two products of the archipelago: tin and pepper. The age when spices and forest produce were the major products sought by foreigners had passed.[43] In addition to Bugis, Chinese, and Dutch trade, increasing numbers of other foreign traders were coming into the region. Most important among these were the English. These groups were drawn to Riau — first, because it occupied an ideal position in the Straits of Malacca; second, because it enjoyed a reputation as a trading centre, inherited from Johor; third, because it was a favourable alternative to Dutch Malacca; and finally, because of the good management of the trade by the Bugis rulers themselves.

In the years before 1760, the Yang Di-Pertuan Mudas had already made significant innovations which reinforced the economic position of the Bugis at Riau. In the tradition of former entrepot states, they recreated the tight, centralized polity that had characterized Malacca and old Johor. Wealth came from the trade and from the foreigners who brought it. It was necessary to establish a stable economy and maintain regular exchange patterns with foreign traders.

Another important facet of the Bugis resuscitation of the Johor economy was the expanded role the Chinese now began to play. Chinese trading activities had, since the Sung times, been a regular feature of the commerce of Southeast Asia. This trade began to expand greatly during the early years of the eighteenth century. There were major Chinese commercial settlements at Batavia, other places in Java, Malacca, and in Siam. Around the 1730s, a new type of Chinese activity began in the Nanyang. This was of great significance for Riau. Chinese miners and agriculturists began coming to work and settle in certain parts of the region.

The earliest notice of Chinese settlements of this type were those of the gold miners at Pontianak in Western Borneo in the early eighteenth century.[44] In 1732, some miners from Borneo and more from China opened the tin mines of Bangka.[45] In 1734–40, due to the decision of Daing Chelak, the second Bugis Yamtuan Muda of Riau, Chinese coolies were brought in to open up gambier plantations on Bentan, the island on which Riau was located.[46] By the 1780s, there were Chinese pepper growers settled at Brunei,[47] tin miners in Kelantan,[48] and tin smelters in Phuket.[49] These coolies brought an improved technology and helped alleviate the severe manpower shortages faced by many Southeast Asian political leaders. As G. William Skinner has noted, the same things were happening in Siam.[50]

Through their own trading connections, together with those of the Chinese traders and the labour of the coolies, the Bugis leaders of Riau were able to build a prosperous and thriving entrepot. Gambier cultivation was of particular importance in assuring the prosperity and security of the port.

A major concern of all previous entrepot-states in the Straits had been the food supply. These trading centres drew large numbers of people together, sometimes as many as 100,000. Ships needed food supplies as well. Yet, there were no good rice-lands in the immediate vicinity of the Straits of Malacca which could have been put under direct political control from the entrepot. The Malay ports had always found it necessary to depend on Java and Siam as major sources of food. Lewis reports that "a thriving trade had also developed between Riau and the ports of Java, which supplied foodstuffs to the Johore ports, probably in return for cloth and opium."[51]

The *Tufhat* indicates that a major exchange commodity for Javanese rice was gambier: "Then for several years everyone was happy. The country was prosperous, food was cheap and everyone traded with great profit. For instance, gambier was priced at two *jaktun* at Riau and was sold for eight and sometimes ten *jaktun* in Java. And Javanese rice was only three Bengal rupees a pikul."[52] Until the 1830s, Java was the major market for Riau's gambier. The *Tufhat* notes that "ships came from Java and Celebes and they traded the produce of Java for the gambier."[53] Gambier, however, did not just go to Java. It seems that most of it went first to Java and then to China, which explains to some extent the role of the Chinese in its cultivation.

At some time early in the eighteenth century, the Chinese evidently began to use gambier as a tanning agent on a significant scale. The first definite word comes from Milburne in 1813. He noted that gambier was being purchased in Batavia by the Chinese "along with hides, in the tanning of which it was destined to aid".[54] The *Tufhat* hints that it was being so used as early as 1784, when it notes that there were Chinese coolies in the jungles gathering hides.[55]

Gambier production had been a traditional Malay occupation and, in the mid-seventeenth century, was established in Sumatra, the west coast of the Malay Peninsula, and in west Java. The gambier "lozenges" which the Malays produced were an item of trade at that time. Gambier's astringent properties made it useful as a medication and it was also chewed as a component of the betel quid.[56]

The establishment of the cultivation at Riau by Daing Chelak marked two important innovations in the traditional production and use of gambier. The first was in the use of Chinese coolies to cultivate the crop and to extract the commercial gambier. This appears to be among the earliest recorded instances of a settlement of Chinese agriculturalists in the Malay world. The second innovation was the joint cultivation of pepper. Ultimately, it was gambier's leather-tanning property that made it important to the West; however, this did not occur until 1835.

Since the Dutch do not appear to have been very interested in gambier during the eighteenth century, there is little mention of these developments in the Dutch sources for this period but, to date, an exhaustive study of these records has yet to be conducted. What we know of it comes from the *Tufhat* and other odd comments in contemporary European sources, mostly from later dates. These show, however, that the gambier trade was obviously of great importance to the Bugis rulers of Riau. The profits contributed substantially to the prosperity of the Riau entrepot in the mid-eighteenth century.

By 1784, gambier cultivation and trade had become an important part of the indigenous economy of Riau. In fact, it appears that gambier was the only crop that Riau ever produced. More importantly, the cultivation and trade were significant because they facilitated the relatively permanent settlement of large numbers of Chinese coolies in the Malay world. In 1784, there may have been as many as 10,000 Chinese settled on Bentan Island.[57]

The Bugis, by opening gambier plantations at Riau, had created an item which was always certain of a market in Java and Siam.[58] Together with hides, gambier assumed an important place in the new exchange pattern. Riau produced gambier which was traded for Javanese or Siamese rice by Bugis or Chinese traders. Merchants in these countries then sold hides and gambier in exchange for Chinese products such as porcelains, silk, and tea.

Viewed in this light, the gambier cultivation at Riau was a significant part of the Bugis power structure. It assured the port of a food supply, yet one which was under the control of the Bugis. It brought wealth to both Malays and Bugis, partly from the trade, partly from the plantations (some of which were Malay-owned), and finally from the fact that a stable food supply ensured a successful entrepot. In addition, the agriculture and commerce brought allies for the Bugis *peranakan* at Riau — these were the Bugis *jati* and the Chinese. The cultivation was a tool or lever which the Bugis used in their struggle for dominance within the maritime polity.

The development of this new pattern of commercial agriculture, despite the rather limited objectives of the Bugis, had wide repercussions for the maritime state. From this time until the beginning of the twentieth century, it remained the major prop of Riau's economy. It would also be of even greater importance to Singapore and the new Malay state of Johor in the nineteenth century.

Thus with the defeat of the Malays and the success of gambier, Bugis domination of the state was secure by 1762. At this time another element entered the picture. In the 1760s, British country traders began to enter the archipelago with cargoes of what rapidly became the most sought-after item in the Asian trade — opium. These traders made the third and perhaps most important addition to the complex of economic forces that were gathering around Riau, the other two being those represented by the Bugis and the Chinese.

The opium traffic quickly became the mainstay of Riau's international as well as local commerce. The *Tufhat* mentions ships carrying opium from Bengal as early as 1740.[59] By the 1760s, it was so well-established that Daing Kemboja obtained half the cargo of a British opium ship on credit in order to pay the Dutch indemnities demanded for the Linggi wars.[60] The proceeds from that sale amounted to $77,754.[61]

It is revealing to note the speed with which this trading pattern developed. According to Diane Lewis' findings in the Dutch archives, "in the first half of the century, no more than ten private English merchant vessels had ever called at Malacca in any one year; in 1769 the number had increased to twenty-six. Ten years later it had more than doubled again. Many of these European vessels were known to visit Riau."[62]

An important repercussion of the expanded country trade was that it brought a new group of Europeans to the archipelago. These men were the forerunners of British expansion in the Malay world. Not only were their cargoes of opium extremely valuable — opium was worth its weight in gold at this time — but they brought a weapons technology which rivalled that of the Dutch. Through the British, the Malays and Bugis were able to purchase arms in order to continue their wars against each other and the Dutch. In addition, the Bugis were producing some of their own armaments, including gunpowder and bullets, at Riau with the aid of Chinese and Indian or Arabian craftsmen.[63]

The Dutch had reason to be worried about the military threat posed by the Bugis. The Malacca authorities were involved in the politics of the Malay states of the Peninsula, particularly Perak, where they had a vital interest in the tin. One Dutch source reports that the Bugis had gained a virtual monopoly over the tin trade in the Straits.[64] In addition, the Bugis had already fought the Dutch to a standstill when they laid siege to Malacca in 1757.[65]

Naturally, the Dutch were very concerned about the commerce in arms and opium. They were running rival entrepots in Java and at Malacca and had been the dominant European power in the Straits for almost a century. Since 1760, they had monopoly treaties with many of the Malay and Bugis states in the region covering the sale of tin, pepper, and spices. Riau was one of these. Lewis notes that "though the terms of the 1757 treaty stipulated that no foreign Europeans should be allowed to come to trade in the ports of Johore, Riau soon became a favourite port of call for many of the English private merchants who now began to trade regularly between India and China."[66]

Writing in 1785, the Dutch governor of Malacca, P. G. de Bruijn, described with envy the flourishing trade which favoured Riau under the Bugis.[67] This commerce involved in part the exchange of four basic commodities: opium, piece goods, tin, and pepper. Opium, which he considered the mainstay of the trade,[68] was brought by English and Portuguese country traders to Riau.[69] They also brought piece goods from Bengal, Coromandel, and Surat. These textiles had been a major item of the India–Southeast Asia trade for centuries. The opium traffic, however, had quite recently become of much greater significance. Especially since the 1760s, it had increased considerably in volume.

From the east came Chinese junks, bringing tea, ceramics, and silk. At Riau, they exchanged these goods for Indian opium and piece goods as well as for the tin and pepper of the archipelago. De Bruijn noted that most of the tin sold at Riau came from Palembang and Bangka. In addition, some of the tin was "smuggled" from the tin and pepper producing states on both sides of the Malacca Straits and Borneo.[70]

The trade at Riau was brisk and this added to the profits. De Bruijn noted that between 20,000 and 30,000 pikuls of tin were imported to Riau annually. Tin arriving before August was carried away by foreign European ships sailing via the Straits [to China on the southwest monsoon] or by Chinese junks which visited Riouw; that which arrived after then was bought up by the English and Portuguese returning from China and making for India. Consequently the tin seldom lay longer than six months at Riouw."[71]

De Bruijn's account of the Riau trade is both confirmed and supplemented by the *Tufhat Al-Nafis*: "… the trade of Riau became great. Many *perahu* came from afar and ships large and small came from Bengal by the scores carrying the trade goods of Bengal. From China came red and green junks, also by the score. Ships also came from Siam bringing rice and other things and *perahu* came from Celebes and Java."[72]

The author of the *Tufhat* points to the quantity of foodstuffs and everyday necessities as indices of Riau's prosperity. Such items as rice, sugar, and cloth were not only readily available at Riau but were also very cheap.[73] He also lists the names of many different kinds of vessels as some indication of the cosmopolitan character of the port. These ships, it is said, were "strung like fish on a line at Sungai Riau from the river mouth to far up-stream".[74] De Bruijn was such an admirer of Riau's trading system that he wished to copy it at Malacca.

In his report to Java he stated that the Siamese, Malays, and Acehnese who frequented Riau could be drawn to trade at Malacca if they could easily buy tin, pepper, opium, and piece goods there. He also requested that an unlimited number of Chinese junks be permitted to trade at Malacca. If this were done, then great profits would accrue to Malacca.[75] The Batavian officials, however, were much more concerned about the prosperity of Batavia and could see no benefits from Malaccan prosperity; thus his recommendations fell on deaf ears.

In her recent study of the country trade, Lewis remarks on the ease with which trade was conducted at Riau. Duties were low, trade was brisk, and the wide-ranging Bugis traders provided Riau with a selection of goods available at no other entrepot in the region. For these reasons, it is easy to see why Riau became the centre of the country trade in the archipelago.[76] The Bugis had thus duplicated the pattern of successful Malayan entrepots of the past. Like Srivijaya, Malacca, and old Johor, they had made Riau the principal meeting-place of the commerce of China, the west, and the Malayan Archipelago.

In about 1780, Riau stood on the brink of achieving great political power in the Malay world. The empire of Johor had been fragmented for almost sixty years. Raja Haji now began to put it back together again. He is one of the great heroes of the *Tufhat*. Since about 1760, he had been sailing around the Malay world, fighting wars and generally exercising his influence militarily.[77]

He fought for the rulers of Jambi and Indragiri and married their daughters; he intimidated the Sultans of Palembang and Perak. He and Daing Kemboja defeated Siak. He forced Sultan Mahmud of Perak to give a daughter to his brother, the ruler of Selangor, in marriage. He fought for, and installed, the ruler of Pontianak as Sultan. Although he would have been considered a Bugis upstart by many Malay rulers, he was beginning to make an impact. A measure of his power was the Dutch fear of him. If he could have gained Siak and Trengganu as allies, Raja Haji could have wiped out Dutch Malacca altogether.

The Dutch were aware of this, however, and abandoned their traditional policy towards Johor. As described by retiring Governor Thomas Schippers in 1773, this policy was two-pronged. The first "prong" was to prevent the combination of "pirate" bands. The second was to maintain neutrality in the conflicts between Siak, Riau, and Trengganu.[78] Raja Haji appears to have combined the "pirate" bands. The Dutch grew fearful of a repeated Bugis attack on Malacca, and so they invaded Riau in 1784. They very nearly lost. The siege of Riau lasted about three months and failed. The Dutch then lifted the siege and returned to Malacca only to find themselves under attack by both Selangor and Riau. The Dutch national fleet from Holland was needed to break the Bugis blockade.[79] They then killed Raja Haji and drove the Bugis out of Riau.

One of the reasons for this diversion into the history of Riau under the Bugis is to show how galling the situation must have been to the Malays and *orang laut* of Riau and Johor. Their state was again rising to pre-eminence, but they themselves were losing power. When Riau fell, the reverberations were felt throughout the archipelago. Pirates and marauding bands began roving the seas, and the Malays of Riau rose up with a vengeance to reclaim their state.

Another reason is to note the structure of economic patterns that Riau brought together. However, with the Bugis gone, the trading patterns also fell apart. The trends which had sustained the pre-1784 commerce were blocked by a number of events in the archipelago which included the Bugis defeat, the upsurge of piracy, and the resurgence of Siak and Trengganu. Unrelated to these but also having an impact were such occurrences as the Napoleonic Wars and the Thai-Burmese wars. Thus, the attempted Malay resurgence at Riau, which marked the period 1784–1815, came at a time of general disorder throughout the world. This meant a decline in trade. Malay prosperity was hindered by generally poor international conditions as well as local warfare. Economic prosperity only returned after 1815, when favourable trends resumed again in the Straits of Malacca. However, the Malays of Riau did not profit from this. These trading patterns were ultimately drawn together at Singapore, under the British. And once again the Malays and *orang laut* of the region found themselves left out.

The situation of the Malays at Riau and Johor had a direct bearing on the foundation of Singapore and the manner in which this event was seen by the Malays. Engku Muda, the son of Temenggong Abdul Jamal, grew to middle age at Riau between 1762 and 1784. He must have been about forty years old when the Dutch fleet drove the Bugis out. The family's status had probably been slipping. What status he had probably came through his mother, Raja Maimunah. Winstedt notes that Engku Muda's two brothers generally used the Bugis title "Daing".[80] Through this connection, he may at least have been able to maintain a certain status and wealth. Perhaps he was one of the Malay chiefs who went into gambier planting.[81] Whatever the case, he appears to have had little in the way of official status. In 1784, he suddenly found himself in a position to reclaim power and office. Three years later, in 1787, he proclaimed himself "Sultan of Riau".[82]

The events that led to his rise began with the Bugis departure in 1784. Sultan Mahmud III (then about twenty-three years old) found himself surrounded by the new leaders of the Malay faction: the Bendahara (Tun Koris), the "Temenggong" (Engku Muda, or Daing Kechil), Raja Indera Bungsu, and Raja Tua Enche Andak.[83] The five of them signed a treaty with the Dutch in 1784. In 1787, they were forced to sign a new treaty which placed even more restrictions on them. Dissatisfied with the treaties, the Malay chiefs invited a group of Illanun sea rovers from Tempasuk in Northern Borneo to drive out the Dutch. The raid was successful but the Malays realized that the Dutch would return; so they all left, except for Engku Muda.[84]

Just how much time he spent at Riau is uncertain. The times were troubled. The political structure had entirely broken down. The forces of Malays and Bugis who had fought the Dutch under Raja Haji were scattered throughout the archipelago, making a living from piracy which was the only way they knew. The Illanuns did not go home but stayed in the Riau-Lingga Archipelago to continue raiding.[85] A prince from Siak, Sayed Ali, organized a fleet and roamed the archipelago for three or four years, staging raids from Kedah to Singgora.[86] The Yang Di-Pertuan Muda, Raja Ali, was in Siantan. The Sultan went to Trengganu.[87] Engku Muda took the opportunity to rebuild his own power. He seems to have become a formidable power in the region between 1787 and 1795. In the latter year, Sultan Mahmud returned and gave Engku Muda control of Riau.

He was so strong that it took almost ten years for Raja Ali, the new Bugis Yamtuan Muda, to dislodge him and allow the Bugis to reoccupy Riau. Between 1795 and 1805, Engku Muda was a dominant force at Riau. The whole Malay-Bugis feud erupted again around this new pair of antagonists.[88]

With the English in power at Malacca, the Malays no doubt expected a return to prosperity.[89] However, the feud dragged on. Engku Muda was extremely reluctant to allow himself to be pushed out as his father had been. He dug in his heels and hung on, either at Riau or Bulang, until about 1804. After that time he simply retired to Bulang and seems to have held his following intact. He accepted a peace with the Sultan but refused the title of Temenggong and insisted on that of Raja Muda. But he allowed his nephew, Abdul Rahman, to accept the title of Temenggong from Sultan Mahmud in about 1806.

Engku Muda's own words, as quoted by Winstedt from the *Hikayat Kerajaʾan*, an unpublished Johor manuscript, perhaps best show his attitude and feelings. These set the family's stance for the next century.

> But Engku Muda had the rank of Temenggong and governed Riau and Johore, refusing however the title of Temenggong. "If I can't be Raja Muda, I don't want a title. But all the islands and islets and Johore are under me and certainly Pahang belongs to my 'father', Dato' Bendahara Abdu'l-Majid: for today the Sultan no longer heeds Malays but lives at Lingga and gives Riau to the Raja Muda. Look at our case. We ought to own the country because we are co-inheritors with the Sultan. Why should he do as he likes? Like him we are descended From Sultan Abdu'l-Jalil and custom ordains we rule the country and how can he stop us? Although I am not installed, who shall object to my rule? If Engku Abdu'r-Rahman wants to be called Temenggong, let him seek audience at Lingga. I won't. If I die, you, Engku, will rule the islands and never lose Johore because to my mind if the Sultan behaves like this we've got to look after ourselves or be worsted."[90]

Engku Abdul Rahman did take the title of Temenggong and shortly thereafter succeeded Engku Muda as the ruler of the island peoples. As we can see from Engku Muda's words, the status of the Sultanate was at a low level. The office had been undergoing pressures of an unprecedented magnitude since 1784. Driven from Riau, Sultan Mahmud III had made a valiant effort to gather the Malay and Bugis forces for a stand against the Europeans. The attack never materialized. After 1795, the Sultan returned to Lingga and began to try to get the entrepot at Riau started again. Prosperity, however, did not return. The Malays and Bugis did, and they spent much of their effort fighting one another.

Another significant repercussion of the catastrophic events of 1784–87 was the change which now took place in the status of the Chinese. Prior to the fall of Riau, possibly as many as 10,000 Chinese had settled there to grow pepper and gambier on plantations owned by the Malays and Bugis. When they deserted Riau, the Chinese remained. "All of the rajas, the important men and the masses of the people had scattered each in his own direction and there was no one left at Riau except for the Chinese who were in the jungle getting hides for the Malays and Bugis who had gambier plantations. There were also many Chinese who had been their coolies and such from the beginning. Because there were many Chinese who had come, they stayed and did not flee."

The returning Dutch, under Admiral Jakob Van Braam, were confronted by a delegation of Chinese who asked for support from the Dutch now that the Malays and Bugis had gone: "All of the dark-skinned people will become pirates. We Chinese cannot live here at Riau any longer. What will we eat? We cannot go to sea now for fear of the pirates. In Riau, all of our food comes from outside."[91]

Van Braam ordered one Dutchman to remain at Riau as Resident and commanded the Chinese to return to work on the plantations which the Malays had deserted. He also promised to send Javanese ships to Riau with rice to trade for gambier.

As far as the available evidence shows, the Chinese did in fact remain at Riau. They were still there in 1818 when the Dutch returned to take possession of the island once again. In the intervening years, they became largely autonomous and militarily self-sufficient.[92] The lone Dutch Resident certainly could not have exercised much influence over their internal affairs, and even he left in 1795 when the British took over the Dutch possessions in the Straits. Engku Muda, from his base at Bulang, could not have exerted anything but a sporadic type of control over Chinese affairs. The result was that the Chinese appear to have developed their own institutions of political and economic control. For them this was a period of virtual independence.

The unsettled conditions of the time affected the entire Malay Archipelago. The American naturalist, Thomas Horsfield, who accompanied Raffles to Java in 1810, has left a detailed report of the manner in which the Chinese tin miners of Bangka reacted to the situation.[93] They relocated their settlements and constructed stockades for their own defence against the Illanun and *orang laut* pirates. Although production certainly dropped, the settlements managed to establish supply lines with the outside and survived. Something very similar appears to have happened at Riau during these years.

In terms of Malay history this development was of crucial importance. Not only did the Chinese now come to represent yet another autonomous force putting additional strain on the already enfeebled Malay polity but they had developed institutions which made it possible for them to operate with virtual independence on a permanent basis. It is against this background that the subsequent aggressiveness and prosperity which the Chinese displayed at Singapore and in Malaya in the nineteenth century must be understood.

This appears to have been the germinal period for the peculiar variety of Chinese secret societies which later became of such great significance in the

Malay world. In addition, so far as Riau and Johor are concerned it was during these years that the foundations of the Kangchu system were laid down. P. J. Begbie's description of the gambier cultivation at Riau, which is based on Dutch sources dating from 1818 to 1825, shows that it had become a purely Chinese enterprise.[94] In 1825, there were over 13,000 Chinese settled on five different rivers on Bentan Island. They were grouped in settlements ranging from a few houses to over 1,000 people. In the larger villages revenue "farms" were maintained. These included monopolies for the sale of opium, spirits, and pork and for gambling and pawn-broking. Another important item is that the Chinese terms *kang* and *chukang* were already being used to refer to the river-mouth settlements where the farms were located.[95] Begbie himself never uses the term Kangchu, but it is possible that the Chinese themselves were already using the term to refer to the headmen of these settlements.

At this time, the *chukang* appears to have been the lowest level in the hierarchy of a purely Chinese power structure that centred on the town of Riau. At the top, and located in Tanjong Pinang or across the harbour at Senggarang, were the two *Kapitans China* of Riau. There were two communities of Chinese there, the Hokkien, often called "Amoy" in contemporary sources, and the Teochew, often styled "Canton".[96] At some periods each *kampong*, as their port settlements were called, had its own Kapitan; at other times one Kapitan governed all Chinese. It seems likely that all of the pepper and gambier cultivators were under the Kapitan of the Teochew community.[97]

Netscher has described a hierarchy of "military" officials under the Kapitan Tan Hoo in 1818. This included two "military commanders" called *toeahania*. Presumably there was one for each community. Then, over each district were two lesser officials styled *abooi* and *toeabak*. The district officials were appointed by the Kapitan, while the Kapitan and the *toeahania* were appointed by the Yamtuan Muda. At this time it seems that all except the Kapitan received a salary.[98] It is interesting that Netscher makes no mention of Kangchu, thus leaving open the question as to whether or not the term was in use at this time. It may be that Kangchu was an alternative term for the *abooi* or *toeabak* or, perhaps, the Kangchu was not a part of this hierarchy. Whatever the case, we should also assume that the secret societies were an integral part of this power structure and that the main focus of the system would have been the control and protection of the revenue farms which were held under the Kapitan.

The significant point of this discussion is that the independence and economic unity which the Chinese had now achieved made it possible for them to deal with the Malay chiefs on an individual basis. The high degree of factionalism at Riau between 1800 and 1820 indicates that no single Malay chief governed the market-place as had been the case in the pre-1784 period. Thus we note that Temenggong Abdul Rahman, the successor of Engku Muda, had settled groups of his own Chinese at Singapore by 1818.[99] The *Tufhat* mentions at least one dispute between rival chiefs at Riau which arose because of the Chinese.[100] It is also noteworthy that for the post-1800 period the *Tufhat* makes hardly any mention of either the Chinese or the gambier cultivation (which persisted and flourished throughout the nineteenth century). This is in contrast to numerous references for the pre-1784 period. This rather conspicuous silence may be taken to indicate that the Malay and Bugis rulers of Riau had lost control of the cultivation, the Chinese, and, to a large extent, the market-place itself. It is not impossible that the Chinese themselves represented a more cohesive unit than did the Johor/Riau government. This must certainly have been true in the economic area. There was probably an interlocking system of debts and financial arrangements among the Chinese of Riau and Malacca that cut across Malay political boundaries. This was also reinforced by a parallel system of secret society relationships.

It was because of this foothold which the gambier planters and merchants had established at Riau in the 1787–1818 period that they were able to move with such speed when Raffles founded his settlement at Singapore in 1819. In the later years of the century, these developments would be of crucial importance in the foundation of the new Malay state of Johor.

There were also external reasons for the domestic strife and the lack of prosperity that characterized Riau between 1795 and 1819. By 1795, there were two English settlements in the Straits of Malacca. Penang had been founded in 1786 and Malacca had been taken over in 1795. These events had knocked away one of the props of Riau's formerly advantageous economic position. Riau no longer held a virtual monopoly on the British trade in the region. No Malay entrepot could successfully compete with two British centres, no matter how favourable its location. This had serious consequences for the Sultanate.

Between 1760 and 1784, Riau had been important to the British as a major distribution point in the archipelago for their opium. It was also a collection point for tin and pepper. The country traders frequented Riau in order to avoid the Dutch and their taxes. For the English, eighteenth-century Riau was almost a free port.[101] There was a need for such a place as Riau so long as the Dutch held Malacca.

The fall of Riau in 1784 left a gap that was partly filled by the founding of a settlement at Penang in 1786. After 1795, the need for a native port such as Riau — so far as the country traders were concerned — had been filled. The British East India Company held both Penang and Malacca. In fact, the country traders themselves now began to disappear or, rather, they began to transform themselves and establish offices in these settlements.

Not only did the British no longer need a Malay or Bugis entrepot — their whole style of trade began to change. With both native and Chinese trade gravitating to the British ports, there was less need for the individual English trader to frequent all the smaller archipelago ports. The British, like the Chinese, were no longer mere passers-by but had also become permanent residents. This circumstance made a crucial difference. One reason for Riau's lack of commercial success after the Dutch were driven out in 1795 must have been the mere presence of the British settlements. These became the major supply centres for the opium trade in the archipelago.

Riau was still in a favourable position for native trade. Given domestic peace, it might have managed to draw a substantial number of native and Chinese traders. But even under the best circumstances, it would still have been economically dependent on the British settlements. They were the source of Riau's supply of opium. The best that any chief could have hoped would have been for guaranteed consignments of opium, at slightly reduced prices, from European or Chinese merchants at Malacca.[102] However, the Malay rulers would have had to stop forcing native trade into their ports. If they continued this practice they would have been considered pirates. In effect this meant that the Malay chiefs would have been forced to halt their traditional exercise of political power. The poverty of Riau at this time no doubt aggravated the conflict between Engku Muda and Raja Ali. British political involvement may have contributed to the unsettled state of affairs as well. The conflict at Riau drew the attention of most of the other Malay states in the region. Between 1795 and 1806, while Sultan Mahmud tried to make peace between Engku Muda and Raja Ali, chiefs from Selangor, Siak, and Pahang travelled to Riau to aid or interfere with his efforts.[103] The British were involved as well.[104] No one was totally disinterested.

In 1805 there was a period of calm, or so it seems.[105] In that year Raja Ali, the Yang Di-Pertuan Muda, died. His chief antagonist, Engku Muda, died the following year. The former was succeeded by Raja Ja'afar, a son of Raja Haji, and Temenggong Abdul Rahman took over from Engku Muda at Bulang.[106] The factions continued intact, but the fighting seems to have stopped and some prosperity may have returned. This was perhaps because the British were favourably disposed towards Raja Ja'afar.[107] Also, Sultan Mahmud was in a stronger position with these younger men. The period of calm ended, however, in 1812 when Sultan Mahmud died. He left two sons — Abdul Rahman was the younger and less forceful individual; the older was Hussain, or Tengku Long. He had married Enche Puan Bulang, a daughter of Engku Muda, and enjoyed the support of the Temenggong. In 1812, when his father died, he was in Pahang marrying the Bendahara's daughter, thus forging another alliance.[108] Raja Ja'afar took advantage of his absence to appoint Abdul Rahman as Sultan. This was naturally opposed by the Temenggong, the Bendahara, and Hussain, who were supported by another of Mahmud's wives, Tengku Putri, who held the regalia.

The Bugis, however, were also fighting among themselves. A quarrel developed between Engkau Karaeng Talibak, the wealthy and influential Bugis merchant, and Raja Idris, a brother of the Yang Di-Pertuan Muda Raja Ja'afar.[109] Thus rivalry was rife.

In 1818, the Dutch resumed control of Malacca as a result of arrangements made at the end of the Napoleonic Wars. They sent Adrian Koek, a long-time Dutch merchant from Malacca, to negotiate a treaty at Riau. When he arrived there, the various power-holders had reached an armed stand-off. The *Tufhat* quotes Koek's letter to Raja Ja'afar:

> ... all of the other (chiefs) hold power equal to yours. With yourself there are two or three equal powers in the state and each is a rule unto himself. You have one rule; Engkau Karaeng has one rule; the Temenggong has another which has kept the government in confusion for some time already. Your brother Raja Idris has one rule; and Tengku Long has yet another. Finally they have fallen to fighting and quarrelling such as the dispute between Engkau Karaeng and your brother. Does all this not bring you great loss? Therefore, the Dutch Company wants to aid you in all of these things, wherever correct. And if there remain any deputies, they will be your slaves; and neither the glory of your name, nor the revenues of your government will be lost.[110]

Charmed by these "sweet words", Raja Ja'afar allowed the Dutch to reoccupy Riau. They gave him the promise of military support with which he could overcome his enemies. This was a blow to the Temenggong who then retired to Singapore.[111] For British commerce the future was equally obscure. The situation of 1786–95 had been restored to a certain extent. The Dutch now controlled Malacca and the entrance to the Straits at Riau. Penang was cut off from much of the valuable trade of the archipelago. Farquhar and Raffles had already begun looking around for an alternative British settlement before Malacca was returned to the Dutch.[112] It was for this purpose that Farquhar had made a Treaty of Commercial Alliance with Raja Ja'afar[113] in 1818 just a few months before the Dutch arrived. The British may also have made some kind of arrangement with the Temenggong even before the Dutch came back to Riau.[114] In any case, the Temenggong was their most logical choice for an ally after 1818. In January 1819, Raffles and Farquhar met him at Singapore and signed their first treaty.

The scene of our story now shifts to Singapore, and we must consider the question of relations between the Malays and British. Riau, now under the Dutch, continued as a port and a seat of Malay power, but from 1819 it had a very strong rival at Singapore and was quickly outstripped. Singapore took over all the functions that Riau had once performed. It was a centre for the Indian opium traffic, and it drew the native and Chinese trade. It also became the centre for the gambier trade. There was no need for a Malay entrepot in the Straits. With the entrepot in foreign hands, the ecological niche that the Sultanate had once occupied was destroyed.

The entrepot had traditionally been the major source of financial support for the Sultanate. Even though the Bugis Yang Di-Pertuan Mudas had controlled the entrepot in the eighteenth century, they still needed the Sultan; so they supported him. He was given a palace and was symbolically elevated to give legitimacy and status to the state.[115] The Bugis may have exploited the Sultanate, but they also preserved it.

Sultan Mahmud may have had little in the way of military power after 1784, but he had strength of character. The *Tufhat* gives a sympathetic picture of him as an able statesman working against insurmountable odds.[116] His failure was not for want of skill and courage but rather from his lack of money and guns. Munshi Abdullah also attests to the good qualities of Mahmud as a ruler.[117] He had, unfortunately, lost the respect of the Europeans. The Dutch saw him as an outlaw, and the English as only a petty and ineffectual chief. But if he had lived until 1819, our story might well have been very different. He could possibly have played off Raja Ja'afar against the Temenggong on the one side and the British against the Dutch on the other. His death, however, left no ruler with an unquestioned claim to legitimacy at a time when Europeans were restoring and expanding their economic position in the archipelago.

In occupying Singapore with the co-operation of the Temenggong and Hussain, the British founded a new entrepot on the doorstep of Riau. As the major economic force (the wealthiest), they also dominated the political situation. Their installation of the ousted Tengku Long as Sultan Hussain of Singapore was their first step towards active involvement in Malay politics.

From this time on, Europeans became the primary source of legitimacy in the Malay political system. A conscious awareness of this reality of life was one of the greatest advantages the Temenggongs of Johor would have during the nineteenth century. They did not readily realize this. Rather, they had to suffer additional set-backs in their relations with Singapore before they began to make any gains. Their experiences with the Bugis at Riau in the eighteenth century may have taught the family the art of perseverance in the face of adversity. The British would reinforce these lessons.

NOTES

1. The capital of the Johor kingdom was moved about twenty times between 1512 and 1682, generally because of Portuguese or Achehnese attacks or because of the installation of a new ruler. From 1513 to 1526, it was at Bentan (Riau). From 1526 to 1618, it was at various sites on the Johor River. In 1618, it was moved to Lingga and then to Tambelan. From 1637 to 1673, it was again located at various places on the Johor River, generally Batu Sawar. It was again at Riau in 1673–85. It was back on the Johor River at Kota Tinggi from 1688 to 1700. From 1722 to 1819, it was at Riau.
2. Richard O. Winstedt, *A History of Malaya* (Singapore, 1935). First published as *JMBRAS*, v. 13 (1935), pp. 1–270. All references are to the first edition.
3. R. O. Winstedt, "A History of Johor 1365–1895 A.D.", *JMBRAS*, v. 10, pt. 3 (December 1932), pp. 1–167, with appendices. His treatment of post-1819 Johor is contained in Chapters 10, 11, and 12 of this work (pp. 86–120).
4. Riau (also Rhio, Riow, Riouw, Rio, etc.) refers to the seat of the Johor empire during the eighteenth century. It was located near the present site of Tanjong Pinang, but during our period there were also establishments (i.e., markets, fortresses, palaces, etc.) at Sungai Riau, Pulau Biram Dewa, Pulau Bayan, Pulau Penyengat, and Sungai Galang Besar. All these places are in the vicinity of Tanjong Pinang in the western part of the Bay of Bentan.

   Bentan is the largest island in the Riau-Lingga Archipelago and occasionally it is referred to simply as Riau. The term Riau is also sometimes used to refer to the entire Riau Archipelago.

   In this study, Riau will refer only to the Port and the island of Bentan itself. Otherwise the term Riau Archipelago or Riau-Lingga Archipelago will be used to indicate the entire island group.
5. Winstedt, "A History of Malaya", Appendix.
6. Winstedt, "The Bendaharas and Temenggongs", *JMRRAS*, v. 10, pt. 1 (January 1932), p. 60. This genealogy indicates that these two offices were generally held by brothers of the ruler. For example, two brothers of Sultan Abdul Jalil (d. 1719) are known to have held both offices. Likewise, Tun Abbas, Tun Hussain, and Tun Tahir, all of whom were brothers of Sultan Sulaiman (r. 1723–59), held both offices. Finally, the elder brother of Temenggong Abdul Jamal, Bendahara Abdul Majid (d. *c.* 1802), had previously been Temenggong.
7. Ibid., p. 58.
8. Ibid., pp. 60, 66.
9. Ibid., pp. 63–66.
10. Ibid., p. 64. Winstedt reports that Engku Muda in 1801 styled himself "Raja of Bulang and Bintang [Bentan], ex-Sultan of Riau".
11. Munir bin Ali, ed., *Tufhat Al-Nafis*, Al-Marhum Raja Ali-Haji Riau, Romanized edition (Singapore, 1965), hereafter referred to as the *Tufhat*. This romanization is based on the *jawi* text published by Winstedt in *JMBRAS*, v. 10, pt. 2 (1932). According to Virginia Matheson "The Tufhat Al-Nafis: Structure and Sources",

Bijd, 127, v. 3 (1971), pp. 375–95, neither of these texts is without errors and omissions. The romanization is reported to be inaccurate in a number of passages. However, authoritative versions are not in print and are therefore useless to the average scholar, let alone the average reader. The romanized version is followed as the authority in this study simply as a matter of convenience in terms of reference and general availability. All passages and information quoted from this version have been checked against Winstedt's for accuracy, but the page references are to the romanized edition. There is now an authoritative English translation of this text: Ali Haji ibn Ahmad, Raja. *The Precious Gift (Tuhfat al-Nafis)*. Translated by Barbara Andaya and Virginia Matheson (Kuala Lumpur, Oxford University Press, 1982).

12. R. O. Winstedt, "A History of Johore 1673 – *c.* 1800 A.D.", *JMBRAS*, v. 10, pt. 1 (January 1932), pp. 164–70. This also includes the 31-page *jawi* transcription of the manuscript and Winstedt's summary of the manuscript. Matheson, in "The Tufhat Al-Nafis", identifies the *Hikayat Negeri Johor* as the "Siarah Selangor" referred to by the author of the *Tufhat Al-Nafis*.
13. Winstedt, in "The Bendaharas and Temenggongs", pp. 60–66, describes and quotes from this manuscript.
14. T. J. Newbold, *Political and Statistical Account of the British Settlements in the Straits of Malacca*, v. 2 (London, 1839), pp. 312–13.
15. O. W. Wolters, *The Fall of Srivijaya in Malay History* (London, 1970), pp. 11–12.
16. Paul Wheatley, *Impressions of the Malay Peninsula in Ancient Times* (Singapore, 1964), p. 163. Wheatley discusses the amount of arable land under the direct control of Malacca: "Despite the wealth and importance of Melaka, the immediate hinterland of the port appears to have been very little developed. At the time of Tome Pires' visit it was clothed with an almost uninterrupted mantle of forest, diversified only occasionally by an isolated *kampong*. Muar and Batu Pahat were small farming communities; Singapore was practically deserted ... Northwards the country was more closely settled. The *Sejarah Melayu* relates that an unbroken line of villages stretched from Kampong Kling, the Tamil quarter of Melaka, to the Linggi River, and there was no need for travellers journeying even as far as Jenggera to take firing with them, for wherever they stopped on the way there would be a settlement. Sungai Ujong, Klang, Perak, Selangor and Bernam, all under the direct rule of Melaka, were small coastal villages of from 200–400 persons."
17. R. O. Winstedt, *Malay–English Dictionary*, Fourth edition (1964), p. 189.
18. Winstedt, *A History of Malaya* (1962), p. 51.
19. M. A. P. Meilink-Roelofsz, *Asian Trade and European Influence in the Indonesian Archipelago Between 1500 and about 1630* (The Hague, 1962), p. 41.
20. *Sejarah Melayu* [Malay Annals], trans. C. C. Brown (1953). Reprint in Oxford in Asia Historical Reprints (Kuala Lumpur, 1970), p. 127. Original text, p. 160.
21. Winstedt, "The Bendaharas and Temenggongs", p. 57.
22. Leonard Y. Andaya, *The Kingdom of Johor 1641–1718* (Kuala Lumpur, 1975).

23. Leonard Y. Andaya, "Raja Kechil and the Minangkabau Conquest of Johor in 1718", *JMBRAS*, v. 45, pt. 2 (1972), pp. 59–60. Andaya notes that the Laksamana was thought to have been Raja Kechil's grandfather.
24. Andaya, *The Kingdom*, pp. 116–21. Continuing political disturbances in south-west Celebes in the late seventeenth and early eighteenth centuries made the presence of numerous roving bands of Bugis refugees a common phenomenon in the island world of Southeast Asia. Their settlements were to be found in Java, Borneo, Sumatra, and the Malay world of the Straits during this period. These adventurers formed a ready source of manpower for the rulers of the area, particularly as mercenaries.
25. Andaya, *The Kingdom*, p. 323.
26. Ibid., p. 312.
27. These genealogies are based on Winstedt's genealogical charts in "A History of Johor, 1365–1895 A.D.", *JMBRAS*, v. 10, pt. 3 (December 1932).
28. The leadership of the so-called Malay faction was held by Sultan Mansur (known as Yang Di-Pertuan Kechil) of Trengganu, also a descendent of Sultan Abdul Jalil, until about 1760. Siak princes, too, involved themselves in the conflicts between the Malay officials and the Bugis Yang Di-Pertuan Muda. However, the group of officials most immediately affected by the Bugis take-over appears to have been the Bendahara, the Temenggong, and the Raja Indera Bungsu.
29. No notice is given in the *Tufhat* of Temenggong Abdul Jamal's death nor is the appointment of his successor mentioned. This text does not mention any Temenggong at all for the years between 1762 and 1784.
30. There appears to have been a streak of insanity running through this family. According to Winstedt, in "A History of Johor", p. 60, Temenggong Tun Abbas went mad in 1736. The *Hikayat Johor Serta Pahang* (see note 35 below) reports that his son Abdul Jamal was also insane. In addition, one of Temenggong Abdul Rahman's sons, Abdullah, was reputedly an imbecile.
31. Raja Maimunah was apparently the only major Bugis princess to marry a Malay. (See Figures 3.3 and 3.4a.)
32. The *Tufhat*, p. 138.
33. Ibid.
34. Ibid., pp. 142–47.
35. R. O. Wintsedt, "Abdu'l Jalil, Sultan of Johore (1699–1719), 'Abdu'l-Jamal, Temenggong (*c.* 1750) and Raffles' Founding of Singapore", *JMBRAS*, v. 11, pt. 2 (December 1933), pp. 161–65, Winstedt here summarizes the text entitled *Hikayat Johor Serta Pahang*, although he does not give the title in this article. A romanized typescript of this manuscript is available in the Johor Archives and is on microfilm in the University of Singapore Library.
36. The *Tufhat*, pp. 10–11.
37. Winstedt, "A History of Johor", p. 12.
38. Buyong bin Adil, *Sejarah Johor* (Kuala Lumpur, 1971), p. 388. This follows the official genealogy of Johor, a copy of which is in the Johor Archives. Presumably

both are based on the one which Winstedt got from Kampong Glam which he titles "Kampong Glam Variant" (Winstedt, "A History of Johor", pt. 3, Preface). There is a copy of this on microfilm in the University of Singapore Library, and perhaps in the Johor Archives, but I never saw it there. Winstedt himself, rejects this version of events and states (ibid., pt. 3, pp. 64–65): "Daing Kechil (alias Tun Ibrahim) never was Temenggong, but Netscher agrees with the Johore authorities in saying (p. 243) that Engku Muda was the son of a Temenggong." The *Hikayat Negeri Johor* also confirms this (pp. 28–29).

39. Andaya, *The Kingdom*, p. 297.
40. It should be understood that there was a growing distinction between the Riau Bugis and more recent arrivals. As the founding generation died off, their children who had been born at Riau were known as *peranakan* or locally born. Natives of Celebes were known as Bugis *jati*.
41. The *Tufhat*, p. 189.
42. Ibid.
43. Two articles put forward the view that the rise of the Dutch in the archipelago created an increased demand for tin and pepper. Graham W. Irwin, "The Dutch and the Tin Trade of Malaya in the Seventeenth Century", in *Studies in the Social History of China and South East Asia*, ed. Jerome Ch'en and Nicholas Tarling (Cambridge, 1970), pp. 267–88; and John Bastin, "The Changing Balance of the Southeast Asian Pepper Trade", *Essays on Indonesian and Malayan History* (Singapore, 1965), pp. 19–52.
44. More recent scholarship on Borneo include: Wang Tai Peng, *The Origins of Chinese Kongsi* (Selangor Darul Ehsan, Malaysia, Pelanduk Publications, 1995); and Yuan Bing Ling, *Chinese Democracies: A Study of the Kongsis of West Borneo, 1776–1884* (Leiden, The Netherlands, Research School of Asian, African and Amerindian Studies, Universitiet Leiden, 2000).
45. Thomas Horsfeld, "Report on the Island of Bangka", *JIA*, v. 2 (1808), pp. 299–376, 373–427, 705–25, 779–824. See especially pp. 302–14 for a discussion of the rise of Bangka's tin industry and the role which the Chinese settlers played in it. See also Barbara Watson Andaya, *To Live as Brothers: Southeast Sumatra in the Seventeenth and Eighteenth Centuries* (Honolulu, HI, University of Hawaii Press, 1993).
46. The *Tufhat*, pp. 96–97.
47. Thomas Forrest, *Voyage to New Guinea* (London, 1972), p. 381. See also J. R. Logan, "Notices of Chinese Intercourse with Borneo Proper prior to the Establishment of Singapore in 1819", *JIA*, v. 2 (1848), p. 615.
48. H. Marriot, trans. and ed., "A Fragment of the History of Trengganu and Kelantan", *JSBRAS*, no. 72 (May 1916), pp. 3–23.
49. G. E. Gerini, "Historical Retrospect on Junkceylon Island", *JSS*, v. 2, pt. 2 (December 1905), p. 55.
50. G. William Skinner, *Chinese Society in Thailand: An Analytical History* (Ithaca, 1957), pp. 80 and 97.

51. Diane Lewis, "The Growth of the Country Trade to the Straits of Malacca 1760–1777", *JMBRAS*, v. 43, pt. 2 (1970), p. 116.
52. The *Tufhat*, pp. 188–89. It has not been possible to find out what a *jaktun* is.
53. Ibid., p. 221.
54. William Milburne, *Oriental Commerce* (etc.), v. 2 (London, 1813), p. 312; also, I. H. Burkhill, *A Dictionary of the Economic Products of the Malay Peninsula*, v. 2 (London, 1935), p. 2201.
55. The *Tufhat*, p. 97.
56. Burkhill, *A Dictionary*, v. 2, p. 2201.
57. This is only a rough guess. However, Begbie (p. 305) reports a population of over 13,000 in 1825. While there had no doubt been substantial growth in this population since 1818, there had clearly been settlements which had survived since the earlier period. Thus, one must assume that the overall population at the worst of the period of piracy never went below 5,000. The *Tufhat* (p. 189) mentions a Chinese merchant population of 800 and claims a Malayo-Bugis population of 90,000 for about 1780. Even if it was only half that, 10,000 Chinese is still a plausible estimate.
58. There also appears to have been an exchange of gambier for rice with Siam. During the late Ayuthaya period (until 1767) and early Thonburi-Bankok periods (especially after about 1780), Siam was sending gambier to China as tribute. *Ch'in Ting Ta Ch'ing Hui Tien Shih Li* (钦定大清会典事例), 1898 edition (Taiwan, 1963), reports that gambier (also referred to as cutch) was sent to China from Siam in 1729 (p. 11768), in 1766 (p. 11772), and in 1795. I am grateful to Dr. Jennifer Cushman for this information. The *Tufhat* reports that Siamese "topes" frequented Riau (p. 97) and that Siamese rice sold for ten Spanish dollars a koyan (a koyan is 5,333.33 lb). $10.00 Spanish was worth about £2 sterling at the time. Since most Siamese trade at this time was in the hands of Chinese (Skinner, *Chinese Society*, p. 41), it would seem that all the elements for a thriving rice-gambier traffic to China via Siam were present. Gambier was not produced in Siam at this time.
59. The *Tufhat*, p. 97.
60. Ibid., p. 135.
61. R. O. Winstedt, "Outline of a Malay History", p. 158.
62. Lewis, "The Growth", p. 117, no. 27.
63. Ibid., p. 115, no. 5; see also the *Tufhat*, pp. 143, 232.
64. John Bastin and R. W. Winks, eds., *Malaysia: Selected Historical Sources* (Kuala Lumpur, 1966), p. 102: "Memorandum handed by Governor Wilhem Bernhard Albinus, on the occasion of his departure to Batavia, to Senior Merchants and Governor-elect Pieter van Heemskerk for provisional reference." (Reprinted from Brian Harrison, *JMBRAS*, v. 27, pt. 1 (1954), pp. 24–34.)
65. The *Tufhat*, pp. 118–19. The Linggi war resulted in a Bugis siege of Malacca which was only broken when reinforcements came from Batavia.
66. Lewis, "The Growth", pp. 114–15.

67. Brian Harrison, trans., "Trade in the Straits of Malacca in 1785, Memorandum by P. G. de Bruijn, Governor of Malacca", *JMBRAS*, v. 26, pt. 1 (July 1953), pp. 57–58.
68. Ibid., pp. 58–59.
69. The so-called country traders were private merchants based in India who traded with the archipelago and China. Originally, these had included Indians, Portuguese, Dutch, and British shippers. By the 1760s, however, the English came to dominate the country trade. They specialized in carrying opium from Calcutta to Canton. See Holden Furber, *John Company at Work*, Ch. 5 (Cambridge, Mass., 1948); also D. K. Bassett, "British Commercial and Strategic Interest in the Malay Peninsula During the Late Eighteenth Century", in *Malayan and Indonesian Studies*, ed. John Bastin and R. Roolvink (Oxford, 1964), pp. 122–40.
70. Lewis, "The Growth", p. 115. "One of the staples of the trade there was tin, but this was no longer brought mainly from the peninsular territories of Johore, for foreign merchants had begun to call at the mouth of the Selangor River itself. Riau's supplies came increasingly from Ujong Salang and Palembang. Bugis trade to the former place flourished between the 1740s and the end of the 1760s, when the island became involved in the Thai-Burmese wars. Bugis vessels also brought pepper annually from the Manpauwa, Passir and the further North Coast of Borneo … to Riau."
71. Harrison, "Trade", p. 59.
72. The *Tufhat*, pp. 141–43. The colour of the junks signified the province of origin of the craft. For purposes of registration and identification, the Chinese government stipulated that the hulls of the junks of each province should be painted a different colour. The red were from Guangdong and the green from Fujian; Jennifer W. Cushman, "Fields from the Sea: Chinese Junk Trade with Siam during the Late Eighteenth and Early Nineteenth Centuries" (Ph. D. Thesis. Cornell University, Ithaca, N.Y., 1975), p. 69.
73. Ibid., pp. 188–89.
74. Ibid., p. 97. These included: *kapal* — ship; *perahu* — Malay canoe, 6–8 ton burden; *kichi* — ketch; *selob* — sloop; *wangkang* — Chinese junk, about 150 tons burden; *tob Siam*, or *tope* — a small-sized junk used in the Gulf of Siam; *santi* — unidentified.
75. Harrison, "Trade", p. 58.
76. Lewis, "The Growth", pp. 115–16.
77. The *Tufhat* (pp. 163–85) gives a long account of Raja Haji's conquests between about 1754 and 1777. Winstedt's version of these events is to be found in his "A History of Johor", Ch. 8, and *A History of Malaya*, 1962, pp. 148–53.
78. "Two Dutch Governor Reports", in *Malaysia*, ed. Bastin and Winks, p. 107.
79. The *Tufhat* (pp. 197–211) gives a good description of this war from the Bugis viewpoint. See also Reinout Vos, *Gentle Janus, Merchant Prince: The VOC and the Tightrope of Diplomacy in the Malay World, 1740–1800*, *Verhandellingen*

van het Koninklijk Instituut voor taal-, land- en volkenkunde (Leiden, KITLV Press, 1993).

80. Winstedt, "The Bendaharas and Temenggongs", pp. 64–65. "Superficially everything about Engku Muda suggests Bugis descent. The old Malay honorific 'Tun' has gone; in place of it we get Che Engku and for his 'brothers' the Bugis title 'Daeng'."

81. The *Tufhat* (pp. 96–97) states that Bugis and Malays owned gambier plantations which were worked by Chinese coolies. Temenggong Abdul Rahman had introduced gambier planters to Singapore before 1819; thus one concludes that the family had some previous experience in this kind of enterprise. W. Bartley, "Population of Singapore in 1819", *JMBRAS*, v. 11, pt. 2 (December 1933), p. 177.

82. Winstedt, "A History of Johor", p. 71. Winstedt cites the diary of the Dutch Resident, F. G. Smidt: "Since 1784 when the Dutch had ousted the Bugis, Riau had been the possession of the Malays in the persons of Raja Maimunah and Engku Muda (son of her and of the Temenggong of Johor) who, according to the diary of a Dutchman, F. G. Smidt, then at Riau, styled himself Sultan of Riau." See also Winstedt, "The Bendaharas", pp. 64–65.

83. The *Tufhat*, pp. 211–14. Winstedt has covered these events in Ch. 8 of "A History of Johor". The Malay text does not identify the Temenggong by name.

84. The *Tufhat* makes no mention of his presence at Riau at this time. Rather it reports that the Sultan went to Lingga together with Raja Indera Bungsu, and about 200 *perahu* of Malays and *peranakan* Bugis accompanied them. The Bendahara went to Pahang with about 150 *perahu*, and about half of the Malay *suku* went to Trengganu. No mention is made of Engku Muda, or the Temenggong; rather, the *Tufhat* simply notes some Malays set up a base at the Bulang Strait to "seek their livelihood" (*menchari rezeki*), suggesting that they became "pirates", pp. 221–22.

85. Ibid., pp. 220–21, The *Tufhat* claims that the Illanuns went back to Tempasuk (Kota Belud, Sabah), but hints that a few remained at Riau. Other sources indicate that most of the Illanuns stayed, set up bases and began raiding. Horsfield describes how Illanuns and *orang laut* from Lingga destroyed the tin-mining settlements at Bangka, "Report", pp. 315–16. They also joined Malay princes such as Sayed Ali of Siak (see below) and attacked many other places in the Peninsula. See R. Bonney, *Kedah 1771–1821: The Search for Security and Independence* (Kuala Lumpur, 1971), pp. 90–94. Winstedt, in "A History of Johor", p. 71, notes that about half of Engku Muda's fleet was composed of Illanuns in 1801. They remained a force in the region until the mid-nineteenth century.

86. Sayed Ali bin Othman was a son-in-law of Mohammad Ali, Yang Di-Pertuan Muda of Siak. In about 1788–90, he set out from a base at Bukit Batu and raided for about three or four years. Eventually he returned to Siak, ousted the ruler, and made himself Sultan in about 1795. The *Tufhat*, pp. 224–29, 248–53. See also Timothy Barnard, *Multiple Centers of Authority: Society and Environment*

in Siak and Eastern Sumatra, 1674–1827, Verhandelingen van het Koninklijk Instituut voor Taal-, Land- en Volkenkunde (Leiden, KITLV Press, 2003), p. 210.

87. Ibid., pp. 223–38.
88. Ibid., pp. 236–40, 244–48 and 253–55. The *Tufhat* describes this conflict between Engku Muda and the Yang Di-Pertuan Muda, Raja Ali. Winstedt has also discussed it in his "A History of Johor", pp. 71–72. In addition, his article "The Bendaharas and Temenggongs" gives perhaps the most comprehensive treatment of Engku Muda in English.
89. The British took Malacca from the Dutch in 1795 following Napoleon's conquest of Holland.
90. Winstedt, "The Bendaharas and Temenggongs", p. 63.
91. The *Tufhat*, pp. 221–22.
92. P. J. Begbie, *The Malayan Peninusula* (Madras, 1834), p. 315.
93. Horsfield, "Report", pp. 314–81. He describes how the Chinese tin-mining settlements here came under pirate attacks after the fall of Riau in 1784. The Chinese, unable to depend on the Sultan of Palembang for protection, were forced to relocate and build fortresses to protect themselves.
94. Begbie, *The Malayan Peninsula*, p. 315.
95. Ibid., pp. 304 and 306. He mentions settlements named "Sinkang" and "Pitjukang".
96. Begbie, *The Malayan Peninsula*, p. 344.
97. E. Netscher, "Beschrijving van een Gedeelte der Residentie Riouw", *Tijdschrift voor Indische Taal- Land- en, Volkenkunde*, v. 2 (1854), p. 159.
98. Ibid.
99. W. Bartley, "Population of Singapore in 1819", *JMBRAS*, v. 11, pt. 2 (1933), pp. 177.
100. The *Tufhat*, p. 269.
101. Lewis, "The Growth", p. 115.
102. The *Tufhat* (pp. 224 and 268) indicates that the Yang Di-Pertuan Muda Ja'afar (1805–29) had very cordial relations with the English at Malacca.
103. Winstedt, in "A History of Johor", p. 71, reports on the involvement of Sultan Ibrahim of Selangor and Bendahara Abdul Majid of Pahang. The *Tufhat* (pp. 238–43) reports Sultan Ibrahim's visit, and (pp. 252–54) tells of Sayed Ali's (of Siak) involvement.
104. The *Tufhat* mentions British involvement in a peripheral way at this period. Certainly one of the considerations in allowing Raja Ja'afar to take over the post of Yang Di-Pertuan Muda in 1805 was his friendship with the Malacca authorities (ibid., pp. 156–57). The British attempt to stop Sultan Ibrahim from going to Riau in about 1800 also indicates their interest. John Anderson, *Political and Commercial Considerations Relative to the Malayan Peninsula and the British Settlements in the Straits of Malacca* (Prince of Wales Island, 1824); reprinted as *JMBRAS*, v. 35, pt. 4 (December 1962), pp. 193–95.

105. The *Tufhat* (pp. 255–56) speaks of prosperity at Lingga and a final settlement over Riau. The Yang Di-Pertuan Muda, Raja Ali, was installed and built himself a palace, and Riau is said to have become populous — all in about 1804. But Winstedt, in "A History of Johor", p. 72, reports that he was not settled there until 21 December 1804; and the *Tufhat* reports his death the following year. He was succeeded by Raja Ja'afar in 1806.
106. Winstedt, "A History of Johor", p. 72.
107. The *Tufhat*, pp. 156–57.
108. Winstedt, in "A History of Johor", pp. 73–77, recounts the basic outlines of this very complex incident.
109. The *Tufhat*, p. 269. "There was a misunderstanding with Raja Idris, the brother of Raja Ja'afar, over the governing of the Chinese (pepper and gambier cultivators)."
110. Ibid., pp. 272–73. See also, C. H. Wake, "Raffles and the Rajas, The Founding of Singapore in Malayan and British Colonial History", *JMBRAS*, v. 48, pt. 1, pp. 50–52.
111. Ibid., p. 275. Other sources suggest that he may have set up the base at Singapore as early as 1812, but no matter where his base was, he obviously continued to exercise some influence at Riau until 1818.
112. *SSFR*, v. 67, 182, and 182a, contain most of the British correspondence dealing with the activities and views of Raffles and Farquhar in the year or two which preceded the founding of Singapore. See also, Wake, "Raffles and the Rajas", pp. 52–58, for the most recent discussion of this period.
113. John Anderson, "Political and Commercial Consideration", pp. 24–26, gives a translation of this treaty.
114. The *Tufhat* (p. 275) claims that there had been some arrangement made between the Temenggong, Hussain, and Farquhar shortly before the founding of the colony. British sources, however, which are based on Raffles' writings deny any such arrangement.
115. Ibid., pp. 189–90.
116. Ibid., pp. 219–56. This covers the period 1787 to 1803. During part of this time Sultan Mahmud was a refugee without a state, and the rest of the time he was trying to patch up the feuds at Riau. The incident in Trengganu where he is said to have prevented a war between Siak and Trengganu (pp. 225–27) is largely a statement of his legitimizing power.
117. Abdullah bin Abdul Kadir, *The Hikayat Abdullah*, trans. A. H. Hill (Oxford, 1970), pp. 271–72.

2

The Prince of Pirates

1819–1825

From 1819 on, the major theme of the history of the Temenggongs is that of their relationship with the British at Singapore. The native chiefs of Singapore, Temenggong Abdul Rahman and Sultan Hussain, did not sever their connections with their relatives in Riau, but these links became less critical. The survival of the Temenggong and his descendants came to depend almost exclusively on the goodwill and tolerance of the Singapore government. However, even though the scene of their story had shifted, there was a great deal of carry-over from the past.

It is necessary to define here the foundations on which the association between the Malays and British was built. A major historiographical problem of this period has been that the founding of Singapore was treated almost exclusively as a chapter in British colonial history. Until recently, virtually no attempt has been made to examine the indigenous viewpoint.[1] That the Temenggong and the Sultan had any legitimate aspirations or expectations in permitting a British settlement at Singapore is given very little consideration in the school of Malayan history originated by Raffles and Crawfurd. The following discussion of the relationship between the British and the Malays will thus attempt to present, as completely as possible, the case for the Temenggong.

The relationship was not a smooth one. It began with misunderstanding and moved quickly to conflict, almost open warfare. The Malay chiefs of Singapore immediately lost ground before the British advance. In 1826, seven years after the settlement of Singapore was founded, there was not even a Temenggong. The fortunes of the family had hit a new low point. For the next ten years their forces were in disarray. After 1836, however, their fortunes began to improve and they gradually regained a position of power and importance in Singapore. By 1850, a certain amount of mutual understanding had grown up between a new Temenggong and the British. It was on the basis of this understanding that the new state of Johor was founded by Temenggong Daing Ibrahim.

It is important to recall that, between 1819 and 1850, Johor was no more than a geographical expression. It is difficult to say exactly when the term *Johor* came to mean only the southern tip of the Malay Peninsula. In the sixteenth century, the *Sejarah Melayu* refers to the area as simply *Ujong Tanah* (Lands-End).[2] The *Tufhat* uses the term *Johor* to refer to the whole kingdom, including the Riau-Lingga Archipelago, up to about 1822 or 1823. The same is true of the *Hikayat Negeri Johor*, where the term *Tanah Johor* clearly includes Riau.[3] The identification of only the southern peninsular region as Johor seems to have been, at least partly, a function of European perceptions. The first instance in the *Tufhat* where the term *Johor* is used to refer only to the mainland comes in 1823 when the Riau chiefs, probably at the urging of their Dutch sponsors, attempted to lay claim to a portion of the mainland. The Yamtuan Muda ordered the Shahbandar to erect a flag in the "country of Johor" (*negri Johor*).[4] Abdul Rahman was indeed Temenggong of Johor, but of which Johor? And what was the significance of his office in 1819? There are no unequivocal answers to these questions. This was a period of such sweeping change that even the meaning of words was altered.

Even in the 1830s there is little evidence that a comprehensive term for what we now call Johor was in common usage. Rather, the region was seen as a collection of tiny principalities, each one known by its own name. Writing in about 1836, Newbold described Johor as being made up of Muar, Padang, Batu Pahat, Pontian, Benut, Johor (that is, Johor Lama), and Sedili. Outside of Muar, these were little more than small villages of about 300–400 people at the most. The Temenggong was said to rule only the portion from Benut to Sedili.[5]

Muar, which was said to have a population of about 2,400, was under a Temenggong of its own. It is not clear whom he recognized as his overlord. Newbold claims that all of these "petty states" were under the "Sultan of Johore", but he does not say whether he means Abdul Rahman of Lingga or Hussain of Singapore. Winstedt, in one article, follows Newbold in stating that Engku Konik, Temenggong of Muar (1801–30), had been installed by Sultan Mahmud III and that his successor was installed by Sultan Hussain of

Singapore in 1830.[6] However, in his "A History of Johor", Winstedt takes a different line. "The immediate sway of the Temenggong of Johor ran from Pontian round Cape Rumenia to Sedili Besar. But Engku Konik, Temenggong of Muar from 1801 to 1830, was appointed by 'Abdu'r-Rahman, Temenggong of Johor and Singapore".[7] This discrepancy is probably indicative of the fact that these territories were not very important at this time.

It is of interest that no contemporary account (*c.* 1800–30), whether Malay, English, or Dutch, has much to say about the Temenggongs' government on the mainland of Johor. This is probably because there really was not one to speak of. In addition, neither Newbold nor Begbie indicate that the Temenggong exercised authority in the islands to the south. But Dutch reports and those from other British colonial officials do connect the Temenggong with the sea peoples and the off-shore islands.

Legitimate authority on the mainland, whoever held it, did not change the fact that outside of Muar there was hardly anything worth governing. In 1826, some Europeans from Singapore travelled up the Johor River as far as Kota Tinggi and found only three settlements.[8] The account of Crawfurd's circumnavigation of Singapore Island in 1825 reports that along the entire southern coast of Johor, from Tanjong Ramunia in the east to Kukub in the west, "the country is one dreary forest without human habitation or apparently the marks of there ever having existed any." Outside of a few "wretched and temporary" woodcutters' huts on Pulau Ubin and a few small villages up the Johor River, the party found only jungle and swamp.[9] Newbold's statement that the population of Johor in 1835–36 was about 25,000 is somewhat doubtful.[10] The area may have been one of considerable settlement in earlier years and only recently depopulated as a result of the pirate raids after 1784. Munshi Abdullah notes that the area around Padang (modern Parit Jawa), on Johor's west coast, had once been heavily populated but that the "depredations of petty rajas" had left it deserted.[11]

In 1818, Temenggong Abdul Rahman was primarily concerned about his island possessions. His dominion, the *satu perentah* that Adrian Koek mentioned, was made up primarily of sea peoples. Ethnically, these people were a mixture of Bugis, both *peranakan* and *jati*, *orang laut*, and "Malays", whatever the word meant at the time. Politically, economically, and socially, their lives were organized around boats, maritime activity, and trade. They probably patrolled the coasts of Johor and collected trading commodities from the *ulu* dwellers. This was the extent of their connection with peninsular Johor. It was only a coastline which, together with the many straits, shoals, swamps, and islands, made up their territory. They drew a living primarily by policing small-scale sea-borne trade. This following of maritime peoples was the foundation of whatever power Temenggong Abdul Rahman exercised at Riau before 1818. When he was at Riau, the Temenggong was primarily a maritime chief. His major concerns were the politics of the capital, the entrepot, and the court. He led a group of subsidiary chiefs[12] many of whom controlled small flotillas of war *perahu,* perhaps as many as ten or twenty each. The *nakhoda,* or captain, of each boat was in charge of a crew of twenty to forty men, some fighters, some rowers. The latter were often slaves and sometimes *orang laut.* This was the "military" side of his following.

In about 1824, the Temenggong's following of maritime peoples numbered anywhere from 6,000 to 10,000. This figure includes his kampong at Singapore which had about 1,000 people, including 500 Bugis who fled from Riau in 1820 under their chief, Arong Belawa.[13] Beyond this, or perhaps with this, the Temenggong controlled the whole western section of the Riau Archipelago. Taken together, various contemporary accounts show that the Temenggong controlled the islands and populations shown in Table 1.

These islands, together with Johor and Singapore, gave the Temenggong a chain of strategically located bases which made possible the control of all traffic moving between the Straits of Malacca and the South China Sea (see Map 1). Whether or not the population figures are accurate (Begbie does not give his source), the variation in the several accounts indicates that the size of

TABLE 1

The Temenggong's Maritime Following, c. 1823[14]

Island	*Suku**	*Population*	*Boats*
Karimon	?	1,250	?
Buru	Buru	670	3
Galang	Galang	1,300	20
Moro	Mora	560	15
Batam	Trong	?	10
Sugi	Sugi	1,600	6
Bulang	Pekaka	1,050	?
Timiang	Timiang	1,100	30
Singapore	……	1,500	?
Johor	……	1,000	?
		10,030	84

* Tribe name

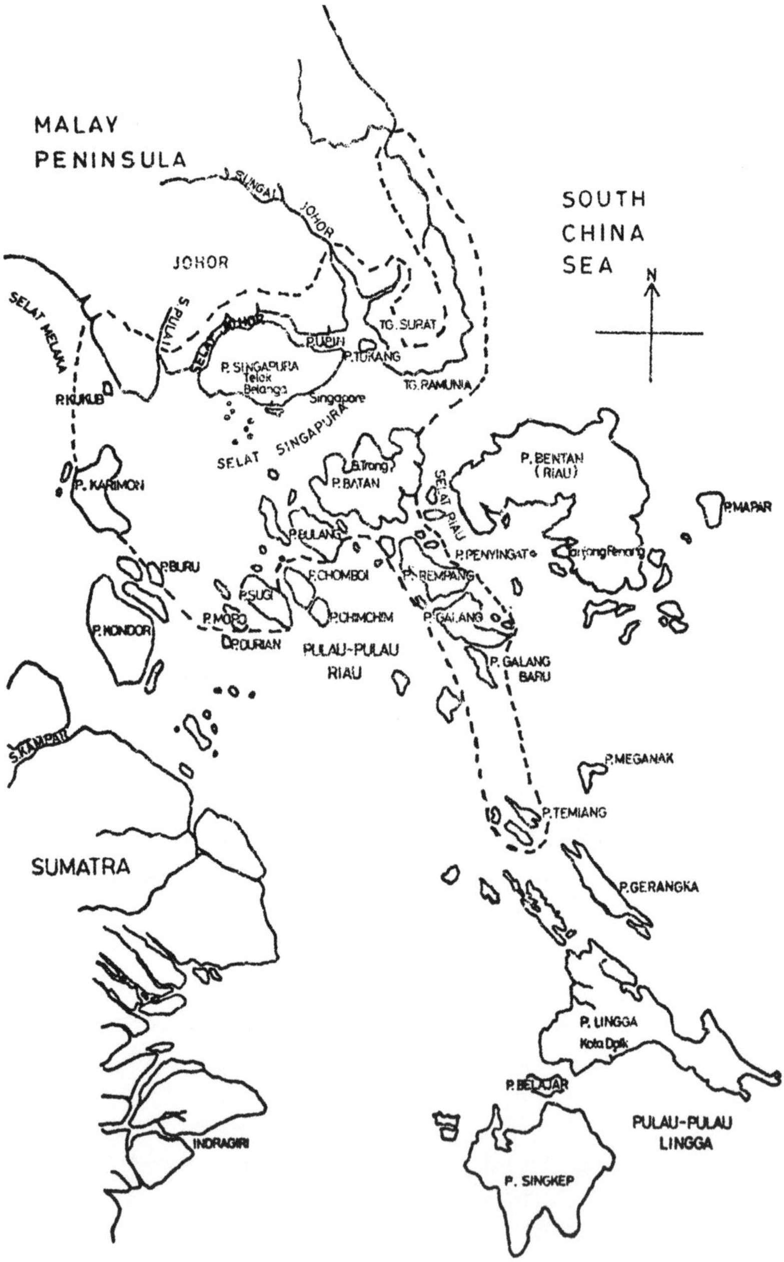

Key: Estimated boundary _ _ _ _ _ _

MAP 1

The Temenggong's Domain, c. 1818–1823

the population under his control was probably quite fluid. It grew or diminished according to the general prosperity and the strength of his position in the entrepot.

The Temenggong and his people left Riau in 1818 when the Dutch gave their support to the Yamtuan Muda, Raja Ja'afar. This move denied them a share in the economic benefits of the port. They went to Singapore and became "pirates", according to the Dutch. In fact, they probably continued their former occupations but without the benefit of recognition from Riau. Originally, the Temenggong's establishment at Singapore was probably meant to be very much like the one Engku Muda had maintained at Bulang in earlier years (that is, the headquarters of the opposition).

The coming of Raffles and William Farquhar in 1819 was a godsend for the Temenggong. It gave him a chance to enter into a privileged relationship with another important European power. The Temenggong thus aspired to a prominent role in the Singapore entrepot, as he had previously done at Riau. As before, he sought power at the centre. He appears to have begun trying to carry out the traditional functions of his office, which included managing the trade, collecting taxes, and policing the harbour and surrounding seas. There is every indication that after 1819 the Temenggong and Sultan Hussain continued to consider Singapore as their state and expected substantial political and economic benefits as a result of their position. The series of agreements that these chiefs signed with the English in 1819 gave them a great deal of power at Singapore.

For about five-and-a-half years, Singapore was governed under a unique set of conventions. Although these arrangements were altered in 1823, and entirely cancelled by a new treaty in 1824, the original treaties give an accurate picture of the expectations of the Malay chiefs in 1819.[15] Between 1819 and 1823, Singapore was under tripartite rule. Authority was shared between the East India Company, the Temenggong, and Sultan Hussain. The 1819 agreements gave equality to all three parties.

On 30 January 1819, Temenggong Abdul Rahman was recognized as the "Ruler of Singapore, who governs the country of Singapore in his own name and in the name of Sree Sultan Hussein Mahummud Shah …" The Temenggong allowed the settlement of the East India Company in return for "protection" and an annual pension of $3,000.[16] A week later, Hussain was brought from Riau, installed as Sultan by Raffles, and a formal treaty was drawn up. Sultan Hussain approved the earlier agreement in exchange for protection and a pension of $5,000 annually. Both princes were bound to "aid and assist the Honourable East India Company (E.I.C.) against all enemies that may assail the Factory or Factories of the said Company" in their territories. The port was to be under the authority of the British government, and all persons belonging to the factory were under the protection of the British. The Temenggong, however, was to receive half of all duties levied on "Goods, Merchandise, Boats or Vessels ..."[17] The question of authority was stated very ambiguously. The Temenggong was the "Ruler of Singapore" but the port was under the authority of the E.I.C. It is also noteworthy that the Temenggong was able to claim such a potentially large revenue entirely for himself to the exclusion of Sultan Hussain. The British considered him the more powerful of the two chiefs. Hussain was but a legal necessity.

A further agreement, on 26 June 1819,[18] did little to clarify matters, although that was its stated purpose. The "Arrangements made for the Government of Singapore" fixed the boundaries of the factory,[19] but it guaranteed the autonomy of the kampongs of the Sultan and the Temenggong which were within the factory territory. It also formalized the tripartite rule under which the settlement was to function: "No Duties or Customs can be exacted, or farms established in this Settlement without the consent of the Sultan, the Tumungong and Major William Farquhar, and without the consent of these three nothing can be arranged."[20]

John Crawfurd has summarized the implications of these treaties. His remarks also reflect the attitude of Englishmen of the time towards such dealings with Malays.

> In the first agreement with a native Chief, the arrangement amounted to little more than a permission for the formation of a British factory and establishment, along two miles of the northern shore, and inland to the extent of the point-blank range of a cannon shot. There was in reality no territorial cession giving a legal right of legislation. The only law which could have existed was the Malay code. The native chief was considered to be the proprietor of the land, even within the bounds of the British factory, and he was to be entitled, in perpetuity, to one-half of such duties of customs as might hereafter be levied at the port. In the progress of the settlement, these arrangements were of course found highly inconvenient and embarrassing, and were annulled by the subsequent treaty of August, 1824.[21]

The authority of these chiefs was so broadly and ambiguously defined by these treaties that even Raffles and Farquhar, who together made the treaties, did not share a common idea of what they meant. During the period when Farquhar was in charge of the settlement,[22] the Temenggong and Sultan gained additional economic benefits. In November 1819, Farquhar established tax farms for opium, liquor, and gambling. One-third of the proceeds of these were to be paid to each of the chiefs. The chiefs also received presents from the captains of Chinese and native craft that came to Singapore.[23] These arrangements ran counter to Raffles' aims. When Raffles took charge of the settlement in October 1822, he ran into conflict with both Farquhar and the native chiefs. He condemned Farquhar's implementation of the 1819 agreements and was dissatisfied with the extent of the authority which had been vested in the Temenggong and the Sultan.

> … the extraordinary principle assumed by Lieutenant-Colonel Farquhar, and maintained by him in opposition to my authority, that the disposal of the land was vested in the native chiefs, that the government of the country was native and the port a native port, rendered indispensable that these points should be fully explained and more clearly defined, and as that officer had also permitted various exactions and privileges to be enjoyed by their Highnesses incompatible with the freedom of the port, I have availed myself of the opportunity offered in negotiating with their Highnesses for the payment of an equivalent for the port duties, to stipulate such arrangements as seem essential to form the bases of the good understanding to be maintained for the future.[24]

Munshi Abdullah, one of Raffles' Malay scribes who had followed him there from Malacca, has described the influence which the Temenggong exercised at Singapore during Raffles' absence:

> All the inhabitants were dismayed by frequent incidents, houses catching fire, robberies taking place in the high noon, people getting stabbed. When morning came people would be found stabbed and wounded to death. The Temenggong's men, the Sultan's men and the foreigners of all races went about fully armed; some of them robbed people in broad daylight, some broke into houses and stole people's property, for they were afraid of nothing … Every day it was the Temenggong's men who started brawls, for their attitude towards the Malacca men was like that of tigers towards goats. The Malacca men were unarmed, knew nothing of dagger tactics, and had never seen bloodshed. In any kind of clash between the Malacca born, whether Chinese, Malays or Indians, and the Temenggong's men, Colonel Farquhar always took the side of the former for he realized that their nature made them shy of fighting with weapons … The two sides were always at loggerheads, and on many occasions violent quarrels flared up between them, not individual combats but free-for-all fights, when a man of one side harboured a grievance against a man of the other. If they had not all been afraid of Colonel Farquhar they would have gone on killing each other every day without stopping.[25]

Raffles's contention that Singapore was being run as a "native port" was at least partly true. The Temenggong was clearly trying to exercise his authority.

Early in 1823, matters came to a head. On 11 March, Farquhar was stabbed by an *amok*, Sayed Yassin.[26] This event happened immediately after Raffles' proclamation forbidding the carrying of arms in the Settlement. The stabbing brought out all the hatred and suspicion that had grown up between the Malays and Europeans. Since it was dark and the assailant had been so badly slashed by Farquhar's men, immediate identification was impossible. The few Europeans panicked and suspicion fell on the Temenggong.

> Then some three or four hundred armed soldiers came running up ... Behind them a squad of soldiers ran past pulling twelve guns already loaded. All the soldiers surrounded the fence which ran around the Temenggong's enclosure and mounted the guns on the side facing his house. Other soldiers rushed up holding flints in their hands and stood there only waiting for the order to touch off the guns ... Not a single one of the Malays was to be seen, all of them having been chased away by the soldiers.[27]

Raffles, although he too suspected the Temenggong, kept his head and did not give the order to fire. He then discovered that the assailant was Sayed Yassin and not one of the Temenggong's men. However, the animosity did not end there. The general ill-feeling continued, and Singapore remained in a state of tension for some months. Raffles had decided to make an example of the incident — he had the body hung on a scaffold and dragged around the town. A Dutch visitor left a record of those days:

> The Lieutenant-Governor Raffles, who was in possession of the body of the murderer, had that, notwithstanding all the objections of the natives, hung on a gallows guarded by soldiers, which had the effect that all the natives adopted a threatening attitude and awakened considerable fear amongst the citizens. Settlers and traders, as well as the Chinese who took the side of the Europeans, were night and day under arms. And this unsettled state of affairs lasted just so long as the body was hanging up, terminating on the third day, when Mr. Raffles considered it wiser to hand over the body of the misdoer to his friends and compatriots for burial. Since this upset there has been no very great sense of security amongst the merchants of Singapore ...[28]

As if to challenge the Europeans, Sayed Yassin's body was buried by the Sultan and became a local shrine and place of pilgrimage.[29]

The problem was clearly more than a question of mistaken identity; there was a struggle for power. The Temenggong and the Sultan were acting as if Singapore was their entrepot, and they did as they would have at Riau. As maritime chiefs, they had traditionally been entitled to a share in the wealth and status that came with the entrepot. To them, Singapore was simply a slight adaptation of the typical Malay port which had sustained their ancestors for centuries. Raffles, although he must have been aware of this, saw things from quite a different viewpoint: "I have had everything to new-mold from first to last; to introduce a system of energy, purity and encouragement … Singapore is now perhaps the only place in India where slavery cannot exist."[30]

To Raffles, Singapore was new; it was his own creation. Yet to the Malays, it was simply one more variation on a very old theme. Practically every Malay state known to history had been based on a trading city. In the maritime world, the entrepot was the major political structure. If a ruler sought power, his aim was to control the port. The Malay chiefs at Singapore were fully aware of the significance of the port, and the treaties reflect the demands they must have made on the Europeans. The trading city had always been the focal point for the political forces of the Malay world. The Malay chiefs may not have foreseen the extent of Singapore's success, but they must have known that the city would soon dominate the region. From the beginning, it was their intention to have a share in its power.

It is difficult to decide whether Raffles himself was aware that he was founding the centre of a new empire. He had been in the Malay world for almost fifteen years by the time he founded Singapore,[31] and he must have had some inkling of the power such a city could have. Regardless of Raffles' statements we must question John Bastin's contention that Raffles' idea of a free port was anti-imperialistic. "Aware of the disfavour which further territorial expansion would bring, Raffles had no idea of these ports becoming colonial establishments. They were rather, he said, to 'be looked upon as so many outposts … for the convenience and security of our … commercial interests, and not as governments intended for the rule and detailed management of a dominion'."[32]

There was a gap between "Raffles' idea" and the reality of the situation. It is ironic that, in attempting to avoid the establishment of an empire, Raffles patterned his settlement on the classic model of the Malay maritime empire. For the next half-century, Singapore continued to imitate the traditional political pattern that such states had followed in the past. It controlled only commerce, but commerce was the only source of political power that Malays had ever known. It did not undertake "the rule and detailed management of a dominion", but the earlier maritime empires had not done so either. Srivijaya, Malacca, and Johor had controlled their empires by managing commerce. The entrepot was the great juncture of the communications and transportation systems of the archipelago. Control of the entrepot gave the ruler economic and every other kind of power over the riverine states of the Peninsula and Sumatra. The ruler of the maritime state limited his political influence to the legitimization and recognition of "tributary" chiefs. Rule was traditionally indirect. From its inception, Singapore was locked into the classic patterns of traditional Malay politics.

The Sultan and the Temenggong were aware of this, and refused to step down from their position when Raffles offered them a chance to become merchants. Munshi Abdullah has described a meeting which took place between Raffles and the two Malay chiefs sometime in 1823. The chiefs came to Raffles, complaining that their allowances were insufficient. Raffles countered by offering to obtain goods on credit for them from an English merchant in India. He would even give them money and draw the plans to build warehouses. Then they could conduct business with the native traders who came to Singapore and could earn a commission on sales. Raffles, however, had overplayed his hand — the chiefs just laughed and said, "It is not the custom of rulers to engage in trade for they would lose dignity before other rulers."[33]

Although he failed to buy off the chiefs in this manner, Raffles sought other ways to limit their power at Singapore. He had no intention of allowing the city to remain a "native port". However, he could not change the original treaty, because he still needed the Malays. The dubious legality of Sultan Hussain's title was the only basis of the Company's claim to Singapore. In 1823, the Dutch remained firm in their contention that the British occupation of Singapore was illegal since it rightly fell within the territories under Sultan Abdul Rahman of Lingga and thus ought to have been Dutch. Because of this situation, Raffles was more or less required to allow the original treaties to stand. The fact that both chiefs had been in contact with the Dutch and the Riau chiefs after the foundation of Singapore justified Raffles' concern that they might yet go over to the Dutch.[34]

Instead, Raffles only tried to modify some of the privileges originally given to the Sultan and the Temenggong with another agreement on 7 June 1823. By this treaty, the chiefs gave up their rights to port duties and their share in the revenue farms. They could no longer receive presents from the captains of Chinese and native vessels, and they were relieved from attendance at court. In compensation, the Sultan received a pension of $1,500 per month and the Temenggong $800. The Temenggong was given an additional sum to finance the removal of his kampong to Teluk Belanga. The chiefs also gave up their authority over Singapore Island: "With the exception of the land appropriated to their Highnesses for their respective establishments, all land within the island of Singapore, and islands immediately adjacent, to be at the entire disposal of the British Government."[35]

Even these concessions were not really enough for the British. However, as Raffles put it in his letter to the Indian Government: "I did not deem it prudent in any way to alter or revise the original treaty, but the conventional agreement now made may be considered equally binding on the parties, and may of course be hereafter adopted as the basis of any more definite treaty to be entered into after the permanency of the Settlement has been established."[36]

The "permanency of the settlement" was contingent upon the Dutch claims. This problem was resolved by the Anglo-Dutch Treaty of London on 17 March 1824. The agreement provided for the recognition of the British position at Singapore. In addition, Malacca was given back to the British, and the Dutch promised to make no treaties with the Malay states of the Peninsula. The British agreed to forgo any treaties with the Sumatran states and withdrew from Bengkulu. This treaty split the Malay world through the Straits of Malacca and Singapore, the middle of the Temenggong's domain.[37] With Dutch recognition of the British settlement at Singapore, the English were no longer dependent on the tenuous arrangements they had made with the native chiefs.

Raffles was unable to guide the fortunes of Singapore by this time. Following the signing of the 1823 agreement, he returned to England and never returned to Singapore. The settlement was taken over by the Resident, John Crawfurd. The new Resident expressed the view that the native chiefs had contributed nothing to the success of Singapore: "It does not appear to me that the influence of the native chiefs has in any respect been necessary or even beneficial in the formation, maintenance, or progress of this settlement, the prosperity of which has rested solely and exclusively on the character and resources of the British Government."[38] It was in this spirit that Crawfurd negotiated a new treaty with the Sultan and the Temenggong on 3 August 1824. The Malay princes were forced to make a full cession of Singapore and the adjacent islands to the East India Company in exchange for a cash settlement. They were allowed to maintain their establishments at Singapore under British jurisdiction: the Sultan at Kampong Gelam and the Temenggong at Teluk Belanga. They were also committed to help suppress piracy.[39]

As a result of the 1824 treaty, the Malay chiefs lost all legitimate claim to status and political power in Singapore. This was the second time in six years that they had experienced such a set-back. For the Temenggong, the situation of 1818 when he had been forced out of Riau was now repeated. This time, however, he had nowhere else to go. Both the new treaty signed with the English and the Anglo-Dutch treaty had deprived him of his former domain in the islands.

> The Carimon Islands and the Malayan Settlement of Bulang are two of the principal possessions of the Tumongong of Johore or Singapore, and his claim

> to them is not only allowed by the rival chiefs [the Yang Di-Pertuan Muda at Riau and Sultan Abdul Rahman], but more satisfactorily ascertained by the voluntary and cheerful alliance yielded to him by the inhabitants. By the present treaty, however, he must either forgo all claims to these possessions, or removing to them, renounce his connexion with the British Government.[40]

There was no future for him at Riau with Raja Ja'afar and the Dutch. All that was left was Johor, and there was nothing there to attract him. Singapore, despite all its troubles, had become a populous and successful port. There were many reasons which compelled the Temenggong to remain there, beyond the fact that he had no alternative.

While Crawfurd's argument regarding the success of Singapore as being the responsibility of the British may have some validity, he appears to have ignored certain realities which his successors ultimately were forced to recognize. Singapore's size and prosperity left many opportunities for the Malay chiefs to augment their wealth and power. They had agreed to aid in the suppression of piracy by the treaty of 1824, and there was really no way that the British alone could police the many channels and straits of the region. In the past the sea peoples under the Temenggong had carried out the function of patrolling these waters. However, since they were not allowed to collect presents or port duties from the native and Chinese vessels, who would pay to suppress the pirates? The allowances given to the Sultan and the Temenggong were insufficient to pay their followers. The only recourse for these people was to continue in their former occupation on a free-lance basis — they became pirates.

We should define the word *pirates*. As long as the Malay political system of the region was operative, the activities of the sea peoples had been violent but perfectly legitimate pursuits. The sea peoples possessed the seas and what floated on them by hereditary-feudal right from the Sultan of Johor. So long as their chiefs held a valid title from the Sultan, their "patrol" activities regarding trade were a legitimate naval operation.

Some groups of *orang laut*, however, did not come under recognized chiefs. These were *perompak* — wanderers and renegades who included hereditary outlaw bands with no fixed abode.[41] There were also *perompak* who were temporary bands of outlaws under down-on-their-luck rajas and foreign adventurers. At this time, certain groups were disorganized and in a turbulent state because of recent economic difficulties. They too had a traditional role in Malay politics, supplying much of the dynamic of political history in the region.[42] During the years 1787–95, when there was no legitimate ruler resident in the archipelago, everyone was a *perompak*. But it should be understood that this was an exceptional period in Malay history.

Generally, Malays recognized a distinction between legitimate and outlawed sea peoples. The *Tufhat Al-Nafis*, even though written from a pro-Bugis, anti-Temenggong point of view, never calls the Temenggong's people *perompak*. Before 1818, the Temenggong's and Engku Muda's people were referred to as *suku-suku Melayu*, "the Malay tribes". The Dutch turned these people into "pirates" by aiding Raja Ja'afar in dispossessing them of their traditional rights at Riau. However, even after 1818, the *Tufhat* did not consider the Temenggong's authority over the Karimons as illegitimate. Commenting on the effect of the 1824 Anglo-Dutch treaty, the author remarked on the Temenggong's position in the islands: "In addition, the Karimon Islands and Buru Island were included under the government of Sultan Abdul Rahman and the Yang Di-Pertuan Muda of Riau. But in this affair, the Yang Di-Pertuan Selat [Sultan Hussain], and the Temenggong and his dependents and people continued to hold them according to the old custom."[43]

The Dutch, who had been instrumental in ousting the Temenggong from Riau, seem to have been the first to accuse him of piracy. The earliest printed reference which connects the Temenggong with "pirates" is that of Colonel Nahuijs, a Dutchman who visited Singapore in 1823. He charged that before 1819, Singapore "was a cavern and hiding place for murderers and pirates" and suggested that Singapore "would have remained the same den of murderers as it was in the past had it not been taken over by the English". He went on to describe the activities of the Temenggong at Singapore during the early years of the settlement:

> This Tommagung is generally said still to have a very good understanding with his elder brothers, the pirates, and to maintain an active correspondence with them, giving them regular news of the comings and goings in Singapore harbour and the destination, cargo and strength of the different ships. The Tommagung lives with his dependents a short distance away from the European town on a site allotted to him by the British Government of Singapore, on account of the frequent quarrels and murders for which his dependents have been responsible. Over all these people as well as over the Bouginese settled in Singapore, the British Resident has not the least authority, even when they attack Europeans.[44]

These charges may provide a clue to the structure of the Temenggong's government. Traditionally, the Temenggong was a "police chief". Colonel Nahuijs makes a distinction between the Temenggong and his "elder brothers, the pirates". There also seems to have been another group, "his dependents". Together with Munshi Abdullah's remarks, this suggests that these dependents were going around the town trying to "collect taxes" and "police" the port.

They checked cargoes and sailing information and fixed the value of presents and port duties. In particular, they tried to govern the Malacca people who had come to Singapore under Farquhar. These people, numbering from 500 to 1,200, were the Temenggong's dependents at Singapore and lived in his kampong/capital; they were a kind of "administrative" group. Before he was forced to leave Singapore town in 1823 and to move to Teluk Belanga, the Temenggong's kampong was hardly distinguishable from the commercial part of the town. Physical movement of the Temenggong's kampong to Teluk Belanga was the only way to remove the many "fingers" of his dependents from all the economic "pies" of the port. These included everything from presents to prostitution; port duties, trade monopolies, coolie-broking, and the usual revenue farms on liquor, opium, gambling, ganja, and the like. The Temenggong's dependents included both blood relatives and certain employed aliens such as Chinese, Arabs, Bugis, and Indians. At sea, outside the port, were the *orang laut* (the "elder brothers") who made up the bulk of the 10,000 people under the Temenggong's government, or *perentah*. The Temenggong's town followers gathered intelligence on shipping and walked the streets. Through the authority of the Temenggong, the port people passed information to their "elder brothers" at sea. The information concerned those who had or had not paid their taxes, who should be attacked, and how much they should be worth. The trouble that they caused the British government is in some respects an index of their relative strength and efficiency. It took Raffles more than three years to get the Temenggong to agree to move to Teluk Belanga — in August 1824, he still had not left the town. But finally he did move at Crawfurd's insistence.[45]

This was the final blow to his authority. Combined with the 1824 treaties, this expulsion blocked the communications system that was the life of his government. He was physically removed from the port and its population. In addition, the treaties recognized a dividing-line which split the Temenggong's island territory in half. Now the most important of his possessions were on the Dutch side of the line, legally separated from the Temenggong and the entrepot. Crawfurd remarked that the effect of this division "virtually amounts to a dismemberment of the principality of Johore, and must thus be productive of some embarrassment and confusion".[46]

The Temenggong had failed in his scheme to have the best of both worlds — to continue to exercise his power as a Malay chief while, at the same time, governing the port of Singapore from under the British umbrella. He may have already been elderly, but it is possible that his death, coming only sixteen months after he signed away Singapore, was connected with his demotion.

A less resilient polity might have collapsed altogether. Something, however, was salvaged of the apparatus of the old political system. The new Temenggong, Daing Ibrahim, eventually took over what remained of his father's state and combined it with new elements to lay the foundation for an agricultural state in Johor. It is hard to say just how much he had inherited from his father. In 1825, Ibrahim was only fifteen years old. He was too young to effectively manage the affairs of his father's government. From 1825, the state went into a period of interregnum and disintegration. There was a power vacuum in the area around Singapore. It was ten years before the Temenggong's successor began putting the pieces back together again. From 1826 to 1836 politics were in abeyance and "piracy" reigned.

NOTES

1. The outstanding exception to this is the recent article by C. H. Wake, "Raffles and the Rajas".
2. Brown, trans., *Sejarah Melayu*, pp. 190–91.
3. Winstedt, "A History of Johor (1673–*c.* 1800 A.D.)", *jawi* text of *Hikayat Negeri Johor*, p. 293.
4. The *Tufhat*, p. 293.
5. Newbold, *Political and Statistical Account*, v. 2, pp. 41–44.
6. Winstedt, "The Temenggongs of Muar", *JMBRAS*, v. 10, pt. 1 (1932), p. 31. See also Newbold's article in J. H. Moor, *Notices of the Indian Archipelago and Adjacent Countries* (Singapore, 1837), Appendix, pp. 73–76, "Sketch of the State of Muar".
7. Winstedt, "A History of Johor", p. 90.
8. "Trip to the Johore River", *Singapore Chronicle*, August 1826, in Moor, *Notices*, pp. 264–68. The Temenggong did exercise authority on the Johor River to some extent. The writer claims he had appropriated some old cannons from Bukit Seluyut (p. 266). However, the Bugis of Johor Lama were apparently under a Suliwatang in Singapore (p. 264).
9. "Journal of a Voyage Round the Island of Singapore", *Singapore Chronicle*, November 1825, in Moor, *Notices*, pp. 268–69.
10. Newbold, *Political and Statistical Account*, v. 2, p. 54.
11. A. H. Hill, trans., *The Hikayat*, pp. 271–73.
12. Three of the major Malay chiefs under the Temenggong were the Panglima Perang, who was living at the Temenggong's kampong on the Singapore River in 1823 (C. B. Buckley, *An Anecdotal History of Old Times in Singapore* (Singapore, 1969), p. 85), and Raja Lang of Bulang ("Report on Piracy by Registrar of Imports and Exports Edward Presgrave", *SSR*, 20 January 1829, p. 71), and, to control the Bugis, Arong Belawa (see below).

13. Arong Belawa apparently took over the following of Engkau Karaeng Talibak (see p. 43 above). His wives included a daughter of Yang Di-Pertuan Muda Raja Ali (1784–1805) and a daughter of Karaeng (Begbie, pp. 283–84). The *Tufhat* has a long account of his expulsion from Riau, claiming that he eventually returned to Riau and made his peace with the Dutch and Raja Ja'afar (p. 279). However, Gibson-Hill reports that he was buried in the Temenggong's cemetery at Teluk Belanga. C. A. Gibson-Hill, "Singapore, Old Strait and New Harbour", *Memoirs of the Raffles Museum*, no. 3 (December 1956), p. 80.
14. Population figures based on Begbie, *The Malayan Peninsula*, pp. 270–72. Boats based on Presgrave, "Report on Piracy", p. 71. See also Appendix A.
15. The authoritative source for these treaties, as well as all of those made by the British with other Malay states, is W. G. Maxwell and W. S. Gibson, ed., *Treaties and Engagements Affecting the Malay States and Borneo* (London, 1924), pp. 115–22. Buckley, in *An Anecdotal History*, Chs. 1–14, also gives these treaties together with prints of a great deal of closely related primary source material from the Straits Settlements Records, as well as his own experience (pp. 36–39) in bringing to light the last remaining original copy of the first treaty.

    The major engagements were between the Temenggong and Raffles, dated 29 January 1819 (Buckley, *An Anecdotal History*, p. 36); between the Temenggong and Sultan Hussain and Raffles, dated 6 February 1819 (ibid., pp. 38–40); between the Temenggong and Sultan, and Raffles and Farquhar, dated 25 June 1819 (ibid., pp. 58–59); between the Temenggong and Sultan, and Raffles, dated 7 June 1823 (ibid., pp. 106–7); and between the Temenggong and Sultan, and John Crawfurd, dated 2 August 1824.
16. Ibid., p. 36.
17. Ibid., pp. 38–40. See Articles 2, 4, 6, and 9.
18. Ibid., pp. 58–59.
19. Ibid., p. 58. Article 1: "The boundaries of the lands under the control of the English are as follows: from Tanjong Malang on the west to Tanjong Katang on the east, and on the land side, as far as the range of cannon-shot, all round from the factory. As many persons as reside within the aforesaid boundary, and not within the campongs of the Sultan and Tumungong, are all to be under the control of the Resident, and with respect to the gardens and plantations that now are, or may hereafter be made, they are to be at the disposal of the Tumungong, as heretofore; but it is understood that he will always acquaint the Resident of same."
20. Ibid., p. 59. Article 7.
21. Crawfurd, 1828, quoted in Buckley, *An Anecdotal History*, p. 40.
22. Lt.-Col. William Farquhar, Governor of Malacca (1803–18), was the Resident at Singapore from its foundation until May 1823, when he was deposed by Raffles. He had ruled the port while Raffles was absent from Singapore, discharging his duties as Lieutenant-Governor of Bengkulu.

    After founding Singapore and drawing up the initial treaties in January and February 1819, Raffles left for Penang. He returned in June to sign the third agreement and then left shortly thereafter for Bengkulu. He did not return again until 10 October 1822, by which time the settlement had become well established under the government of Farquhar (ibid., pp. 48, 73.).

23. Ibid., pp. 63–64.
24. Ibid., pp. 120–21. Raffles to Supreme Government, 7 June 1823.
25. A. H. Hill, trans., *The Hikayat*, p. 159.
26. Ibid., pp. 169–75.
27. Ibid., p. 172.
28. H. E. Miller, "Letters of Colonel Nahuijs", *JMBRAS*, v. 19, pt. 2 (October 1941), p. 195.
29. A. H. Hill, trans., *The Hikayat*, p. 174, fn. 9.
30. Quoted in Winstedt, "A History of Malaya", p. 218.
31. Raffles first arrived in Penang in 1805 where he served as Assistant Secretary. He quickly learned the Malay language and was soon recognized as an expert on Malay affairs. In 1811, he accompanied Lord Minto, the Governor-General of India, during the invasion of Java and, when Minto left, he was appointed Lieutenant-Governor of Java. In 1816, after the British withdrew from Java, he returned to England where he was knighted and returned to Sumatra to become Lieutenant-Governor of Bengkulu in 1817.
32. John Bastin, "Raffles and British Policy in the Indian Archipelago", *JMBRAS*, v. 27, pt. 1 (May 1954), p. 82.
33. A. H. Hill, trans., *The Hikayat*, p. 163.
34. Buckley, *An Anecdotal History*, pp. 50–51. Buckley gives copies of letters from the Temenggong and Sultan to Yang Di-Pertuan Muda Raja Ja'afar, claiming that the British had forced them against their will to allow the settlement. Raffles also had an adversary in his colleague, Governor Bannerman of Penang, but the latter had died in 1819.
35. Ibid., pp. 106–7.
36. Ibid., p. 121. Raffles to Supreme Government, 7 June 1823.
37. C. D. Cowan, ed., "Early Penang and the Rise of Singapore, 1805–1832: A Series of Documents from the Manuscript Records of the East India Company", *JMBRAS*, v. 23, pt. 2 (March 1950), pp. 145–47.
38. Crawfurd to Governor General, 10 January 1824, quoted in Buckley, *An Anecdotal History*, p. 163.
39. "A Treaty of Friendship and Alliance … etc.", quoted in Buckley, *An Anecdotal History*, pp. 168–70. See also A. H. Hill, trans., *The Hikayat*, pp. 218–20, which gives an interesting, if unsubstantiated, account of the manner in which Crawfurd was said to have coerced the chiefs into signing the treaty.
40. Crawfurd to Calcutta, 1 October 1824, quoted in Buckley, *An Anecdotal History*, pp. 178–79.
41. Begbie, *The Malayan Peninsula*, pp. 271–73. Begbie describes some *suku* as being perpetual wanderers, while most lived more or less ashore or at least had bases on the islands from which they drew their names. There were also the Illanuns, whom everyone looked on as pirates.

42. The *Tufhat*, pp. 224–29, 248–53. The account of Sayed Ali of Siak (1784–1805) is a classic version of the outcast raja as a pirate state-maker. Engku Muda perhaps represented the same tradition.
43. Ibid., p. 296.
44. Miller, "Extracts", pp. 192–95.
45. Crawfurd to Supreme Government, 10 January 1824, quoted in Buckley, *An Anecdotal History*, p. 160. "The demand made by the same chief for a residence in the town of Singapore has placed me in the same awkward position as his pecuniary one. The matter was never hinted to me, either verbally or in writing, from the source of my instructions on other points, and it was with a good deal of surprise that I first heard the demand. The residence of the Tumongong and his numerous and disorderly followers was a nuisance of the first magnitude. Three thousand dollars had actually been paid for his removal. Three thousand are demanded for the same object, and yet he wished to preserve a temporary residence in the very same spot, and to occupy all the ground which he had ever occupied. This would have perpetuated every nuisance, for abating which so large an expense had been incurred. The matter would probably have been aggravated, when the followers of the Tumongong were living in his enclosure removed from the control of their chief."
46. Crawfurd to Calcutta, 1 October 1824, quoted in Buckley, *An Anecdotal History*, p. 178.

3

The Temenggong of Singapore

1825–1848

Temenggong Daing Ibrahim[1] was the founder of modern Johor. He was a transitional figure who bridged the gap between the ancient maritime and the modern landed state. When he was left with the responsibility for the family's fortunes, he had very few resources. If he was to survive as a ruler, he was faced with two apparently mutually exclusive alternatives: the way of the English or the way of his own followers and Malay tradition. He could be a puppet or a pirate. He managed a compromise.

In 1826, his only tangible resources were his father's pension, which the Straits government continued to pay to him, and his own kampong at Teluk Belanga. Cut off from the Riau court and the Sultan, he had no title.[2] He was not officially installed as Temenggong until 1841. The period between Abdul Rahman's death and his own installation was one of trial and testing, during which the young chief made his own way in a changing and dangerous world.

His father's death had very nearly brought about the disintegration of the Temenggong's government. Many of Abdul Rahman's followers drifted off and went their own way; some may have rallied briefly around Tengku Yahya, a follower of Sultan Hussain. In 1826, he is reported to have sent people to work the tin mines which had been opened in the Karimons.[3] However, he lost much of his attractiveness as a Malay leader when these followers were driven out. In 1827, a combined force of Dutch and Riau Malays decided to enforce the boundary arrangements of the Anglo-Dutch Treaty of 1824 which put the islands outside the control of the English and the Singapore chiefs.

The Karimons were attacked and Tengku Yahya's men were defeated.[4] From this time on, the Sultan, who shared in the debacle, declined in status among the Malays of Singapore as has been chronicled by Munshi Abdullah. He was forced to flee to Malacca in 1834 and died there in disgrace the following year.[5]

It was perhaps fortunate that Ibrahim was not yet of age and thus escaped involvement in the fiasco of the Karimons. His youth may also have made him a less attractive leader for the sea peoples, many of whom had turned to piracy as a means of support. In 1835 the Governor of Singapore, Samuel Bonham, noted that the increase in piracy had come about as a result of the deaths of Temenggong Abdul Rahman and Sultan Hussain. He expressed the view, contrary to Crawfurd's, that a strong chief at Singapore was necessary if piracy was to be brought to a halt.

> That piracy has increased of late I cannot deny, and I attribute it to these reasons, the deaths of the Sultan and Temenggong, and to the impossibility of our making any adequate provision for these officers; formerly the Rayats or Orang-laut in our immediate vicinity were under the control of these chiefs, but of late in consequence of their deaths, they have split themselves into separate parties, no longer acknowledging the descendants of the late Sultan or Temenggong, but become, to a considerable extent, under the influence of the Sultan of Lingga … The Karimuns, Moro, Sugi, Galang, and other hordes of marauders are all to the southward of the Straits of Singapore and we are therefore precluded by the treaty of London from at all interfering with them, even though we be inclined to do so, in assisting the Temenggong's family in regaining and upholding the authority exercised by their father.[6]

Following the foundation of Singapore, Europeans in the Malay world came to be deeply concerned about Malay piracy. It was generally felt that the continued attacks on the native traders who came to Singapore would destroy the commerce of the port. Throughout the decade from 1826 to 1836, the topic of piracy, its causes, and how it could be suppressed came to occupy much of the thinking of the Europeans at Singapore. Almost every contemporary account of the Malay world dwells at some length on the persistence of piracy as a way of life among the Malays.[7] A book-length treatment of Malay piracy was compiled by Horace St. John in *The Indian Archipelago*. He equated all Malay political activity with piracy.

> The coast dwellers of the Malay peninsula formed in other parts several tribes, each of which, known in the country dialect as *suku* was under the authority of a chief. All these petty rulers were dependent on a prince of superior rank,

> who held his authority direct from the sovereign throne. In this manner the whole political system of the region was founded in piracy. It was thus in former times they obtained from some petty princes of Borneo and Sumatra supplies of rice, munition, and arms, on condition that all their booty should be divided into three portions — two for the pirates themselves and one for their ally. A proverbial saying among them exhibits the whole rationale of this usurious system — "to give two and receive one". From the intercourse held with the freebooters, many chiefs amassed wealth in gold and silver, in pieces of artillery, in masses of copper ore, and in beautiful women to be sold as companions for the pillow of some richer Indian prince.[8]

It is perhaps an exaggeration to say that the Malay political system was never anything more than piracy. The previous discussion of the history of the Johor empire and early Singapore was intended to show that the difference between piracy and political activity, as far as Malays were concerned, was largely one of legitimation. The first two decades of the nineteenth century had been a particularly unfortunate period for the maritime empire. By 1824 the Sultanate had been deprived of its last shreds of legitimacy, the empire had been cut in half by the British and the Dutch, and the entrepot, which had always served as a focal point for Malay political organization, was firmly dominated by Europeans.

Nicholas Tarling, who has investigated the subject of Malay piracy at some length, suggests that Europeans were inclined to classify most Malay political activity as piracy. He has offered a reasonable explanation of the general shape of maritime Malay states. Generally, these were founded by petty chiefs who established outposts at the mouths of rivers and drew a living by taxing trade between visiting merchants and upriver communities. The conditions under which business was usually conducted, involving advances, monopolies and competition, offered many opportunities for commercial disputes. In the European settlements, such disputes were often treated as "piracy". Likewise, disturbances arising from conflicts within these states or with other states, which often included attacks on trade, were also considered piracy "rather than interference with neutral trade".

Tarling also discusses the role of maritime empires, such as that of Johor, which rose to power under "warrior-chiefs" who subdued lesser states, taxed their trade, and forced ships into central entrepots. This too was often treated as piracy rather than naval warfare and tax collection. Finally, he points out that the decay of such an empire, as had recently happened in Johor "would leave at its centre an aristocracy and its followers, that, deprived of imperial revenues, resorted to piratical means of subsistence, roaming the seas and attacking traders indiscriminately".[9]

Despite the "excuses" that Tarling offers for the Malays, he ultimately comes down on the side of the suppression. Such activity, no matter what one called it, and what caused it, was violence "which the British might have a duty to suppress … Both sides were caught up here in the prevailing conditions, and their struggle is tragic. A historical impasse existed, and no doubt the only way out was to suppress the marauders. If, therefore, one might find some explanation, even some excuse, for the Malays, one might also find the same for the British."[10] However the fact remains that the marauders were ultimately suppressed. The British declared war on them and, as resources became available, eventually wiped them out. The struggle was particularly tragic for the *orang laut* and for the chiefs who sought to practise politics in the old way.

This had been the mistake of Temenggong Abdul Rahman and Sultan Hussain. In 1819, they had seen Singapore as a base from which to reconstitute the old Johor empire. The disputes with Raffles and Crawfurd between 1819 and 1824 were largely the result of the chiefs' attempts to collect revenues. The treaties of 1824 had cut them off from their traditional territories and had placed the activities of their followers outside the law. The chiefs were also enjoined to aid in the suppression of piracy. The British attitude towards piracy was one of the chief problems facing Ibrahim. He was in a situation where his very legitimacy as a chief depended on British recognition. There was no doubt in the minds of the British that his predecessor had been a pirate, and it was thus incumbent upon Ibrahim to clear the family of any further charges.

And yet, his only political resource, his only subjects, were the pirates themselves. By 1830, the evidence suggests that Temenggong Ibrahim's government was a reconstituted but smaller version of his father's. Ibrahim's state, too, was composed primarily of sea peoples. Despite Bonham's contention that the Temenggong's following had become fragmented, by the time Ibrahim came of age he had already begun to show his strength among these peoples.

In 1835, a report in the *Singapore Free Press* accused the Temenggong and his followers of a number of piracies in the immediate region:

> It is reported that a number of piratical boats manned by people belonging to Tellok Balanga have been and still are lurking in the straits between this and Rio, committing atrocities of more than usual number and daring. In the hope that it may attract the notice of Government, I request that you will publish this list of them in your next paper.
>
> One Pucat which left Rio on or about the 1st inst. bound for this place, captured; crew 25 or 26 in number missing, supposed to have been all murdered.[11]

The account goes on to give details about four more vessels which had allegedly been attacked by pirates from Teluk Belanga.

Bonham's subordinates also suspected the Temenggong of being involved in piracy. In his book, T. J. Newbold recommended "a discreet surveillance over the conduct of the present Tumungong of Johore; who is more than suspected of being the mainspring of the daring system of piracy which has so long been an opprobrium to the eastern extremity of the Straits. A threat of withdrawing the stipend he enjoys gratuitously from the British Government might be useful."[12]

The Dutch, too, cast suspicion on the establishment at Teluk Belanga. In 1836, the Resident of Riau "pointed out that although the population of Rhio and Lingga was altogether bad, it was notorious that a great number of pirates actually lived in the New Harbour and Teluk Belanga districts of Singapore itself — where they got their information and their powder and shot, and where they were able to get rid of their booty without difficulty."[13]

Bonham himself was well aware that Ibrahim had become a rather disreputable character at Singapore. He left the following description of him in 1835:

> His father died in December, 1825, and was succeeded by his eldest son who is naturally imbecile [*sic*] ... his next brother therefore has the management of the monthly sum we pay him ... This young man is about 18 years of age [actually Ibrahim was 25 at the time] idle and completely illiterate; indeed, except by his clothes and consequent personal appearance, not a remove higher on the scale of Civilization than the meanest of his followers. I make these remarks because an opinion exists here that the last is very deeply involved in many of the Piracies which take place in the neighbourhood ... they [the Temenggong and the Sultan] are indeed incapable of restraining their own dependents, among whom, though I have no tangible evidence to prove it, there can be little doubt that there are many who live upon what they get by this mischievous and atrocious way.[14]

Despite the Temenggong's unsavoury reputation, Bonham decided to set a new course in Anglo-Malay relations. In 1836, the Temenggong agreed to cooperate with Bonham in suppressing piracy. This was a turning-point for the Temenggong. For the next thirty years, he came to be considered the primary Malay ally of the British, not only as a controller of the sea peoples but also as a negotiator on behalf of the Straits government in its dealings with other Malay chiefs. In order to do this, Bonham followed his inclinations "in assisting the Temenggong's family in regaining and upholding the authority exercised by their father".

Why did Bonham do this? Tarling considers it a fatal mistake which led the British into a fumbling policy of intervention in the Malay states.[15] Other reports from the period suggest that Bonham had decided on a comprehensive solution to a number of Singapore's chronic problems. Piracy was one of these, taxes were another, and the economic cycle was yet a third. In the years 1835–36, these problems converged on Bonham.

In April 1835, a public meeting was held in Singapore and a letter drafted to India and the King in Council asking for government assistance in suppressing piracy. In reply, the Indian government proposed a plan to levy duties at Singapore to pay for piracy-suppressing expeditions.[16] The Singapore merchants were outraged at this threat to free trade and enlisted aid from England to forestall the proposal. Mary Turnbull reports that the East India and China Association in London brought pressures to bear on the Board of Directors of the E.I.C. The scheme of levying taxes at Singapore was duly scuttled and the Straits Settlements continued as free ports "exempt not only from import and export duties, but also from tonnage and port dues, wharfage and anchorage duties, port clearance and stamp duties". The Singapore merchants, *laissez-faire* capitalists to the core, were willing to put up with anything, even piracy, rather than pay taxes. This situation continued until about 1867, and left the Singapore government in a state of continual poverty, thus forcing it to seek rather extraordinary means in order to make ends meet.[17]

Bonham and the Straits government were thus trapped between the Singapore merchants and the East India Company. The merchants would complain about piracy, but they would not pay for its suppression. Undoubtedly, a certain amount of their reluctance to pay taxes in 1835 stemmed from the current economic crisis. Munshi Abdullah reports that there had been a crash and that many Chinese merchants, who had borrowed heavily from European merchants, had gone bankrupt. The European merchants naturally were forced to absorb substantial losses.[18]

Piracy may or may not have been a contributing cause of the poor economic situation; it certainly did not help. In the early 1830s, not only Malay and *orang laut* traders were being attacked but Bugis, Chinese, and even a few European vessels were victims.

Bonham was thus forced to find a means of ending piracy which would cost the Singapore government nothing. Much of Bonham's success in solving these outstanding problems lay in the fact that he appears to have been an extremely practical man. Buckley reports that he had had long experience in the Malay world by the time he became Acting Governor of Singapore in 1836, and that "Mr. Bonham, afterwards Sir George Bonham, was very popular among the Europeans and natives." Bonham "commenced life in the East in the Civil service in Bencoolen, and had a considerable knowledge of mankind, and, like a sensible man, exerted himself to keep things in easy train and make them pleasant when he could".[19]

We have identified some of the things that must have been uppermost in Bonham's mind at the time. Many Europeans also favoured a more expansive and interventionist policy than Singapore had traditionally pursued. One of these was T. J. Newbold, Bonham's subordinate.[20]

Tarling shows the first evidence of Bonham's new policy with the expeditions of the gunboat *Andromache* in 1836. In May 1836, the *Andromache* arrived in Singapore under Captain Henry Ducie Chads. Chads had a commission from the Indian government to assist in piracy suppression and to deliver a proclamation to the Malay chiefs, informing them of a system of passes which was to be instituted for identifying trading boats. The Commissioners also had authority to communicate directly with the Dutch.

After surprising a number of pirates in Singapore harbour, the *Andromache* with Bonham and Chads headed for Riau in June 1836. They met with Goldman, the Dutch Resident, and informed him of their intentions regarding the pass system stating that they would henceforth hold the local chiefs responsible for piracies committed in their jurisdiction. They also made reference to the alleged pirate settlement on the nearby island of Galang. Goldman pointed out that under the Treaty of 1824, the British Commissioners had no authority in the Riau-Lingga Archipelago. He said he would have to consult with Batavia before he could cooperate with them. Upon this, the *Andromache* sailed straight to Galang and wiped out the settlement there.

The following month, they went to Pahang where some "Johor" pirates had sold as slaves the captives that they had taken from a Cochin-Chinese trading junk. It was at this point that the name of Ibrahim became associated with the anti-piracy campaign, and undoubtedly with the activities of the *Andromache*. Regarding Pahang, Tarling points out that "as force could not be employed in this Peninsular state, Bonham accepted the offer of Temenggong Ibrahim of Johore, still resident in Singapore, to use his good offices with the Bendahara."

Tarling describes this liaison with Ibrahim as a definite departure from the policy which the Straits authorities had followed since 1824. It was also continued by his successor, Butterworth.

> The significant fact here is the close association of Bonham and Butterworth with Temenggong Ibrahim. Through their operations for the suppression of piracy and the slave trade, the Governors were carrying on "intercourse" with the native states. The Temenggong was the first of the reformed princes, and

> he offered his aid, readily accepted, in communicating with other chiefs, particularly the Bendahara of Pahang. The influence of Government and of the Temenggong were thus closely associated.[21]

While Tarling is of the opinion that this association brought unforeseen problems for the Straits government, there can be little doubt that it worked to the benefit of Temenggong Ibrahim. In 1837, the Temenggong's status among the *orang laut* and the Malay chiefs of the region visibly increased.

In April 1837, 270 small boats containing the families of *suku* Galang came to Singapore to seek refuge under the Temenggong.[22] Ibrahim asked the government for permission to receive them and promised that he would be responsible for them. If Bonham's statement about the various *suku* of Riau who had broken away from the Temenggong's control is correct, the *Andromache*'s raid on Galang had had the effect of driving them back into the fold. The Galang people had a very high reputation among other *orang laut*.[23] It is therefore possible that many of the other *suku* followed their example and now looked to the Temenggong for protection, support, and leadership.

A Malay report of the *Andromache*'s cruise indicates that the Commissioners did not limit their attack to Galang but went down through the Riau Straits shooting at every *perahu* they chanced upon: "As they sailed back to Singapore from Galang they kept watch for native craft and whenever they met one it would be destroyed by cannon fire." At that time, Sultan Muhammad was travelling from Lingga to Riau with some other chiefs. "When they arrived at the Sambu Straits, they stopped to let the women go ashore to bathe. There they heard the news that a gun-boat was roving about the sea shooting at all perahus with mat sails."[24]

Fear of the gunboats appears to have driven many sea peoples to Ibrahim for protection. He was the only Malay chief who had a legitimate voice at Singapore. The Galang raid and other excursions of the *Andromache*, together with the coming of the steam-cruiser *Diana* in 1837, and Ibrahim's involvement in the Pahang negotiations seem to have acted as a catalyst for the Singapore chief's prestige among other Malay chiefs. Buckley reports that in July 1837 "the Rajah of Selangor came to Singapore in his own brig, and was received with a salute of 15 guns. The Sultan of Lingga paid a visit to Singapore at the same time, so the *Free Press* remarked that there were 'two crowned heads' in the same place; but both more than suspected of giving countenance to piracy."[25] The *Tufhat*'s report of this visit indicates that some effort was made at this time to patch up the split that had existed between the Riau-Lingga and Singapore chiefs. Sultan Muhammad[26] of Lingga had come to get the body of his aunt, Raja Maimunah, for burial at Riau. While he was there, he also married Tengku Ampuan, a half-sister of Ibrahim.[27]

Ibrahim was able to begin playing an important role in all further contacts between the Straits government and Malay chiefs throughout the region. Under Bonham, the Straits government embarked on a policy of intervention to suppress piracy. This intervention took the form of negotiations and occasional gunboat diplomacy. We may also suspect, although no mention of the topic is found in the sources, that the Temenggong himself must have outfitted patrol boats of his own at this time.[28] Since the Temenggong was not a wealthy man, his source of provisions and arms must have come from the government, or through intermediaries on their behalf.

The most likely sources for such supplies were the European merchants of Singapore. It is thus of great importance that the year 1837 also saw the relocation of two of Singapore's leading merchants to Teluk Belanga. James Guthrie and William Wemys Ker are both reported to have purchased land from Ibrahim and built houses near his kampong.[29] In the case of Ker, this marked the beginning of a long and profitable association between his company and the Johor government. The firm, Ker, Rawson & Co., later known as Paterson & Simons, was the principal European agent for the Johor government throughout the nineteenth century. The exact nature of the association between Ibrahim and these merchants in its initial years must remain a matter of speculation, but by 1843 there were reports of regular business dealings between the Temenggong and Ker.

The year 1837 was a watershed for the Temenggong. The key event was his relationship with Bonham, and everything else followed from that. He aided in the Pahang negotiations and was most likely suspected by other Malays of having had a hand in the Galang raid. This made him a man of importance as far as the sea peoples and many other Malay chiefs were concerned. His relationship with Bonham was also instrumental in the connections that the Temenggong was subsequently able to form with the Singapore mercantile community. This new configuration of relationships did not automatically ensure the Temenggong's success as a ruler; however, it did place him in a position where he could utilize one type of resource to reinforce his influence with other groups and thus acquire access to further resources. None of this was done without fighting and struggle. The next twenty-five years of Ibrahim's life were marked by constant conflict and turmoil. In 1841, the first of his many achievements was gained. He was officially recognized as the Temenggong of Johor by Governor Bonham in the presence of the Bendahara of Pahang.

The Temenggong did not, however, rely solely on the British for recognition of his new position. It is noteworthy that Bendahara Tun Ali of Pahang had been present and had thereby given his approval to the appointment. Since there was no longer a recognized Sultan at Singapore, Temenggong Ibrahim then travelled down to Lingga. The *Tufhat* reports: "... after Daeng Kechil Ibrahim had been installed as Temenggong Sri Maharaja he then went to Lingga to come before Sultan Mahmud Muzaffar Shah and to meet his 'uncle' Raja Ali the Yang Di-Pertuan Muda. Raja Ali was the husband of Ibrahim's sister, Raja Chik. When he arrived at Lingga he was honoured by Sultan Mahmud and Raja Ali according to the prescribed custom followed when rajas meet."[30]

Tarling has discussed at some length the leading role which Temenggong Ibrahim now began to play in this phase of British intervention in the Malay world. He began by negotiating with Pahang. Ultimately, he became involved in the Pahang succession dispute and brought in the British on his side. He and the British lost this war, but the credibility he had gained with British governors of Singapore was not destroyed. According to Tarling, "Trengganu was named as one of the states in which the Temenggong had influence."[31] He goes on to describe a subtle series of manoeuvres which seem to have been initiated by the Temenggong. In 1850, Sultan Omar of Trengganu suddenly started negotiating with the Dutch, much to the alarm of the Singapore authorities. "This was a move in native politics and the Dutch were not instigators. Its cause was undoubtedly Omar's alarm at the extending influence of the Temenggong in Pahang and in the Peninsula as a whole, associated as it appeared to be with the power of the British Government."

The Temenggong also became involved in a struggle with the successor of Sultan Hussain, Tengku Ali.

> In 1852, after describing a visit from the Temenggong, Church analysed the situation of the east coast. "In this neighbourhood, there are two parties, on one side, the Sultan of Lingga, the Sultan of Trengganu, and the young princes of Johore [Tengku Ali]; on the other, the Raja Bendahara of Pahang, and the Temenggong Sri Maharaja." But as yet there were no hostilities to call for British "interference or remonstrance". Another element in the situation, of which Church must have been aware, was that both Ali and the Temenggong had supporters among the merchants of Singapore.[32]

This conflict dragged on until 1855 when Governor William J. Butterworth, in one of his last official acts, recognized Tengku Ali as Sultan. This again, however, was largely a victory for the Temenggong. In order to gain his title, Ali had to surrender all claims to Johor. He was given only the small territory of Muar, lying between the Muar River and the Kesang. He received a lump sum of $5,000 and a pension of $500 per month from the Temenggong. This acknowledgement of his claim to Johor was one of Ibrahim's major achievements, and it was a direct result of the assistance he had begun rendering the Straits government in 1837.

In the official history of Johor, the *Hikayat Johor* of Major Dato Haji Mohamad Said, we are given an explanation of Ibrahim's success. The author notes that Sultan Hussain lost his power to the British because he did not "look after it". "There was a small difference between the Temenggong and the former Sultan. The Temenggong was clever and conscientiously looked after himself. He came to be on good terms with the officials of the Company. Because he helped them in whatever affairs he was able, the English came to like him."[33] This was particularly true of Governors Bonham and Butterworth, both of whom followed a similar policy towards the Temenggong and the other Malay states.

Tarling, who has examined in some detail the conflict between Temenggong Ibrahim and Tengku Ali, has noted that the settlement of the Johor question left the Straits government with additional problems. "The territorial division no doubt avoided much of the confusion of a divided administration over all Johore. But, affected as it was by the obstinancy of the two parties and by the timidity of the Supreme Government, the treaty of 1855 did not attain the real aim of the Straits Government, and the territorial division was one cause of this failure."

He points out that a few years later the tensions which had grown up in the Malay world as a result of the British government's association with the Temenggong led to open warfare on the Peninsula. In Pahang, a succession crisis developed into a full-scale civil war with the Temenggong intervening to support one side and Sultan Omar and Sultan Ali the other. "This war was a profound problem for the Straits Government, anxious as ever to preserve peace between the states. Its methods are illustrated by the history of its relations with Trengganu, and these again are bound up with the operations for the suppression of piracy."

One of the ultimate failures of British policy on the east coast of Malaya was that Trengganu eventually became a tributary state of Siam. Tarling suggests that this unfortunate result was owing to the Temenggong "on whose influence British policy on the east coast was largely founded".[34]

It is difficult to speak of the Temenggong as having pursued an independent foreign policy. Since he continued to keep his residence within the colony of Singapore, his freedom of action was highly limited and ambiguous. Tarling shows him, however, as having played a key role in the manipulating, if not directing, of British policy towards the Malay states. For the British, it appears to have been a relatively unsuccessful policy on the whole. But while the Temenggong suffered set-backs, he also reaped some permanent advantages, not the least of which was the ultimate recognition of his claim to Johor in 1855.

Until the 1840s Johor had remained an uninhabited jungle. As a resource, it was more of a liability than an asset. This was one of the reasons why Ibrahim had first turned to the sea peoples and to piracy when faced with the task of rebuilding the family's political prestige. Although he was successful in gaining allies among the British and respect from his fellow chiefs by this expedient, these offered no permanent solution to the overriding question of his poverty. One of Bonham's considerations in accepting the Temenggong's aid was that it offered a reasonably cheap method at a time when the government was beset with financial troubles. Piracy suppression could never have offered much in the way of financial remuneration for the Temenggong and his followers. If the pirates were to remain dormant and if the Temenggong was to retain his power over them, he needed additional resources, and Johor offered the only possible alternative. It was wide open for agricultural development. However, this demanded both labour and capital, and the Temenggong had neither. At this time, the Temenggong benefited by a stroke of luck. Gutta-percha was discovered in the forests of Johor.[35]

The story of gutta-percha illustrates the benefits which recognition by the Europeans had brought to the Temenggong. Malays had long been aware of gutta-percha and its remarkable properties. There are reports that they had occasionally used the rubber-like substance for making the handles of choppers. However, it was of no great value to them. During the 1830s, some enterprising Malays began to manufacture buggy whips from gutta-percha and sold them to Europeans in Singapore. Some of these found their way back to England.

In 1832, William Montgomerie, an English surgeon, published a paper on the properties and potentialities of gutta-percha. His research, however, did not attract general notice until 1843, when the Royal Asiatic Society recognized the potential of the substance for manufacturing surgical and chemical apparatus. A few years later, with the development of submarine telegraphy, gutta-percha was found to be the only substance capable of protecting underwater cables from the elements.[36]

Ibrahim was able to capitalize on this discovery through his contacts with the European merchants of Singapore. His neighbour, W. W. Ker, seems to have been instrumental in alerting the Temenggong to the value of Johor's gutta-percha.[37] One source reports that the first commercial shipment of gutta-percha to England was sent by Ker, Rawson & Co.[38] The Temenggong declared a monopoly on all gutta-percha in Johor and began employing gangs of labourers to go into the jungles to collect the substance.[39] It soon became clear that there was a market for all the gutta-percha that could be delivered to Singapore.

By 1848 people all over the region had joined in the search for gutta-percha, or *getah taban* as it is called in Malay. "*Menaban*", according to J. R. Logan, now "became the cry throughout the land".[40] Logan reports that news of gutta-percha had spread to both coasts of the Peninsula from Penang to Pahang and throughout the Riau-Lingga Archipelago, Borneo, and the east coast of Sumatra. Most of this was finding its way to Singapore and, oddly enough, to Temenggong Ibrahim. Buckley reports a complaint by the mercantile community of Singapore against the Temenggong.

In 1848, the Chamber of Commerce petitioned the authorities regarding the Temenggong's interference with the freedom of the port. According to them, the Temenggong had been systematically monopolizing the traffic in gutta-percha coming to Singapore. They claimed that his followers had been regularly intercepting boats bringing the substance for sale in Singapore. He is said to have had armed men in boats stationed at various points outside the harbour to intercept boats carrying gutta-percha, intimidate the crews, and purchase the gutta on the Temenggong's terms.

The report also shows the proportions which the trade had reached by this time. The annual trade amounted to between 10,000 and 20,000 pikuls, valued at $150,000 to $200,000. The Temenggong is said to have controlled about ninety per cent of this, "whence it was inferred that extreme influence of some kind was used, or some part of it would have found its way to parties who offered much higher prices for it than that which the native traders received from him".[41]

Thus, it turned out that all gutta-percha belonged to "Johor". W. H. Read, a prominent resident of Singapore at this time, and no friend of the Temenggong, has left an ironical description of the Temenggong's methods. In 1846, a public meeting was called to honour Ibrahim for his services in preventing piracy around Singapore. There was a ceremony on Government Hill when Governor Butterworth presented the Temenggong with a Sword of Honour. "Whilst this 'tamashah' was proceeding at Government Hill I, and the aforementioned merchants, counted several boats stationed outside the island, and manned by the Tumonggong's people, to seize any gutta percha which might be imported from outside places, at arbitrary prices, probably often at no price at all."[42] (See Plate 2.)

There is no indication in the sources that the Temenggong modified his practices regarding the collection of gutta-percha, but complaints were not repeated and so one assumes that he did take some steps in this direction. However, by this time he had become a wealthy man and his fortune enabled him to begin the agricultural development of Johor. In order to pacify the merchants, and to build a better public reputation, the Temenggong gave a grand feast on St. Andrew's Day, 13 November 1848. His guests at Teluk Belanga found that the place had been transformed.

> A few years ago, Telok Blangah only presented the appearance of a very dirty Malay village, the royal residence being merely distinguished from its neighbours by being of brick, and if possible, dingier and dirtier than the rest. Now everything has put on a new face. The money, which has flowed so copiously into the Telok Blangah coffers, through the successful dealings of His Highness and his followers in the gutta trade, has been more judicially applied than is generally the case when Malays become possessed of a little cash.

No longer satisfied with the "rude huts in which they were formerly content to live", the Temenggong and his followers had built themselves neat, European-style bungalows "gay with green and white paint" and tile roofs.[43]

With the dispatching of groups of gutta collectors to Johor, Ibrahim affirmed his claim to the land. These people no doubt acted as sources of information and the ruler became better acquainted with the resources and geography of the state. He also began moving people around. Many groups of aborigines, such as the *orang benua* and the *orang biduadanda kallang*, were resettled by the Temenggong in areas where they could be useful to his ends.

J. R. Logan, in what was one of the first anthropological studies conducted in Southeast Asia, has left an account of the abovementioned peoples.[44] This report gives an interesting picture of the manner in which the Temenggong's government actually operated on land as of about 1848.

The *orang sabimba* had been transported from the island of Batam, near Riau, to Sungai Tamram at the southern tip of Johor. There were about seventy people in the tribe when Logan observed them. They included about twenty-five men, thirty women, and fifteen children. He describes them as "living in a very degraded condition as serfs of the Temenggong". They were under a Malay official known as a *jenang* who employed them in collecting gutta-percha, dammar, rattan, gharuwood, ebony, chandan, and wax. In return, they were given rice, sago, and a little cloth. A number of other Malays were allowed to trade with them as well.

The *orang biduanda kallang* used to live on Singapore Island and, at some time after the founding of the settlement, were transported to Pulai in Johor. Originally there were about a hundred families but, by the time Logan made his observation in about 1847, their numbers had been depleted by smallpox to only eight families. They too were engaged in the collection of forest produce and were under a follower of the Temenggong.

Logan describes the relationship between the Temenggong's "government" and the *orang benua* who inhabited Johor as being only nominal. Judicial matters, law and order, and other such functions were not handled by the government but by the *batin* or traditional headman of the tribe. With regard to the Temenggong's government, he says the "relation to the Binuas is properly that of a maintenance and regulator of the Malayan monopoly of their trade". The representative of the Temenggong at the villages was often called "To Jinnang". Logan states that the *orang benua* of Batu Pahat were under a Bentara or the "Manki Pimanggan of Boko".

In addition to the *orang benua* and other aborigines, Logan says that there were three types of Malays living in Johor in the mid-1840s. These included the *pengulu* who had been posted to the various river mouths to ensure the monopolies on trade with the *orang benua*. They were in the employ of the Temenggong, and were very often Teluk Belanga Malays. There were other Malays from Teluk Belanga who were settled in different areas "enjoying some consideration and influence from their means and connections with Singapore". Then there was a third group of "miscellaneous settlers", presumably Malays but perhaps Chinese as well, who did not have the advantages of the former two groups.

Logan reports that most trade with the *orang benua* was in the hands of the *pengulu* and Johor Malays, as he termed the dependents and followers of the Temenggong. The *pengulu* or *jenang*, or other variously named headmen of each river, was the chief of the trade monopoly with the *orang benua*. Incoming traders were required to visit the head of the river first. Sometimes they had to trade directly with him; other times they were allowed to go upriver and trade directly with the natives. As Logan noted: "This system is enforced with more or less strictness according to the character of the Pangulu, but traffic is always to a certain extent carried on without his intervention. Strangers are absolutely forbidden from trading with the Binuas."[45]

Logan was rather critical of this system. He states that the "industry of the Binua is limited to the acquisition of the necessities which his own land produces". In other words, they were self-sufficient. But the Malays had taught him "to covet things which he knows not how to procure but from them". These included cloth, earthenware, parangs, iron, sugar, coconuts, and rice. The Malays would sell these to the *orang benua* and get them into debt. Being obliged to the Malay traders, the *orang benua* were forced to collect rotan, gharuwood, chandan, camphor, dammar, wax. All these things, Logan stated, were of no inherent value or use to the natives themselves and were collected only because of their debt to the Malay traders.

Naturally, there was a good deal of price manipulation. Logan claimed that the goods sold to the forest people were priced at between 100 per cent and 400 per cent above their value at Singapore. Similarly, the prices of jungle produce were fixed by the *pengulu* at 100 per cent to 400 per cent below the Singapore market price.

Gutta-percha thus appears to have solved a number of the Temenggong's chronic problems. First, it gave him an opportunity to employ his only two resources — the sea peoples and Johor. Also, it finally made possible an alternative to a life of piracy, although this was more apparent than real at the time. Ibrahim was well aware of the disadvantages that continued dependence on the sea peoples would bring him. Thus in 1844, one year after the discovery of gutta-percha, the first pepper and gambier planters were authorized to settle in Johor.

The wealth from gutta-percha, in addition to financing the beautification of Teluk Belanga and gambier planting, also seems to have made it possible for the Temenggong to begin organizing a form of government in Johor. Ultimately, the major task of his government would become the management of the pepper and gambier plantations. However, in 1847, it appears to have been organized along much more traditional lines.

What kind of prince was Temenggong Ibrahim in 1848? In assessing the man, we should try to see him in relation to his predecessors. This is probably how he saw himself — he was "Temenggong", heir to Abbas, Abdul Jamal, Engku Muda, and Abdul Rahman. This conception did not require a great act of imagination. His government, in Singapore and Johor, bears a striking resemblance to those of his ancestors. There are two related reasons for this: one is simply the force of family tradition; the other is that the type of state which Ibrahim inhabited (that is, Singapore) was in certain respects quite similar to eighteenth century Riau. This, too, is probably the result of the force of the tradition of the maritime Malay empire. In 1848, Ibrahim was an exemplar of his ancestors. Like them, he was a kind of "official" of the Singapore government; he was the local "diplomatic" representative of the Malay world. Not all, but much of the Malay policy of Bonham, Butterworth, and Cavenagh was conducted through him. Yet he was not recognized as a ruler in any place outside of Johor and Teluk Belanga. He certainly received a number of "votes of confidence" from the Malays. Among these we can include the Galang refugees and the chiefs of Riau, Lingga, Selangor, and Pahang. In this respect, he occupied a position similar to that which Abdul Jamal had held at Riau. He represented the "*suku-suku Melayu*".

Like the earlier Temenggongs, he was a kind of port official and policeman. He was responsible for the suppression of piracy and he also enjoyed certain trading and tax monopolies, particularly over gutta-percha. Until about 1862, he was also allowed a share in the joint Singapore-Johor revenue farms. The settlement of *pengulu*, traders, and pepper and gambier planters in Johor also appears to have been a traditional type of activity. Government was limited to the protection of economic monopolies.

The Temenggong's relationship with his subjects or followers seems to have been characteristically economic. His state administration, if it can be called that, was largely a tax-gathering operation. Both the *pengulu* on the rivers and the people in boats were enforcers of tax monopolies. With the exception of these, he appears to have had no other subjects.

On the other hand, all the Temenggong's *political* relations were with equals or superiors — the chiefs of Riau and the Peninsula, and the Singapore government. In this sphere of activity, Ibrahim made marriage alliances, acted as a go-between, and applied pressure wherever he could in his own interests. These activities helped him attain recognition as his father's successor and also gave him, in 1855, an unchallenged title to Johor itself. This recognition gave him access to economic resources, and his wealth gave him still greater influence in Malay political affairs.

The Temenggong had yet another sphere of relationships that was both political and economic — his connection with the Singapore merchants. Ibrahim was instrumental in helping certain Singapore merchants gain concessions in native states. Thus, Martin, Dyce & Co. was involved in Siak; and in Pahang the Temenggong's friends, Paterson & Simons, had obtained mining rights.[46]

How close was this pattern of statecraft to that of his predecessors? It is difficult to tell since we know so little about the affairs of earlier Temenggongs. Politically, there seems to be some correspondence. Temenggong Abdul Jamal had married into the Bugis lineage by taking Raja Maimunah as a wife. Yet the *Tufhat* states that he was allied with the Malay faction at Riau. On the other hand, the *Hikayat Johor Serta Pahang* indicates that his popularity among the Malays was not very high. Could a part of his unpopularity have been the result of his ambiguous relationships with both groups, as Winstedt suggests?[47] Temenggong Ibrahim certainly had his share of enemies, but in the long run he was more successful in his statecraft than Abdul Jamal. It appears that this was the real distinction between these two chiefs. Abdul Jamal had been defeated, whereas Ibrahim was victorious.

All the Temenggongs had controlled a following of sea peoples. The family stronghold at Bulang appears to have been the centre of their forces for some four generations, from Tun Abbas to Abdul Rahman in 1824. The size and strength of the following may have fluctuated with general conditions, but it seems to have remained more or less intact. Between 1830 and 1837, Ibrahim engineered a revival of this force. The distinction here was primarily one of location. Bulang was off-limits to Ibrahim, and so he had to relocate the *suku*

PLATE 1
Temenggong Daing Ibrahim
(Courtesy of the Arkib Negara Malaysia)

under his command at Singapore or Johor. The services rendered by the sea peoples to Temenggong Abdul Rahman seem comparable to those done for Ibrahim.

Another area of similarity is in the relationships that these various chiefs maintained with the rulers of the entrepot. Almost all of them seem to have formed an opposition group. Abdul Jamal opposed both the Bugis and Sultan Sulaiman. Engku Muda faced Raja Ja'afar and Sultan Mahmud. Temenggong Abdul Rahman also opposed the Sultan and the Bugis and, after 1818, the Dutch as well. Within a very short time after allying himself with Raffles, he again found himself in opposition. Ibrahim was able to capitalize on this role, and acquired a certain share of power within the Straits government.

It is interesting to note that, in every case, the Temenggong always played a secondary role in the entrepot. In a sense, all such officials were dependent on the ruling group for legitimization, whether it was the Bugis, a Sultan, or Europeans. The chiefs were also economically dependent on the entrepot.

PLATE 2

The Temenggong's Kampong at the foot of Mount Faber, Singapore 1837 — from a lithograph by A. Bertrand and based on a sketch by M. Lauvergne. Mount Faber was originally known as Teluk Belanga Hill. (See pp. 75, 88)
(Courtesy of the National Museum, Singapore)

PLATE 3

Singapore looking south from Government Hill (now Fort Canning) in August 1846 — a painting by J. T. Thomson which had its inspiration from the occasion of the presentation of a "sword of honour" by Gov. Butterworth to Temenggong Daing Ibrahim, at Government House, Fort Canning Hill, on 1 Sept. 1846, in recognition of the Temenggongs' assistance in suppressing piracy. Present at the ceremony were the Resident Councillor, the Sultan of Johore, and representatives of the various communities in Singapore. Butterworth is shown with his wife in the foreground painting. The painting is not the ceremony itself but is based on the event which took place. Thomson took the opportunity to give a view of the town of Singapore and the sea from Fort Canning Hill, illustrating at the same time the various types of people who were in Singapore

They derived whatever wealth they got as a result of the trade which came to the port.

Raffles did not want to see Singapore run as a native state. But the force of tradition was quite strong. Singapore had inherited some of the aristocracy of the former Johor empire. The British port also took over the same trading patterns that had characterized Riau's trade before 1784. Politically, by 1848, the Singapore government was expanding its influence over a number of Malay states. In many cases, it acted as a legitimizing and pacifying force; so too had the earlier Johor sultans. Singapore was the centre of the Malay world, both politically and economically. It was indeed a free port under the government of the East India Company, but for the average Malay everything at Singapore must have seemed quite familiar. There was more correspondence between Singapore and old Riau than there was between Singapore and Dutch Malacca. Except for its European rulers, Singapore was a native port but certainly a bigger and more affluent one than had ever been seen before.

NOTES

1. Temenggong Daing Ibrahim (b. 1810, d. 1862), also known as Daing Ronggek, Daing Kechil, and Tengku Chik, was the younger son of Temenggong Abdul Rahman. The elder son, Abdullah, is reported to have been mentally unbalanced (Winstedt, "A History of Johor", p. 91). Winstedt notes that he was also wrongly called Ganggek and Renggek by Munshi Abdullah. See also Major Dato Haji Mohamad Said bin Haji Sulaiman, *Hikayat Johor dan Tawarikh Al-Marhum Sultan Abu Bakar Johor* (Johor Baharu, 1950), p. 3.
2. Winstedt, "A History of Johor", p. 91. Winstedt suggests: "Probably the delay in installing Ibrahim as Temenggong of sixteen years was due to hesitation on the part of Sultan Hussain of Singapore to usurp the prerogative of the Sultans of Lingga and to the fact that after Sultan Hussain's decease in 1835 there was no Sultan of Singapore until 1855."
3. Moor, *Notices*, p. 272, carries a report by John Crawfurd, "Journal of a Voyage Around Singapore", quoted from the *Singapore Chronicle*, November 1825. Crawfurd noted that mining efforts in the Karimons had begun about 1825. There were about seventy Malays and Chinese engaged in working the tin mines there in October.
4. The *Tufhat*, pp. 306–11. This is a lengthy account of the battle which was fought in the Karimons. It concludes by noting that Ibrahim, or Daing Ronggek, afterwards came to Riau to pay his respects to Raja Ahmad (the father of the author) and reported that none of his people from Teluk Belanga had participated in the occupation of the Karimons since it was against the law. He also said that Sultan Hussain (the Yang Di-Pertuan Selat) had not himself approved the "war", but this had been the work of his wife and Tengku Yahya. See also Nicholas Tarling,

British Policy in the Malay Peninsula and Archipelago, 1824–1871 (Kuala Lumpur, 1969), pp. 23–28.

5. A. H. Hill, trans., *The Hikayat*, pp. 265–79. Abdullah describes the last years of this unfortunate prince, including his forced departure from Singapore in 1834 and his death at Malacca a year later.
6. Cited in Nicholas Tarling, *Piracy and Politics in the Malay World: A Study of British Imperialism in Nineteenth Century South-East Asia* (Singapore, 1963), p. 80.
7. See the following for various opinions regarding Malay piracy: Newbold, *Political and Statistical Account*, v. 1, pp. 36–47; Begbie, *The Malayan Peninsula*, pp. 270–74; Raffles, *History of Java*, pp. 246–62; Buckley, *An Anecdotal History*, pp. 276–82; John Anderson, *Mission to the East Coast of Sumatra in 1823* (Oxford, 1971), pp. 227–28; and finally the lengthy series of articles published under the title, "Piracy and Slave Trade of the Indian Archipelago", *JIA*, v. 3 (1849).
8. Horace St. John, *The Indian Archipelago*, v. 2 (London, 1835), pp. 160–62.
9. Tarling, *British Policy*, pp. 14–15.
10. Tarling, *Piracy and Politics*, p. 11.
11. *SFP*, 12 November 1835.
12. Newbold, *Political and Statistical Account*, v. 1, p. 37.
13. Walter Makepeace, R. St. J. Braddell, and G. E. Brooke, *One Hundred Years of Singapore* (London, 1921), p. 383.
14. *SSR*, R–3, Bonham to Prinsep, 23 April 1835.
15. Tarling, *Piracy and Politics*, p. 61.
16. Buckley, *An Anecdotal History*, pp. 276–77.
17. C. M. Turnbull, *The Straits Settlements 1826–1867* (Kuala Lumpur, 1972), p. 191.
18. A. H. Hill, trans., *The Hikayat*, p. 281.
19. Buckley, *An Anecdotal History*, p. 383.
20. Newbold, *Political and Statistical Account*, v. 1, pp. 40–46.
21. Tarling, *British Policy*, pp. 48–55.
22. Tarling, *Piracy and Politics*, p. 102.
23. J. T. Thomson, "Description of the Eastern Coast of Johore and Pahang with Adjacent Islands", *JIA*, v. 5 (1851), p. 143. Thomson gives evidence of the reputation of *suku* Galang among the other groups of *orang laut.* He reports a conversation with some men from *suku* Buru: "Judging from occasional expressions which escaped from them they appeared to look upon piracy as a highly manly pursuit, and as giving them a claim to the approval of their fellows. Thus Attak would occasionally say, 'the orang Gallang (Men of Gallang) do so and so, or such is the custom with them.' He appeared to think that notorious class highly worth of imitation; when asked to sing, he would say I know none but Gallang songs."
24. The *Tufhat*, pp. 330–31.
25. Buckley, *An Anecdotal History*, p. 315.

26. Sultan Abdul Rahman had died in 1830. He was succeeded by his son, Sultan Muhammad Muzaffar Shah (b. 1803, d. 1841).
27. The *Tufhat,* p. 334.
28. At a later date, there is evidence that the Temenggong did outfit some boats to suppress pirates; see *SPF*, 9 June 1859, which carries a report of the apprehension of some "Galang" pirates by the Temenggong's men.
29. C. A. Gibson-Hill, "Singapore: Notes on the History of the Old Strait, 1580–1850", *JMBRAS*, v. 27, pt. 1 (May 1954), p. 200.
30. The *Tufhat,* p. 338.
31. Tarling, *British Policy*, p. 57–58.
32. Ibid., p. 58.
33. Mohamad Said, *Hikayat Johor*, p. 3.
34. Tarling, *British Policy*, pp. 61–63.
35. Burkhill, *Dictionary*, pp. 1623–25. Gutta-percha (*getah taban*) is the latex-like sap of various varieties of *Blanco Palaquim*. From the time of its discovery in the 1840s, its most important use has been in the coating of trans-oceanic telegraph cables. It is also used for surgical and chemical apparatus, corks, golf balls, and dental fillings. Ordinarily, gutta-percha is a hard, solid, yet slightly elastic, substance. However, it can be softened simply by putting it in hot water and then remoulded into shape. On cooling it resumes its original hardness.
36. Two good accounts of the story of the discovery of gutta-percha are generally available. Buckley, *An Anecdotal History*, pp. 402–5; and Thomas Oxley, "Gutta Percha", *JIA*, v. 1 (1847), pp. 22–29.
37. W. H. Read, *Play and Politics*: *Reminiscences of Malaya by an Old Resident* (London, 1901), p. 14. Read, without giving names, simply notes that the Temenggong was made aware of the value of gutta-percha by "a Singapore merchant".
38. Allister MacMillan, comp. and ed., *Seaports of the Far East, Historical and Descriptive, Commercial and Industrial Facts, Figures and Resources* (London, 1923), p. 224.
39. J. R. Logan, "Range of the Gutta Taban Collectors, and Present Amount of Imports into Singapore", *JIA*, v. 2 (1848), p. 529.
40. Ibid., p. 530. Logan explains *menaban* as "a word which the dictionary of Gitta Teban has added to the Malay language … Menaban, from taban, signifies to collect Gitta taban."
41. Buckley, *An Anecdotal History*, pp. 482–83.
42. Read, *Play and Politics*, p. 14.
43. Buckley, *An Anecdotal History*, pp. 495–96.
44. J. R. Logan, "The Orang Binua of Johore", *JIA*, v. 1 (1847), pp. 261–300.
45. Ibid., p. 286.
46. Tarling, *British Policy*, p. 73, n. 290.
47. Winstedt, " 'Abdu'l-Jalil", p. 161. "It is however now clearer than ever why the children of Temenggong 'Abdu'l-Jamal adopted the title of Daing from their mother. It is just possible that the Temenggong's uncle, Sultan Sulaiman, suspected 'Abdu'l-Jamal of being too thick with Raja Maimunah's Bugis relatives".

4

The Temenggong and the Chinese

1844–1860

The 1840s saw the beginnings of a new model Malay state. This polity was not based primarily on sea peoples and control of trade but rather on commercial agriculture and control of a settled Chinese population. This was not merely a different economic system — it represented a transformation of the classical Malay political unit. The essence of the change was the creation of a new state and a more permanent economic resource in the territory of Johor.

We need not look far for the causes of this new orientation. The beginning of effective piracy-suppression measures in 1836 had, if nothing else, sealed the fate of the sea peoples. Henceforth their political and economic importance began to decline. By 1860, the once proud sea rovers of the archipelago were reduced to a few scattered tribes of shy nomadic peoples. The Keppels, Brookes, and Congaltons had blown them out of their island strongholds.[1] Britannia ruled the waves, and no Malay ruler would ever again build a state based on the *orang laut*.

The indigenous peoples were being outnumbered and outgunned at sea. Two trends which accelerated greatly in the 1840s and 1850s cut very deeply into the structure of the maritime polity. The first of these was the gradual displacement of the native traders by Chinese traders and even larger square-rigged ships owned by Europeans and wealthy Chinese and Arab merchants. Wong Lin Ken reports that by 1842 the proportion of the archipelago trade carried in square-rigged ships had come to exceed that carried by native vessels.

In 1842, the total tonnage of the archipelago trade with Singapore amounted to 109,387, of which 53,112 tons were carried by Malaysian *perahu*, and 56,275 tons were carried by square-rigged ships. By 1865–66, the total tonnage of the trade had increased to 233,465, of which 62,639 tons were carried in native vessels and 170,826 tons in square-rigged ships. Thus the Malaysian traders' share of the traffic had shrunk to a mere twenty-seven per cent of the total.[2]

Piracy was perhaps related to this trend, but the connection is not clear. Wong suggests that the overall decline in native trade may have been due to piracy, particularly the resurgence of Malay and Illanun piracy in 1843–49. However, he points out that native trade had done very well with extensive piracy in the pre-1836 period. Besides, British, Dutch, and Spanish naval attacks on pirates between 1845 and 1851 had broken the backs of the great pirate fleets of the Illanuns and Balininis.[3] Thus he concludes that piracy and native trade were not connected.

This is an interesting argument. Other writers have been unable to resolve the question regarding the connection between piracy and native trade. In 1828, Fullerton made a thoughtful observation on the relation between native traders and pirates: "… as Piracy is concerned, it is difficult to distinguish Pirates from Native Traders. I fear as regards Malay Prahus they not infrequently follow both pursuits as occasion points out prospect of Profit."[4]

Christopher Hooi, who did a survey of piracy between the years 1800–1867, brings us a step closer to a plausible solution. He shows that as trade increased, there was a consequent increase in piracy. Despite remarks about piracy destroying the trade, he points out that there are no statistics to show this.[5] Tarling, quoting Commodore Hay in 1862, comes close to the mark: "It does not appear to be at all clear that the trade on the whole has been affected by piracy. A change has taken place not in any way to be regretted, by which square-rigged vessels have been substituted for native craft in much of the coasting trade. These square-rigged vessels are apparently not generally subject to the attack of pirates who appear to respect their supposed means of defence."[6]

If this were the case, we might refute Wong's conclusion by suggesting that the anti-piracy campaigns had the simultaneous effect of destroying native trade. This was the consequence suggested by an item in the *Singapore Free Press* in 1846, commenting on the raids launched by Brooke and Keppel on the Illanun pirate settlements in Borneo.

> The warlike operations of our men of war in Borneo of late years have produced a disastrous effect on the native trade between that quarter and Singapore. This trade which was steadily augmenting is now all but

> annihilated. Last year there was a falling off in the Exports to Borneo by native vessels of above $85,000 dollars [*sic*] and this year it is almost certain will exhibit a much worse result.[7]

Thus the Malays were on the decline. In Singapore, they were being overwhelmed by sheer weight of numbers as well as by technology. By July 1845, the Chinese had come to make up the majority of Singapore's population. There were 32,132 Chinese in a total population of 57,421.[8] Over the next fifteen years, the Malays actually declined in numbers. In 1849, out of a total population of 59,043, there were 12,206 Malays and 2,269 Bugis. Ten years later, an estimate of the population in the *Singapore Free Press* noted that there were only 10,000 Malays and 2,000 Bugis. During the same period, the Chinese and European populations had doubled.[9]

With their general drop in numbers, the Malays at Singapore declined in status. Economically and politically, their influence was decreasing. Cameron noted that there were no Malay merchants in any of the Straits Settlements: "The Malay never rises to be more than a hawker; and this is the result, no doubt, of that want of ambition to be rich."

On the official level, British and Dutch pressure on the maritime state destroyed it during the mid-nineteenth century. The deposing of Sultan Mahmud IV by the Dutch in 1857 and the terms under which the British at Singapore gave recognition to Sultan Ali in 1855, make the late 1850s a watershed. The breakdown which had been in progress since 1784 was finally complete. These twin moves were merely the *coup de grace*. The Sultanate was stripped of its last shred of legitimacy and fell into the hands of the European powers. Major chiefs under the sultans, such as the Yamtuan Muda at Riau and the Temenggong, who cooperated with the imperialists, managed to make limited gains, but they too could not seek to replace the Johor Sultanate. They were permitted to maintain states at the cost of forgoing the refurbishment of the empire. However, even the attainment of control of a state depended on a productive population which could be taxed. Without control of economic resources, political power meant nothing.

The means by which the Johor ruler first filled his treasury from the state was the trading monopoly in gutta-percha. Here he collected no taxes but simply the profits on his investments. His income was limited by both the strength of the sea peoples and the supply of gutta-percha — both were decreasing. The pirates were being eliminated and the jungles were being depleted of gutta-producing trees. Collection of gutta-percha required the destruction of the tree. Each one yielded about fifteen to twenty catties.[10] It was estimated by J. R. Logan, in 1848, that some 270,000 trees had been felled since 1844. No attempts were being made at this time to plant new trees. In any case, these took about thirty years to mature. At that time, Logan wrote: "The imports from Johore have greatly diminished since last year. The tree in many districts has become so scarce that the taban obtained does not repay the time consumed in searching for it. The chief supplies must now be looked for from Sumatra, the northern countries of the Peninsula, and, above all, Borneo."[11]

With the establishment of pepper and gambier plantations in Johor, the Temenggong embarked on an innovative and risky enterprise. He joined forces with the Chinese pepper and gambier planters who had previously established themselves at Singapore. Between 1835 and 1844, these Chinese opened up large tracts of virgin land in the interior of Singapore Island. In the 1840s, disputes among the planters led to secret society wars in Singapore. The refugees from these conflicts made up the first wave of immigrants to Johor. They cleared the jungle, made the land "live", and produced a new and more stable income for the Temenggong.

Ultimately, this association between the Johor government and the planters brought new problems for the Malay ruler. The Chinese proved as difficult to manage as the British and his own people, the *orang laut*. In addition, the Johor ruler found himself embroiled in Chinese economic conflicts. However, he appears to have had a certain measure of success in avoiding many potential problems. At least there were no secret society conflicts in Johor.

In the 1840s, the Chinese planters represented an indispensable resource for the Temenggong. They and the gambier crops were the only means by which the jungles of Johor could be cut down and the land brought under cultivation. So far, this had been the only form of cultivation which had proved capable of producing a reliable profit from the thin red soil of the region. Where all others had failed, the Chinese pepper and gambier planters had succeeded in Riau and then in Singapore. They were thus the most logical candidates to settle in Johor.

However, if he was to collect revenues and thus support his own government, it was also necessary for Ibrahim to devise means whereby he could control these immigrants. Here again, his resources were very slim. The Chinese pepper and gambier planters were very good at managing their own affairs. They had settled in Singapore with neither help nor permission from the government and had relied solely on their own systems of control.

In looking for guidelines to organize his own government of these people, the Temenggong had few successful examples to choose from. The Riau Malays, the Dutch, and the English all had difficulty in ruling large populations of rural Chinese. Likewise, there was little in his own heritage which would have prepared him to undertake such a task. No Temenggong before him had ever really governed a land area the size of Johor, and none had ever controlled a population of comparable size and energy.

In seeking precedents to organize his government, the Temenggong appears to have fallen back on whatever traditional patterns of rule seemed appropriate. He allowed the Chinese a great deal of freedom to manage their affairs within the state. This was perhaps one of the oldest methods of Malay government, and it was still the basis of control in Riau under the Dutch. At the same time, however, Ibrahim found it useful to borrow some administrative techniques from the British. He introduced a system of written grants of authority made to the headman of each settlement. The Johor government thus began as a minor innovation on a very old theme.

By the end of the nineteenth century, a number of observers noted that the Temenggongs had developed a unique type of economic administration in Johor called the Kangchu system.[12] It drew its name from the term used to refer to the Chinese headman of each river where plantations had been established. The headman was the Kangchu — a Chinese term which, loosely translated, means "lord of the river". The Kangchu received a grant from the Temenggong which was called a *surat sungai* (river document). This document authorized him to open plantations on a certain river and placed in his hands the right to collect taxes, exercise the functions of government, and control cultivation within the river valley covered by the grant.

To administer the settlement, he constructed a large house near the mouth of the river. This was called the *kangkar* ("river foot") and it housed the tax monopolies controlled by the Kangchu.[13]

Our study of this system is based on the collection of *surat sungai* which have been preserved in the Johor Archives. They provide us with the first "modern" written documents produced by a Malay government. Through them we are able to trace the course of settlement in Johor and also describe, in some respects, the evolution of the Johor government itself. The system was, in the final analysis, a unique combination of Malay, Chinese, Dutch, and English administrative practices.

It appears that the system by which the earlier cultivation at Riau was organized provided the model for the Kangchu system which was created in Johor. It is noteworthy that all the settlements were riparian. This was primarily a function of the geography which was common to both Bentan and Johor. Rivers provided the only means of access to the land. A major feature of all of these settlements was the revenue farms which were located there. Begbie describes the settlement of Singkang on the Sebong River thus: "The population in 1825 amounted to about 1,040 souls residing on the banks of the river, and allowing for immigration and births, we might be led to estimate it at present [1834] as not under 1,300." At the time this estimate was made, however, it was stated that there were only forty houses, one arak distillery, one opium, and one gambling farm.[14] Everything was farmed out to the Chinese themselves. In matters of economic administration, they were a relatively autonomous community. This was a typical administrative pattern which the Dutch adopted for ruling their settlements in Southeast Asia. In Riau, at this time, the Dutch had appointed a headman for each Chinese community, who was known as the "captain" or *kapitan*. For example, the inhabitants of the district of Sebong were mainly gambier planters and retail traders who brought the gambier and pepper to Riau. They were governed by an individual selected from among themselves, who was accountable for their behaviour to the Kapitan of the Chinese of the Canton kampong.[15]

Thus the Kapitans at Riau were both administrative officials, policemen, and revenue farmers for the government. When the British founded Singapore, they adopted the practice of farming out the revenues, but no such official as a Kapitan was ever appointed.[16] While this meant that in theory all races of Singapore were under the same legal system, in practice it meant that very often the Chinese were not governed at all. So long as all Chinese resided within the town limits of Singapore, the problems faced by the British administration were apparently manageable; but as soon as large numbers of Chinese began to settle in the interior of the island, they were removed from governmental control altogether.

This attempt at introducing European-style administrative practices to govern a foreign population proved to be a failure particularly in regard to land administration. L. A. Mills devoted an entire chapter of his book to the Malacca land problem. In conclusion, he described the British policy as follows: "It was born of misconception, it lived in travail and tribulation, and it closed in failure. Consistent throughout, it was one unending chronicle of excellent intentions and faulty execution, of disappointed hopes and continual losses — the most depressing chapter in the history of British Malaya."[17]

While the Singapore land problem did not cause quite the same kind of difficulty, other matters produced chaos, confusion, and eventual bloodshed. Here the administrative breakdown was intimately connected with pepper and gambier planting and Chinese secret society conflicts. When cultivation in Johor began, it must have appeared to Temenggong Ibrahim that the British system had little to recommend itself. Thus, we shall find that the Temenggong based his administrative system on the old pattern and appointed a Kapitan.

It should also be recalled that Temenggong Ibrahim's father had dabbled in gambier planting. The first cultivators at Singapore were brought there by

Temenggong Abdul Rahman before 1819.[18] There were twenty plantations on the island when Raffles arrived. However, there is no evidence that this connection of the Singapore Malay chiefs with Chinese gambier planters in any way continued after 1824. In fact, by 1822 all of the original plantations had been sold and became a part of the town. Whether any Malays in Ibrahim's following possessed some particular expertise as a result of this earlier experience is a matter of speculation. It appears that Ibrahim had to relearn everything anew.

Before discussing the settlement of Johor, however, it is necessary to sketch briefly the history of gambier at Singapore. Gambier cultivation became established and spread across Singapore almost without the British noticing it. For the period from 1819 to 1835, Europeans paid little attention to gambier cultivation at Singapore. Crawfurd makes a vague reference to it in a paper published in 1825, so there must have been some contemporary evidence of it.[19] The first European to observe the extent of the cultivation at Singapore was the Resident Councillor, Prince.

Buckley reports that in 1827 Prince visited Bukit Timah to survey the ground before a road was cut: "He went on foot accompanied by the contractor of the roads. They had a five hours' walk … the distance cut through undulating hill, marshes and rills was fourteen miles; three-fourths of it in gambier and pepper cultivation."[20] Thus, by 1827 the planters had already cleared a belt of land ten and a half miles long or even more. But, in 1830 Earl could still write that there was an independent Chinese community in the interior which no European had ever visited.[21]

Before 1835, most gambier was exported to its traditional markets in Java, Celebes, Siam, and China. Although Europeans were aware of gambier's use for tanning and dyeing, a heavy import duty in Great Britain prevented its export to that country. But in 1834 the tariff was lifted and the *Singapore Chronicle* regarded gambier as likely to become a staple article of export from Singapore to Britain.[22]

The rapid expansion of gambier cultivation at Singapore after this time was made possible partly because it was already established, but more importantly because the gambier market itself had been relocated at Singapore. In 1830, Earl reported that the once thriving port at Tanjong Pinang in Riau had degenerated to a sleepy little village. However, the interior of the island had been "brought into a good state of cultivation by a large body of industrious Chinese" who possessed extensive plantations of pepper and gambier. Their numbers were said to amount to forty thousand, but no census had been taken. Only a small part of their produce came through the town of Riau, the greater part being sent to Singapore from the northern part of the island.[23]

This traffic in gambier to Singapore had been going on since shortly after the founding of the settlement. Imports of gambier, most of it probably from Riau and Lingga, between April 1820 and April 1821, amounted to 10,790 pikuls.[24] In August 1821, these ports sent 578 pikuls of gambier and 195 pikuls of pepper to Singapore.[25] In 1825 and 1826, the value of the gambier imports to Singapore totalled $19,313 and $28,057 respectively, but no figures for weight are available.[26]

This traffic was carried on in the *sampan pukat* which plied between Riau and Singapore. The *pukat* trade was entirely in the hands of Chinese merchants at Singapore. Song Ong Siang reports that the wealthy Singapore merchant Seah Eu Chin began his career as a clerk on one of these craft in 1823. The *pukat* trade also took in both shores of the Straits of Malacca and the east coast of the Peninsula.[27]

In 1830, Seah Eu Chin established his own business as a commission agent to supply the traffic between Singapore, Riau, Sumatra, and the Peninsula. In 1835, he went into planting himself and bought a large piece of land which included most of the present Tanglin district of Singapore. He planted gambier and pepper but also experimented with other crops such as nutmegs. Eventually he concentrated on gambier and pepper. As did many other Singapore *taukeh*, he went on to make his fortune in the gambier business.

After 1835 gambier cultivation increased rapidly in Singapore. Jackson has traced the rise of this production: "In 1836 production was estimated to total 22,000 pikuls. This rose to about 48,000 pikuls in 1839 and to 80,000 pikuls in 1848. In the latter year the Singapore plantations also produced 30,923 pikuls of pepper, and these two crops together occupied over three-quarters of the total estimated cultivated area and accounted for nearly three-fifths of the total value of agricultural produce on the island."[28]

Newbold's statistics on the Singapore gambier market in 1836 indicate that large shipments were already being made to the West (Table 2).[29] Evidently, Singapore's gambier production more than equalled the imports which were probably from Riau. This must have been marked by a rather substantial shift in population. The export figures show that Britain, after only one year as a customer for Straits gambier, was one of the two largest consumers. Apparently, the demand for gambier had increased by thirty per cent within a year.

From this time, gambier flourished in Singapore. It involved the largest single group of the local Chinese population. Until the 1890s, gambier was the most important element of Singapore's local economy. This importance was more in terms of employment opportunities than of its share in the total income of Singapore.[30]

TABLE 2
Gambier Imports and Exports (Singapore), 1836

	(pikuls)
Stocked in Singapore:	
Local production (estimated)	22,000
Imports	19,624
Total	41,624
Exported to:	
Great Britain	9,921
Calcutta	7,096
Celebes	9,961
China	1,095
Siam	1,060
Cochin China	3,310
Borneo	2,725
Bali	1,159
Other	979
Total	37,306

Newspaper reports show that European interest in gambier had been aroused. There were several long articles describing the Chinese methods of cultivation and giving some idea as to the average size and productivity of the plantations or *bangsal*, as they were called.[31]

Ideally, a gambier plantation was worked by about three to eight men. According to various reports, the acreage could have been from 50 to 250, but the lower figure is more plausible. The main equipment in a *bangsal* was a large cauldron used for boiling the gambier leaves. After most of the liquid was boiled off, the remainder was filtered and reboiled until it was fairly thick. It was then poured into flat moulds and left to harden. These were cut up into small cubes, wrapped, and prepared for shipment. The dregs were used to fertilize the pepper plants.[32]

Certain natural limitations determined the optimum size and location of a *bangsal*. The astringency of the gambier leaves deteriorated rapidly after picking and within twenty-four hours they were "brown and useless". This meant that harvesting and processing had to be done together. Leaves had to be put into the pot as soon as possible after they were picked.

TABLE 3
Gambier Prices at Singapore, 1831–1861

Date	*Prices (Spanish $ per pikul)*
January 1831	1.30 to 1.75
January 1834	4.00 to 5.00
January 1837	3.00 to 3.25
January 1840	2.70 to 2.80
January 1844	1.50
January 1849	0.90 to 1.00
January 1855	3.15 to 3.20
January 1859	2.67 to 2.70
January 1861	2.85

This technology had already been well developed, both at Riau and Singapore, by 1835. The terrain and soils of Singapore were essentially the same as Bentan Island or Riau. Thus, once the European demand for gambier developed, there was no obstacle to start planting in Singapore. It was simply a matter of getting an adequate supply of labour and equipment for planting operations. Judging from the rapid increase in Singapore's Chinese population between 1835 and 1849, this was no problem. Cultivation expanded rapidly.[33]

By the mid-1840s, after a decade of almost unchecked expansion and prosperity, a number of economic and social problems began to plague Singapore's pepper and gambier economy. These were an important cause of Chinese secret society conflicts which, ultimately, led to open warfare between various groups. These disturbances worked to the advantage of Temenggong Ibrahim, and in 1844 the first groups of planters in Singapore were ready to move to Johor.

Expansion of the cultivation into Johor was only a temporary solution to the economic problems which turned out to be chronic. It will thus be useful at this point to describe briefly the three major problem areas: prices, land tenure, and the financial system which supported the cultivation.

Jackson has given sample prices for gambier during the period 1831–61 (Table 3).[34] The gambier price tended to be very unstable and this made it a highly speculative commodity. Production was very much affected by the laws of supply and demand and tended to alternate between underproduction and overproduction. The high prices of the 1834–40 period encouraged fairly extensive planting and by 1849 large tracts of Singapore island had been brought under cultivation. This drove down the price and put pressure on the planters.

Another problem was that of land and land tenure. In the beginning, there was a great deal of unoccupied land and no legal system of land tenure. Gambier cultivation was ideally suited to these conditions. Jackson has described it as a form of shifting cultivation. A gambier plantation had a productive life-span of only about twenty years. After that, the soil became exhausted and the cultivators moved on. Also, the means by which commercial gambier was produced required large supplies of firewood.[35] The crop used up land very quickly.

By the early 1840s, the supply of available land and forest was becoming exhausted and boundary disputes between the cultivators came to the notice of the government. At this time, the government began to implement a system for registering these rural landholdings. In 1841, J. T. Thomson arrived in Singapore as the first Government Surveyor.

A newspaper article suggested that the new surveyor should immediately begin laying down boundaries of plantations and implementing a system of quit rents and title deeds in order to prevent conflict among the planters.[36] The survey went ahead, but rather than stopping disputes, it created more. These conflicts, according to Dr. Lee Poh Ping, were the fundamental cause of the secret society warfare which then broke out in Singapore.[37]

By 1845 the interior of Singapore had been opened up with the construction of roads, and for the first time the government had access to the gambier plantations.[38] The attempts then made to survey the plantations and register the land caused quite a controversy.[39] Many of the planters objected to paying quit rents, particularly at this time when the price of gambier stood at a relatively low $1.65 per pikul.[40] Other factors also came into play.

To the falling prices and the land shortage must be added problems arising from the nature of the system by which planting was financed. At best, gambier cultivation was a subsistence occupation. The planter, if he was hard-working, frugal, and did not smoke opium or gamble, could net about $300 to $400 per year.[41] All the planters were poor men who had come to Singapore with little or no capital. In fact, they were often in debt from the moment they got on the boat in China. Only a few became wealthy from gambier, and these were not planters. Rather it was the merchants in the town who grew rich. They supplied the planters with provisions, capital, and credit.

> They [the planters] were financed by Chinese shopkeepers and merchants in Singapore town who usually claimed a proportion of the future crops until the debt was discharged. This system of pledging the future plantation and its

> products was on conditions highly favourable to the capitalist. Thus, it was observed in 1841 that "Almost the whole of the Pepper and Gambier plantations have been made, and are now it is believed up-held by borrowed capital — so that the actual cultivators are nearly at the mercy of the Chinese merchants of the Town."
>
> Many of these pioneer planters never cleared their original debt and remained under the control of Singapore financiers; indeed, it was believed that two-thirds of the plantations existing in 1839 were subject to encumbrances of this description.[42]

These shopkeepers were given an additional advantage over the planters with the implementation of the new land laws. Since they were town-dwellers, they were the first to be notified of government policies. They also knew best how to make the laws work to their advantage. The title deeds could only benefit the capitalists by giving them a legal hold over their debtors, the planters. It should be noted that the monopoly purchase and sale agreements alone would never have held up in an English court.[43]

The economic tensions between planters and shopkeepers were exacerbated by dialect differences.[44] Most of the planters and small shopkeepers were Teochews who generally knew very little English. The wealthier merchants who financed the Teochews were Baba, or Straits-born Chinese, many of whom had originally come from Malacca. These were generally Hokkien and most of them spoke some English. The ultimate source of Singapore's capital reserves were the European merchants. Since they had easier access to the European world of Singapore, the Baba merchants were in a position to dominate the flow of capital in the colony.

All the various Chinese dialect groups in the Straits Settlements were represented by secret societies, or *hui*. In 1846, the major groups at Singapore were described in a newspaper article: "The Hoes in Singapore are numerous, the principal being the Tan Tae Hoe (Heaven and Earth Society) otherwise called the Ghee Hin Hoe (Justice Exalted Society) and the Kwan Tec Hoe. The former is said to number from 10 to 20,000 members, the latter about 1,000."[45] In terms of dialect-group alignments, the Ghee Hin (or Ngee Heng) was a largely Teochew society. The Kwan Tec Hoe was the principal Hokkien society.[46]

The major outbreaks of violence at Singapore during the 1840s and 1850s were between the Teochew Ngee Heng and the Hokkien societies. Their struggle appears to have included the gambier-producing areas of both Riau and Singapore. Buckley reports that in 1847 the Yamtuan Muda of Riau had allied with the "Quan Tek Hoe" and that, as a result, the Tan Tae Hoe had gotten the worst of a series of outbreaks there.[47] The *Singapore Free Press* reported that about 1,500 refugees had left Riau and gone to Singapore.[48] Some of these set up a base on the Seletar River under a planter named Neo Liang Quan. In 1847, they launched an attack against Galang Island near Riau and destroyed a large number of pepper and gambier plantations.[49] Buckley's remarks as well as Song Ong Siang's account show a definite connection between secret society conflicts and pepper and gambier planting. Song also reports that the Chinese Christians in Singapore, who were also planters, were likewise involved in these conflicts. They too had their organizations which were called "Hong-kahs".[50]

A series of newspaper letters in March 1846 gives a unique insight into the manner in which the Chinese themselves perceived the situation. On 26 March, the *Singapore Free Press* printed a letter from a secret society headman called Tan Tek Hye, who styled himself "Keeper of the Quinangular Seal". He raised a protest against the assessments then being made on the plantations in the interior by the government. He informed the general public that, in retaliation, the society had commanded about 4,000 pepper and gambier planters to leave for Johor.[51]

In subsequent issues of the papers, letters were printed, supporting or criticizing the stand of the secret society chief. All, however, confirmed that the planters were leaving and that the government policy was the major cause of their departure.

For Johor, these events were of some importance. The 4,000 planters of the Ngee Heng did go to Johor and this marked the beginning of a long association between the Johor ruler and that Chinese secret society. Eventually, it was recognised as the only legal Chinese society in Johor and remained as such until 1916 when the British authorities forced it to disband.

The records of the Johor Archives and Singapore newspaper reports show that gambier planting had already started there before March 1846. Both Mills and Coope have erred in stating that planting in Johor began before 1844. Mills states that "between 1835 and 1840 ... the failure of the spice plantations on the island of Singapore caused many of the Chinese to migrate across the Strait of Johore." Aside from the fact that the influence of the nutmeg failure is problematical, it is also noteworthy that he gives no source for this date. In the following sentence, he mentions the presence of revenue farms in Johor, but his source here is one dating from 1847.[52]

Coope's error is twofold. He notes that "the first surat sungai which I have traced is dated A. H. 1245 (A.D. 1833)".[53] The writer's own researches in the collections of the Johor Archives show that the earliest traceable *surat sungai* was issued on A. H. 26 Muharram 1260 (9 October 1844) for Sungai Sekudai. Coope appears to have erred first in transcribing the *jawi* numerals, which

TABLE 4
Gambier Plantations in Johor, June 1845

Rivers	*Plantations*
Sekudai	20
Melayu	12
Danga	15
Tebrau	3

admittedly are close to illegible, and mistook 1260 for 1245. His second error was in converting A.H. to A.D.: A.H. 1245 began on 3 July 1829 and ended on 21 June 1830, so his statement that A.H. 1245 is the same as A.D. 1833 is likewise incorrect. We must take 1844 as the date of the first known *surat sungai.*[54]

The second grant, made on 22 October 1844, gave the Tebrau River to Kapitan Tan Kye Soon.[55] By April 1845, three more *surat sungai* had been recorded. One of these was for the Melayu River and the other two (apparently duplicates) were for the Tiram, a tributary of the Johor River.[56]

A contemporary newspaper report gives the first notice of planting in Johor. While it does not fully correspond to the information in the Archives, the discrepancies are minor ones. It states that cultivation had begun on four rivers and that, in all, sixty-two plantations were in operation (Table 4). The total population of these rivers was estimated at 500.[57]

This was clearly the start of pepper and gambier planting in Johor. It is interesting to note that, from the beginning, all settlements were made under official grants from the Temenggong. The settlement of Johor was under some form of Malay control from the first. Within a year, five more rivers were opened. Between July 1845 and April 1846, *surat sungai* were issued for the following streams: Chat, Lunchu and Paksi, Tiram Duku, Buluh Besar and Pendas.[58]

The continuing secret society disturbances in the interior of Singapore and the government's efforts to register the Singapore plantations worked to Johor's advantage. The new settlements probably absorbed the 4,000 planters that had been ordered to migrate by the Singapore headman of the Ngee Heng Society. In Johor, these settlers became the nucleus for a local branch of the Ngee Heng. They appear to have come under the direct authority of Kapitan Tan Kye Soon, the Kangchu of Tebrau. He is recognized as the founder of the Teochew community in Johor.

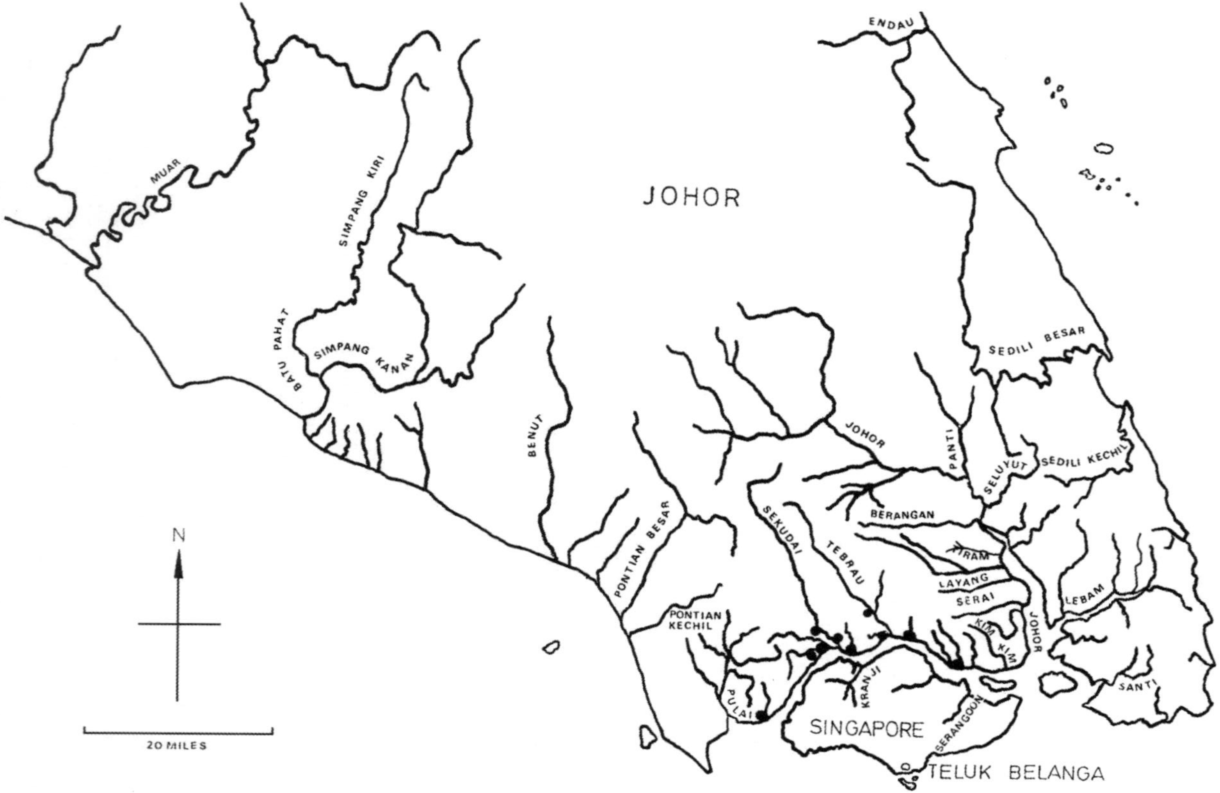

MAP 2

Kangchu Settlements in Johor, 1849

An account of Tan Kye Soon is given in *The Teochews in Malaya*. Part of it is given here in translation:

> The organization of the Ngee Heng was very large. The policy of the local government in early Singapore was one of *laissez-faire*, so they could carry on their activities freely. Later on, however, the government began to restrict them. So, Tan Kye Soon, who was an important leader, felt that the society could no longer stand to operate in Singapore. He made plans to expand into Johor.
>
> At that time, Johor was an underdeveloped place. Tan Kye Soon brought in some workers and proceeded bravely. They first opened Tan Chukang. The cultivation was successful and gradually he initiated the development of Johor Baharu. Today we call Johor Baharu "New Mountain", which means the newly developed place.
>
> After some years, when Muar disobeyed the Sultan, Tan Kye Soon raised an army and went to pacify Muar. Thus, the Sultan came to love and trust him. And he was commissioned by the Johor government to be responsible for the police force.
>
> Since he was the leader of the Ngee Heng, the government specifically permitted their open activities. This is the reason why the Ngee Heng of Johor was different from that of Singapore.[59]

This Chinese report, together with the information from the Archives, indicates that the Temenggong had, in some respects, relied on traditional models in organizing the government of his Chinese subjects. Like the rulers of Riau, both Dutch and Bugis and probably the Malays before them, he had placed the pepper and gambier planters under a Kapitan. It is significant that this Kapitan was probably not a merchant in the first instance, although he no doubt became one later. At the beginning, however, Tan Kye Soon was clearly a secret society chief and a kind of military commander. Most points made in the Chinese account appear to be corroborated by contemporary newspaper reports about secret society activities in Johor and Singapore. The *surat sungai* provide additional confirmation. The building of roads in Singapore and the government's attempts to register the plantations certainly brought Chinese activities in the interior under much closer official supervision.

The Tebrau settlement pre-dated the founding of the Malay government's headquarters at Tanjong Putri by more than a decade. Kangkar Tebrau (or Tan Chukang) seems to have been the centre of local government in Johor for the period between 1844 and 1855. In the latter year, a police station was established at Tanjong Putri. Being the headquarters of Johor's Kapitan China, Tebrau would have been the seat from which the revenue farms of all the Johor

Kangchu were managed. Thus, the statement regarding his military following should be taken at face value. The *surat sungai* identify him as Kapitan and the Chinese account notes that, as the major Ngee Heng headman, he was head of the police force. While there is no mention in other sources about his campaign against Muar, the unsettled state of affairs on that river, as well as the Temenggong's involvement in these conflicts, was noted by other observers. The Chinese account is plausible and reinforces the argument for Tan's role as a "policeman".

This settlement and its role in the cultivation during these years are mentioned only in the Chinese sources. Apart from the relevant *surat sungai*, no Malay or English accounts give further information regarding Tebrau's early prominence. The *surat sungai* suggest, however, that it was an important settlement and, at least until 1869, remained the headquarters of the Kapitan. A *surat sungai*, dated 1859, indicates that Tan Kye Soon had taken a partner who later succeeded him both as Kangchu and as Kapitan. This was his adopted son, Tan Cheng Hung.[60] The latter individual then held the post for several years and then sold off his holdings and disappeared from the scene.[61] In 1873, a *surat sungai* indicates that a new Kapitan had been appointed since 1869. His name was Seah Tee Heng, a Sekudai Kangchu. He may possibly have become Kapitan in 1871.[62] By this time, Tebrau had probably begun to decline in importance with the growth of the new town of Johor Baharu.

There is little definite information about the number of plantations or *bangsals* opened at Tebrau or about the actual population during the period 1844–60. The only figures available refer to the subsidiary holding at Sungai Pandan. In 1864, there were forty plantations on this river.[63] There should have been many more, further up the Tebrau itself beyond the *kangkar*. The nature of the evidence in the Archives, however, does not give information on acreage, produce, or population. The *surat sungai* merely authorized the opening of an area. To the Johor government, the Kangchu was primarily a concessionaire whose major role was the collection of taxes.

While the Kangchu must have had some responsibility for ensuring that the planters' debts with the shopkeepers were paid, there is little evidence that such transactions were a matter of government record. The government's concern, as seen in the *surat sungai* and related documents, was with revenue farms and the collection of taxes. In matters of tax-farms, as with the financing of the planters, the economic life of Johor was determined by Singapore.

The arrival of the 4,000 Chinese in about 1846 coincided with the first mention of revenue farms in Johor. Buckley carries a quotation by Mr. Thomas Church, the Resident Councillor of Singapore, regarding an assault on one Ang Ah, a Chinese merchant of Singapore, in July 1846: "The assault we have reason to believe was prompted by a wish to annoy Ang Ah,[64] because he has recently become renter of the Opium Farm lately established in Johore by the Tomoongong, whose Chinese settlers daily increase, to the serious detriment of the Singapore Revenue Farmers ..."[65]

Even though there was a Kapitan in Johor, the farms of the state were still held from Singapore. By 1847 the major Singapore tax-farmer, Cheang Sam Teo, held the Johor farms as well. At that time he paid $300 per month for them.[66] From this time, whether officially sanctioned by the Singapore government or not, the Johor and Singapore farms were generally held jointly by the same syndicate.[67] So the revenue collection for Johor was, from the beginning, based on and financed from Singapore. The Singapore farmer supplied the capital and the opium, and the Kapitan and other Kangchu in Johor were presumably responsible for the local administration of this monopoly as well as for final processing and distribution. It is important to stress the continuing connection between Johor and Singapore and to note that Johor never became economically independent of the British settlement throughout the nineteenth century. A major preoccupation of the Johor government was the regulation of the relationship between the Johor Kangchu and the Singapore tax farmers.[68]

Even in the case of the Malay government itself, the centre remained in Singapore at Teluk Belanga until the 1860s. The first moves at actually setting up any kind of government establishment in Johor did not get underway until 1855. One obstacle, besides the generally unsettled condition of the state before that time, was the fact that the Temenggong's claim to Johor was not fully recognized. The treaty of March 1855, by which Tengku Ali, the son of Sultan Hussain, was recognized as Sultan of Johor, also (strangely enough) recognized the Temenggong as sovereign ruler of the state. Ali's title was an empty one, and the only territory which remained under his control was the narrow strip of land between the Muar and Kesang Rivers.[69] This settlement removed all legal impediments to the establishment of a formal governmental apparatus in Johor by the Temenggong.

The only eyewitness account of the beginnings of the Johor government is the *Tawarikh Dato Bentara Luar*, the biography of Dato Mohamed Salleh bin Perang, one of the major officers of the Johor government. Writing in 1894, he recounts the first settlements in Johor:

> ... around 1855, Al-Marhum Ibrahim began to open Johor and make it a state. At the place called Tanjong Putri, where the state's capital is now located, he built a factory [*gedung*]. It was situated on the hill where the military base is today, Bukit Tambatan. The flag pole of the government was erected there and

> the place was named Iskandar Putri. No trading was done there as yet, nor were any merchants settled there. The only other buildings were one or two houses for the people who worked there. The chief was my uncle, Enche Dapat bin Mohamad Salleh. The Chinese pepper and gambier planters were already quite numerous in Johor. The head of each river had his own place.

He reports that in 1855 his own father was taken into the Temenggong's employ in Johor. About this time, he claims, Cheang Sam Teo, the Singapore opium farmer, bought the Johor farms. It was the job of the Dato's father, Enche Perang bin Mohamed Salleh, to guard these farms. He was empowered to arrest anyone bringing illicit opium into the state or anyone manufacturing debased opium in Johor.[70]

However, Singapore remained the centre of government. The Temenggong's court and palace remained at Teluk Belanga. Until 1858, all the government correspondence dealing with Johor (for example, licences, summonses, warrants, etc.) were issued from the government offices at Teluk Belanga. The Singapore kampong was also the base for the Temenggong's minister (*menteri*), Enche Long. Apart from the abovementioned factory, there was only a jail at Iskandar Putri. Dato Mohamed Salleh himself first joined the Temenggong's government in 1856, when he became a clerk under Enche Long. His work included writing out licences for planting and cutting timber.[71]

In about 1855, Ungku Abu Bakar, Temenggong Ibrahim's eldest son, was named heir-apparent. As his father was growing old, the young prince began to take over many of the functions of government. "He had spent three or four years studying in the English school.[72] At that time he was over twenty years old and had already begun to take over some of the work of government … all of the government business conducted with Europeans was under his direction. In all of these affairs, he was prudent, sharp-tongued and clear headed. He gained many friends among the Europeans and merchants." Abu Bakar then continued the work of building up the government in Johor.

> In 1858, His Highness Ungku Abu Bakar requested permission from his father to move all of the offices of the Johor government to Iskandar Putri. He appointed his cousin, Raja Ahmad, also known as Raja Kechil, to be the Resident at Iskandar Putri. But Abu Bakar was also there and together they put in order all of the things necessary to set up a police station and made the laws which are still in use today. Since Johor was very close to Singapore, all of the legal measures followed the system set up in Singapore. This was done in order not to upset the people who came to live in Johor. They were made to feel that it was the same type of law that they had been accustomed to in Singapore and Malacca.[73]

TABLE 5
Rivers for which Surat Sungai Had Been Issued by 1862

Straits	*Johor River*	*West Coast*
Sekudai	Tiram	Pontian Besar
Tebrau	Layu	Pontian Kechil
Melayu	Papah	
Tiram Duku	Kering	
Chat	Pecha Periok	
Lunchu	Tembaga	
Paksi	Chemarang	
Buloh Besar	Lebam	
Pendas	Chemak	
Danga	Redan	
Tajun Galang Patah	Ayer Puteh	
Choh	Santi	
Pulai (*ulu*)	Bukit Berangan	
Sengkuang	Panti	
Ulu Sekudai	Seluyut	
Semenju	Temon	
	Renggit	
	Punggai	
	Nipah	

Towards the end of 1858, Dato Mohamed Salleh reports that his own office was moved to Iskandar Putri. Enche Long had him appointed as chief secretary to the Resident, Raja Ahmad. His duties included those of chief clerk, court recorder, and treasury agent. He had three or four clerks working under him, but the business of the government was rather light at this time. The court was generally open for business only two or three days during a week. Abu Bakar himself frequently returned to Teluk Belanga to visit his father and the rest of his family who continued to maintain their residences in Singapore.

By the time of Temenggong Daing Ibrahim's death in 1862, the cultivation in Johor had become well established. The Johor Archives records show that about forty *surat sungai* had been issued between 1844 and March 1862 (Table 5). The greater majority of these were for rivers flowing into the Johor Straits which separated the mainland from Singapore. Another major area of settlement was the watershed of the Johor River. As an estuary, the river was

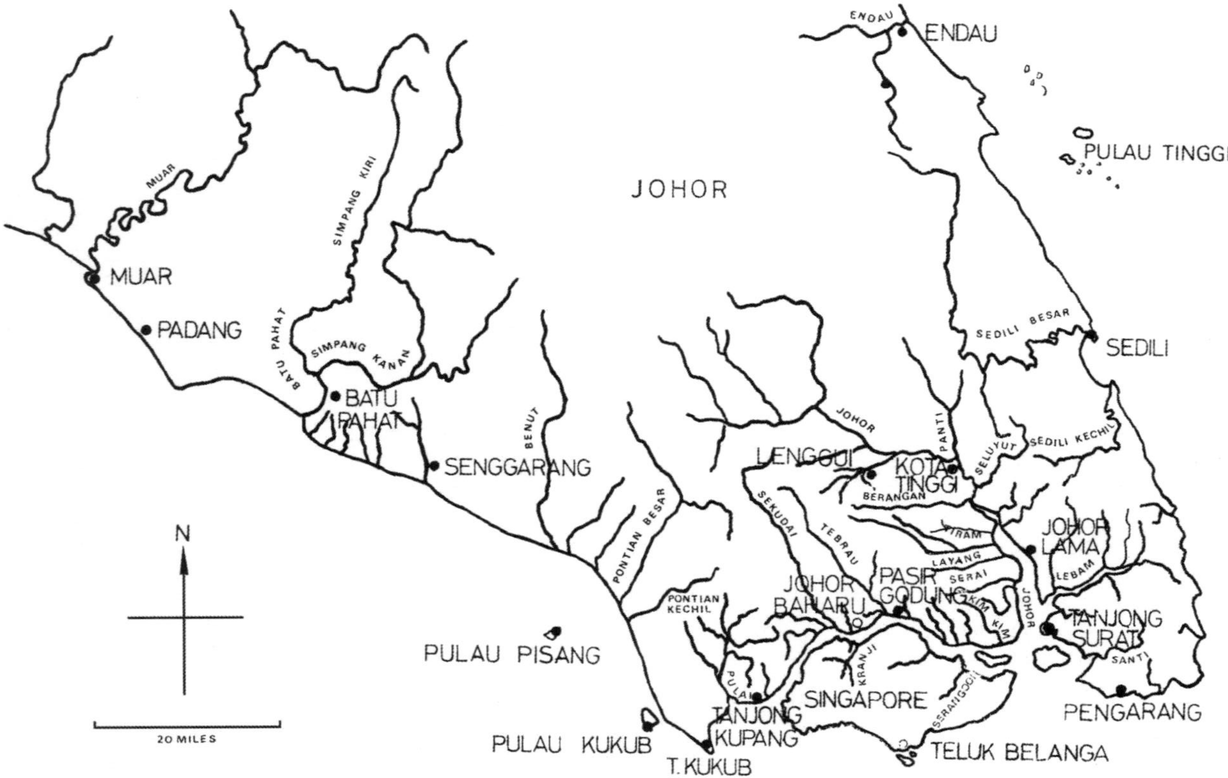

MAP 3
Kangchu Settlements in Johor, 1859

TABLE 6
Settlements in Johor, 1844–1862

	Surat Sungai	*Rivers*	*Kangkar (c. 1862)*
Johor Straits	18	16	14
Johor River	18	19	16
West Coast	4	2	2
Total	40	37	32

administered more as part of the sea rather than as outflow from the land. Its banks were treated as a sea coast, not a river bank. The *surat sungai* for the many small tributaries flowing into it were given out individually and there was never any *surat sungai* for the entire river.

Eventually, one man came to control most of one entire bank of the Johor River, but that was a rather special case. It should also be noted that no grants had as yet been made for Johor's east coast on the South China Sea, and only two had been made for the west coast. The population was clustered in south Johor. The statistics are shown in Table 6.[74]

What this represented in terms of population, number of plantations, or production is a matter of speculation. According to the figures given by Begbie, and this is confirmed by later evidence, the *kangkar* generally had populations ranging from 200 or 300 up to about 2,000. *The Singapore Free Press* published an estimate of Singapore's population in July 1859. This was a letter and it included an estimate for Johor as well. The writer claimed that the number of Chinese in Johor was estimated, "by those who have the best means of knowing it", at about 60,000.[75]

This figure strikes one as excessive. If we use a rough average of about 1,000 to a *kangkar* (which is probably still somewhat high), 30,000 may be more likely. It is possible that the writer of the letter got his information from the Temenggong. The latter would be inclined to give an inflated figure so as to justify the percentage of the joint Singapore-Johor revenue farms which he received from the Singapore government.

Apart from this, there are no other records of Johor's revenue which would give us an indication of how much money the state was receiving. A tax on gambier was collected, but there is no indication of the amounts of money or gambier exported. The gambier was all sent to Singapore and shows up on the record as an unknown percentage of Singapore's exports.

As a gambier cultivating area, Johor was one of three major producing centres at this time. The other two were Riau (Bentan Island, Galang Island, and perhaps a few others) and Singapore itself. In terms of agricultural population, the three regions seem to have been of more-or-less equal size, depending on local conditions. Politically, these were "separate" entities: the Malay state of Johor, the Dutch Residency of Riau under the Netherlands East India Company, and the Straits Settlement of Singapore under the British East India Company.

If this entire territory is seen from the viewpoint of the gambier economy, the political boundaries within it become much less defined. Gambier represented a unified economy which blanketed the three political zones. The economy was capitalized and controlled by a handful of wealthy *taukehs* in Singapore such as Seah Eu Chin, and his son Seah Liang Seah, Tan Seng Poh, Cheang Hong Lim, and Tan Hiok Nee. They were at the top of a vast "pyramid" of humanity making a living out of gambier in some way or other.

The gambier economy included a mixture of interdependent relationships. There was the debtor-creditor arrangement between the planter and the shopkeeper, which governed the exchange of produce and provisions. There was a legal arrangement between the Kangchu and the Malay rulers (in Johor and Riau). There was the military hierarchy of the secret societies. There was a merchandizing arrangement between the Kangchu and the Singapore opium farmer or some smuggler — a dealer who was not a part of the syndicate which held the farms. The Kangchu managed the distribution of opium in his river valley. He probably controlled a group of coolies as well and owned a share in the boat which serviced his *kangkar*.

Everything converged on the Kangchu. He managed the planter-shopkeeper relationship. He was the basic government concessionaire. He was also the local military chief and undoubtedly the wealthiest man in the district. At this period (*c*. 1860) most Kangchus in Johor and Riau were probably residing in their respective *kangkar*, although this was changing. Perhaps many of the Singapore Kangchus were already beginning to live in the town rather than at their settlement. Their military role appears to have been declining at this time as the local governments organized more effective official police forces.

Our evidence suggests that most Kangchus had initially been secret society chieftains in charge of a small body of fighters. Conditions in Johor during the 1840s had not changed much since 1787 and were none too secure. Such settlements would necessarily have to be able to defend themselves, protect their revenue concessions, prevent gambier smuggling, and keep the planters and coolies at work. In both Johor and Riau, these Kangchus were under the authority of a Kapitan who was appointed by the Malay ruler. It is impossible to outline with any certainty the relationship between the hierarchy of the secret societies and the distribution system for the opium, but one would suspect that these were quite closely linked particularly at the lower level. There likewise would have been a close connection between these groups and the coolie brokers who supplied the human resources which they exploited.

The system was changing however. As conditions became more secure in the 1860s, the need for the Kangchu's military role decreased. This meant that the Kangchu himself often changed in status. There was an increasing tendency for the Kangchu to be primarily a capitalist or, in local terms, a *taukeh*.

This then was the situation in Johor at the beginning of 1860. Iskandar Putri, a small but functional administrative centre, had been established in Johor and a corps of Malay administrators were beginning to exercise control on the spot. As shown on Map 3, most of the small rivers flowing into the Johor Straits had been opened to cultivation, as well as some of the tributaries of the Johor River.

The Johor of about 1860 was largely the creation of Temenggong Ibrahim. He had begun in 1825, without title or estate, but only as the heir to his father's leadership of the Teluk Belanga community. He did not begin to attract attention until about 1834, when he emerged as a suspected pirate chief. In many ways, his career began like those of hundreds of Malay rajas before him — he was a disinherited prince forced to claim a state by conquest.

His battleground was, however, British-controlled Singapore and he faced a power that greatly outweighed anything he could hope to muster. Thus, in 1836, he took the only opportunity available to him and joined forces with Bonham against the pirates. On the basis of this alliance, he gained power and received recognition from Europeans as well as his brother chiefs at Riau and on the Peninsula, and he finally received his title in 1841.

He began to build a state in Johor shortly after this. The discovery of gutta-percha and the development of difficulties among the Chinese pepper and gambier planters of Singapore supplied him with the wealth and manpower to begin agricultural settlements on the empty land. His government here was of a very traditional style and seems to have amounted to no more than the collection of taxes and management of trade monopolies. The Temenggong did not see Johor as a sphere for political administration. For him, politics were in Singapore and the Malay world which centred around it. Johor was simply an economic resource.

There was little need for him to exercise the actual powers of government over the Chinese. He merely appointed a Kapitan, as had been done at Riau, and took the precaution of excluding all secret societies with the exception of the Ngee Heng. The Kapitan and the Kangchus were the major administrators of the cultivation and whatever law and order was maintained on the plantations. They were also responsible for the collection of taxes and the Temenggong's revenues.

From a strictly pragmatic point of view, the Kangchu system made possible the initial development of large tracts of virgin land in Johor. As a pattern of social, political, and economic organization, it was admirably suited to the resources and requirements of the period. Efforts were concentrated on the cultivation of two crops which were in high demand throughout the nineteenth century — pepper and gambier. Successful cultivation and initial processing of these crops required a minimum of technological sophistication and equipment. They drew primarily on the most readily available resources of the area: Chinese labour, the unoccupied land and ample forests of Johor, and the many small but navigable rivers which gave access to them.

At the same time, minimal and appropriate demands were placed on the available capital and on the existing social and economic institutions. The family-run Chinese businesses of Singapore, the Chinese clan and secret society structures, and the Malay political organization of the Temenggong were admirably suited to finance, manage, and control this system of agricultural production. Moreover, they were able to do so at a profit.

It would be incorrect, however, to presume that such a task as that of opening up the Johor wilderness to cultivation could have been done without the British presence in Singapore. It is doubtful that such an enterprise would have been undertaken were it not for the entrepot. As we saw with Riau, this cultivation had long been a part of the entrepot complex. In the nineteenth century, British Singapore provided a market at which the produce could be gathered, sold, and exported. It was at Singapore that the monetary resources, the supplies, and the labour force were concentrated. Without the entrepot, the development of commercial agriculture in Johor would have been impossible.

Singapore's dominant position in the pepper and gambier business long pre-dated the opening of Johor. Singapore remained the financial and commercial centre of the industry throughout the nineteenth century. Johor was destined to continue its existence as a state which, though politically independent, was economically totally dependent on Singapore.

Until the end of the 1850s, Johor was largely governed *in absentia*. The Temenggong and his more important followers remained at Teluk Belanga. On the Chinese side, the merchants and shopkeepers of Singapore financed the planters in Johor. As Temenggong Ibrahim aged and his son Abu Bakar began to assume control over the state, they set out to build a state administration in Johor. By the mid-1860s, Iskandar Putri had become a prosperous little village and much of the administration of the state was conducted from there.

However, the Chinese and the gambier and pepper market remained at Singapore. Johor was tied to the entrepot. The story of Abu Bakar's government in Johor begins with his attempt to end this economic dependence. This move brought him into direct conflict with the Singapore government and the Chinese merchant community of the colony. Although the attempt itself failed, it brought about a move to place the state's administration on a much more orderly basis. This in turn resulted in the growth of a Malay bureaucracy which became the core of the future government of the state.

NOTES

1. Tarling's *Piracy and Politics in the Malay World* is a good guide for the major piracy suppression campaigns launched from Singapore against the Malays of the Riau-Lingga Archipelago in 1836 by Captain Congalton on the *Zephyr* and Captain Chads on the *Andromache.* The following year, the steamer *Diana* came to Singapore to suppress the pirates. In the 1840s, James Brooke began a campaign against the Brunei Malays, the Ibans and the Illanuns of Borneo. In 1843, he was joined by Captain Henry Keppel and the H.M.S. *Dido*. By the 1860s, Malay "piracy" had ceased to be a major concern of the Straits Government. See Tarling, Ch. 2 and 3, pp. 67–145.
2. Wong Lin Ken, "The Trade of Singapore, 1819–1869", *JMBRAS*, v. 33, pt. 4 (December 1960), pp. 82, 293, Appendix C, Table xxiii.
3. Ibid., pp. 82–83.
4. *SSR A–57*, pp. 10–11.
5. Christopher Hooi, "Piracy and Its Suppression in Malayan Waters, 1800–1867", Academic Exercise (University of Singapore, 1955), p. 66, Appendix D.
6. Tarling, *Piracy and Politics*, p. 173.
7. *SFP*, 4 August 1846.
8. *SFP*, 21 August 1845.
9. *SFP*, 30 July 1859.
10. G. F. de Bruijn-Kops, "Sketch of the Rhio-Lingga Archipelago", *JIA*, v. 8 (1854), p. 400.
11. J. R. Logan, "Range of the Gutta Taban Collectors", pp. 532–33.
12. Coope, "The Kangchu System", pp. 247–63. See also Tan Tek Soon, "Chinese Local Trade", *SCM*, v. 6, no. 23 (September 1902), p. 91. Coope was the first to use the term "Kangchu system". Not being aware of Tan Tek Soon's article at the time he wrote, he apparently considered his article the first published description of the system under which Johor's cultivation was managed. Included in this article is a translation of several samples of Kangchu correspondence: a *surat sungai*, a *surat tauliah* (Kangchu letter of authority), and a translation of the *Kanun Kangchu* or the "Law of the Kangchus".

13. Since it was primarily a Chinese system of cultivation, Chinese terms were used by Malays as well to describe its institutions. Spelling of the terms is based on their pronunciation in the Teochew dialect. The most commonly encountered terms are: *Kangchu* 港主 — lord of the river; *kangkar* 港脚 — river foot; and *chukang* 厝港 — generally this term was used with a proper name such as Tan or Lim (e.g. Tan Chukang or Lim Chukang) and signified "the place of the Tan (or Lim) river".
14. Begbie, *The Malayan Peninsula*, p. 305.
15. Ibid., p. 308.
16. No Chinese Kapitan was ever officially appointed at Singapore. However, there were a number of respectable Chinese merchants who held posts in the government. At first, Raffles placed the various kampongs of Chinese under their own headmen, but there is no record of these or other appointments. Prominent Chinese merchants did however function as headmen. These included such individuals as Tan Che Sang, Tan Tock Seng, Tan Kim Ching, Tan Kim Seng, Tan Jiak Kim, Seah Eu Chin, and others whose names frequently appear on the pages of Song Ong Siang's book.
17. L. A. Mills, *British Malaya 1824–1867* (Kuala Lumpur, 1966), p. 114.
18. Bartley, "Population of Singapore in 1819", p. 177.
19. John Crawfurd, quoted in J. R. Logan, "Agriculture in Singapore", *JIA*, v. 3 (1849), p. 509.
20. Buckley, *An Anecdotal History*, p. 198.
21. G. W. Earl, *The Eastern Seas* (London, 1971), p. 353.
22. James C. Jackson, *Planters and Speculators: Chinese and European Agricultural Enterprise in Malaya 1786–1921* (Kuala Lumpur, 1968), p. 9.
23. Earl, *The Eastern Seas*, p. 142.
24. Cowan, "Early Penang", p. 112.
25. Ibid., pp, 119–20. Riau — 164 pikuls of pepper and 170 of gambier; Lingga — 16 pikuls of pepper and 8 of gambier; and Sebong — 400 pikuls of gambier and 15 of pepper. Cowan incorrectly identifies Sebong as "Sabon, Island just South of Carimon" (p. 120, fn. 79.). This is clearly the Sebong River in northern Bentan, also known as Singkang, which was shipping its produce direct to Singapore.
26. Ibid., p. 176.
27. Song Ong Siang, *One Hundred Years' History of the Chinese in Singapore* (Singapore, 1967), p. 90.
28. Jackson, *Planters, and Speculators*, p. 8.
29. Newbold, *Political and Statistical Account*, v. 1, p. 320.
30. Seah Eu Chin, "The Chinese of Singapore", *JIA*, v. 2 (1848), p. 290.
31. *SFP*, 28 March 1839. See also Jackson, *Planters and Speculators*, pp. 19–22.
32. Burkhill, *A Dictionary*, v. 1, pp. 2199–2202.
33. Song, *One Hundred Years' History*, p. 23. In 1835, the Chinese population of Singapore was 13,749. By 1849, it had grown to 24,790.
34. Jackson, *Planters and Speculators*, p. 13.

35. Ibid., p. 10.
36. Buckley, *An Anecdotal History*, p. 353.
37. Lee Poh Ping, "Chinese Society in Nineteenth and Early Twentieth Century Singapore: A Socioeconomic Analysis", Ph.D. Thesis (Cornell University, Ithaca, N. Y., 1974), pp. 120–27.
38. Buckley, *An Anecdotal History*, pp. 363, 440. In 1841, there were two major roads into the interior of Singapore from the town. One went to Serangoon and another to Bukit Timah. Each was about seven miles long. By 1845, the Bukit Timah road had been extended across the island an additional eight miles to Kranji on the Johor Straits.
39. *SFP*, 26 March 1846 and 2 Apri1 1846. These contain a series of letters dealing with the assessment of the plantations. The first purports to be from a secret society chief, one Tan Tek Hye "Keeper of the Quinangular Seal", in the issue of 26 March and the other two in the issue of 2 April.
40. *SFP*, 21 August 1845.
41. *SFP*, 28 March 1839.
42. Jackson, *Planters and Speculators*, pp. 11–12.
43. Since these agreements violated the principle of free trade, it does not seem that, if challenged, an English court would have upheld them. Naturally, they never were challenged since the planters had no idea of their rights under English law nor would they have imagined that free trade (if they understood the concept) applied to any of them. Finally, these agreements, even if they were written (which is doubtful) would have been in Chinese. For the shopkeepers, the institution of title deeds was an ideal solution, since they made the planters the tenants of the shopkeepers. In 1864, when this question again arose in Johor, the shopkeepers demanded that the Johor government issue title deeds, saying that it was too easy for the planters to break the monopoly agreements.
44. Lee, "Chinese Society", pp. 23–62.
45. *SFP*, 7 April 1846.
46. Leon Comber, *Chinese Secret Societies in Malaya: A Survey of the Triad Society from 1800 to 1900* (New York, Locust Valley, 1959), p. 61. See also Carl A. Trocki, *Opium and Empire: Chinese Society in Colonial Singapore 1800–1910* (Ithaca, New York: Cornell University Press, 1990), p. 92, fn. 26.
47. Buckley, *An Anecdotal History*, p. 463.
48. *SFP*, 12 February 1846.
49. Buckley, *An Anecdotal History*, pp. 463–64.
50. Song, *One Hundred Years' History*, p. 35.
51. *SFP*, 26 March 1846.
52. Mills, *British Malaya*, p. 183, fn. 32.
53. Coope, "The Kangchu System", p. 247.
54. *SKMK-I*, No. 57, 23 April 1864, which refers to the original grant and gives the correct date. For a comprehensive discussion of these documents, see Trocki, "The Johor Archives and the Kangchu System 1844–1910", *JMBRAS*, v. 68, pt. 1 (May 1975), pp. 1–46.

55. *SKMK-I,* No. 60, 12 August 1864, cites the original grant as having been made to Kapitan Tan Kye Soon on 22 October 1844.
56. *SKMK-I,* No. 4, 18 February 1849, for Sungai Melayu, and the two Sungai Tiram grants are *SKMK-I,* Nos. 8 and 8a, 17 January 1845 and 7 April 1845.
57. *SFP,* June 1845, quoted in Buckley, *An Anecdotal History,* p. 431.
58. *SJB,* No. 10, 5 July 1871, probably refers to *SKMK-I,* No. 13, undated for Sungai Tiram Duku; Sungai Chat, *SKMK-I,* No. 5, 26 August 1845; Sungai Lunchu and Paksi, *SKMK-I,* No. 6, 27 October 1845; Sungai Buloh Besar, *SKMK-I,* No. 9, 29 November 1845; Sungai Pendas, *SKMK-I,* No. 7, 26 April 1846. All rivers are located in South Johor and flow into the Johor Straits.
59. Hsing Nung Pan, *The Teochews in Malaya* [潘百星晨, 马来亚潮侨通金监] (Singapore, Nan Tao Publications, Ltd., 1950), p. 42.
60. *SKMK-I,* No. 3, 1 August 1859, for Sungai Tebrau is made to Kye Soon and Cheng Hung. A later *surat sungai* (*SKMK-I,* No. 60, 12 August 1864) records the settlement of a dispute over the inheritance of Kapitan Tan Kye Soon. This recognized Kapitan Tan Cheng Hung as Kangchu.
61. *SJB,* No. 74, 8 May 1883, reports that the Dato Bentara of Johor, Ja'afar Haji Mohamed, had purchased the Kangchu rights to Sungai Tebrau from Kapitan Tan Cheng Hung on 24 June 1869. The original bill of sale is missing.
62. *SKMK-I,* No. 99, 19 October 1873, is the first mention of Seah Tee Heng as Kapitan. However, *SJB,* No. 8, 26 March 1871, records the sale of Sungai Telor by Tan Cheng Hung. Cheng Hung was not styled "Kapitan" in the bill of sale. He was however, in 1866, when he first acquired the rights to Sungai Telor, *SKMK-I,* No. 74, 4 June 1866.
63. *SKMK-I,* No. 60, 12 August 1864.
64. This appears to be a reference to Sim Ah Nga, who later appeared as an agent for Heng Bung Soon, the Singapore opium farmer in 1863. Carl A. Trocki, *Opium and Empire.*
65. Buckley, *An Anecdotal History,* p. 430.
66. Mills, *British Malaya,* p. 183.
67. Until 1862, the Singapore and Johor farms were rented jointly under an arrangement between the two governments. The British became dissatisfied with the share which the Temenggong received under this agreement and it was terminated. *SKMK-I,* No. 59, 11 September 1863, reports that Tan Hiok Nee was made the opium farmer for Johor Baharu and, one presumes, for all of Johor. The *SSD* (1876) "Johor", p. 4, reports that the Johor farms were held by Cheang Hong Lim, Major Tan Hiok Nee, and Tan Seng Poh. Hong Lim and Seng Poh were regular members of the syndicate which held the Singapore revenue farms. See Song, *One Hundred Years' History,* pp. 21, 131–33, and 168–69. Also, Song (p. 159) quotes the *Daily Times* report that the opium farms for Singapore, Malacca, Johor, and Riau had been amalgamated in 1870. There is no definite word in any of the sources available to the writer on the status at the Johor farms between 1863 and 1870. It is possible that Tan Hiok Nee held them independently; on the other hand, he may have found it convenient to make some

arrangements with the Singapore farmers as soon as he received the Johor farms in 1863.

68. For a more comprehensive discussion of the relations between the Singapore and Johor opium farms, see Trocki, *Opium and Empire,* Ch. 4 and 5.
69. Winstedt, "A History of Johor", pp. 92–94.
70. Mohamed bin Haji Ilyas, comp., *Tawarikh Dato Bentara Luar Johor, Mohomed Salleh bin Perang* (Johor Baharu, 1928), pp. 67–68. This is an edited collection of some of the Dato's diaries and publications.
71. Ibid., p. 74.
72. This was the Teluk Belanga Malay School founded by the Rev. Benjamin Peach Keasberry around the beginning of 1846. See Buckley's short account of his life, *An Anecdotal History,* pp. 320–22. In addition to his school, Keasberry also ran a printing press and taught printing, bookbinding, and lithography. Others who were either students or teachers at this school included Abu Bakar's brothers and cousins as well as others like Dato Mohd. Salleh, Munshi Abdullah and his sons, especially Mohd. Ibrahim, later Dato Bentara Dalam of Johor.
73. Mohamed bin Haji Ilyas, comp., *Tawarikh,* pp. 76–78.
74. Trocki, "The Johor Archives", pp. 20–23. The figures for these two tables are based on *SKMK-I,* Johor Archives.
75. *SFP,* 31 July 1859.

5

Abu Bakar Takes Command

1860–1873

The period 1860–73 was one of rapid progress for Johor. The state's pepper and gambier agriculture expanded greatly during these years as a result of a rising demand for gambier in the world market. Johor also benefited from the decline of the plantations in Singapore and the increased Chinese immigration to the Malay world. These favourable trends were enhanced through the policies of the young and energetic ruler who succeeded Temenggong Ibrahim in 1862. During the first decade of his rule, he became the single most important Malay political figure of the entire century.

Temenggong Sri Maharaja Abu Bakar was twenty-eight when his father died. In addition to being both fluent and literate in English and Malay, he had already spent several years looking after family affairs and running the newly-established government in Johor, and was thus admirably qualified to take full control. Both mature and experienced, he also succeeded to a secure position. The change of rulers created no lapse in the state such as that which had occurred in 1825. Abu Bakar was able to begin his rule with his father's achievements as an accomplished fact. It is, then, not surprising that he moved on to much greater things.

On succeeding, Abu Bakar inherited the considerable influence which his father had exercised among the other power-holders in the region. His status and position were immediately acknowledged by the officials and the merchants of Singapore as well as by the other rulers on the Peninsula and in Riau. In 1866, he pushed beyond the confines of the Malay world and travelled to

PLATE 4

Sultan Abu Bakar

(Courtesy of the National Museum, Singapore)

England where he was received by Queen Victoria. Later he made many more trips and, according to the *Hikayat Johor*, formed a close relationship with the Prince of Wales, later King Edward VII.[1] During his first five years in office, he quickly pulled together the many interests of his father and recreated a new Johor.

The 1860s were a turbulent period for the young chief. Both he and his state were very much creatures of Singapore. In his quest for power, Abu Bakar maintained stances which occasionally alarmed the Singapore government. He was thus continually forced to act according to either European sensibilities or his own ambitions. The evidence suggests that his aims went far beyond the borders of his own state. There was also a certain ambiguity regarding his status and his relationship to Singapore. It was this open-ended situation that generated much of the activity of the period.

It is important to remember that Abu Bakar's predecessors were technically officials under the Sultan of Johor. The treaty of 1855 had given Temenggong Ibrahim a clear title to the territory of Johor and he was recognized as an independent ruler. On the surface, this agreement marked the accomplishment of the transition from port official to territorial ruler. However, there remained

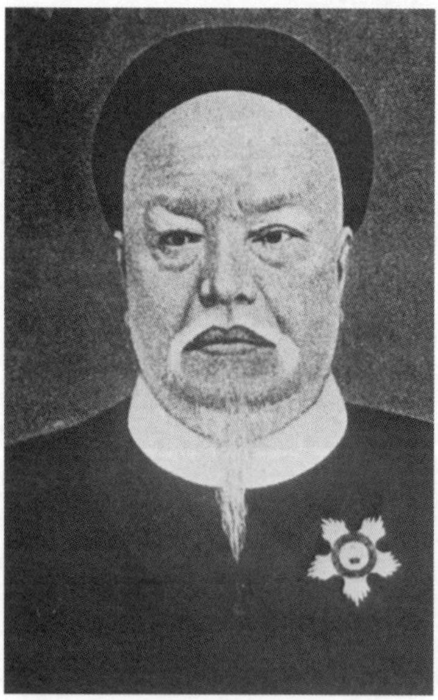

PLATE 5
Tan Hiok Nee
(Courtesy of the Arkib Negara Malaysia)

many ambiguities regarding Abu Bakar's status and role. The idea of the division of the Malay Peninsula into a number of autonomous states was relatively new. Johor, under Ibrahim and Abu Bakar, was the first of the new model Malay states.

In addition to the vaguely defined states and territories of the period, there remained the question of the old Sultanate. As the office decreased in power, the number of "Sultans" increased. There were three in 1860: Sultan Ali of the Singapore line in Muar; Sultan Sulaiman of Lingga who was under both the Yamtuan Muda and the Dutch; and the predecessor of the latter, Sultan Mahmud, whom the Dutch had deposed in 1857. None of them possessed an independent source of wealth or a viable power base. At the same time, there were other, more powerful, territorial chiefs who also traced their lineage back to Sultan Abdul Jalil (d. 1719). These included Abu Bakar, the Bendahara of Pahang, and the Sultan of Trengganu. Among the three, only Abu Bakar had direct access to the immense economic and military power represented by Singapore.

In 1862, there was a wide range of possibilities open to Abu Bakar. He was in a position to try to redefine both himself and his state as he saw fit. The British, however, had their own ideas about the appropriate relationship between Singapore and Johor as well as about that between Johor and the other states of the Peninsula. They became concerned about the growing influence of the Temenggong. John Cameron noted that the Treaty of 1855 had created some problems regarding the Temenggong's status:

> … the present Sultan not long ago sold his birthright of the sovereignty to Johore to the present Tumongong's father, who was his hereditary vassal; but, strange to say, retained as he still does the title of Sultan. It has been a badly managed piece of business, and has given rise to great dissatisfaction among the rajahs of the peninsula, who refuse to acknowledge the Tumongong — because, in point of hereditary rank, his is beneath many of them. With respect to the island of Singapore it is beyond doubt that the Tumongong's family had great claims, both because they so cordially assisted our settlement, and because, though subject to the seignory of the Sultan, the soil appears to have been their property. In point of ability and education, too, the Tumongongs have been far in advance of the Sultans; and, in the affairs of the island, have been the men with whom our Government has invariably had to deal. But, on the other hand, we have done a great deal for the Tumongong's family, which by our occupation has been raised to a wealth and importance it would never otherwise have attained; and it appears to me that the English Government will do wisely to abstain from much interference in the native politics of the peninsula …

Cameron tended to absolve Abu Bakar of consciously seeking power for himself and to put the blame for the ruler's adventures on influences emanating from the Singapore mercantile community. The Temenggongs were known to have close relationships with the agency houses of Paterson & Simons, Guthrie's, and Martin, Dyce & Co. Speaking of Abu Bakar, Cameron noted: "The present Tumongong is an amiable and high-minded gentleman, more desirous, I think, of peace and quiet than of great power; and if difficulties should afterwards arise in our relation with him, it will be very much the blame of those who inconsiderately forced ambition upon him."[2]

The extent to which Abu Bakar was an innocent pawn in the hands of "greedy" English merchants and lawyers remains an open question. We have no record of his intentions nor of the merchants. Turnbull has pointed out, however, that he was very much his own man. "While he still employed Simons and Napier (the lawyers), Abu Bakar did not put himself entirely in the hands of agents and lawyers as his father had done, and he set out to free himself from dependence on either the government or the merchants of Singapore."[3]

The events of the years 1862–66 tend to support Turnbull's statement. They show the young Temenggong attempting to seize both political and economic autonomy for Johor. Ultimately, both official Singapore and the Anglo-Chinese mercantile class combined to oppose him. By 1866, he had been forced to retreat from his initial advances. He did not, however, accept an ignominious defeat. Rather, he beat a strategic withdrawal and graciously accepted a certain amount of political and economic restriction. He even found some ways of turning defeat to his own advantage.

The first check to his power came as a result of his attempts to extend his influence over the adjoining states of Pahang and Negri Sembilan. His father's relations with Pahang, initiated in 1836, had bound Abu Bakar to the Bendahara. Winstedt has described the nature of these ties in 1862: "In 1857 the Bendahara-designate (Muda) of Pahang, Tun Koris, had married one of Abu Bakar's sisters Che Engku Besar. Abu-Bakar himself, before his father's death, had married Che' Engku Chik, a daughter of Bendahara Tahir and a sister of Tun Koris. These alliances had not been without political motive and Tun Tahir had even given Johor the territory between Endau and Sedili Besar in return for a promise of its assistance." The Temenggong also had a mining concession in Kuantan which he held in partnership with William Paterson.

In 1862, the ties between Johor and Pahang were strengthened by a treaty which, despite earlier prohibitions on such relations, was given the approval of the Singapore government. The treaty provided for mutual assistance in case of attack also gave Johor additional territorial concessions. Pahang recognized the Endau as its southern border, and Pulau Tioman and all of the islands to the south of it were given to Johor.[4]

Bendahara Tun Tahir and his son, Tun Koris, were in need of allies. Pahang had been torn by a succession dispute since 1847. The Bendahara faced a strong rival in the person of his brother, Wan Ahmad. By the middle of 1862, Wan Ahmad had allied himself with Sultan Omar of Trengganu and the deposed Sultan Mahmud of Lingga. He was also supported by Abu Bakar's rival, Sultan Ali of Muar. The Siamese, too, had become involved in the struggle.[5]

Winstedt suggests that Abu Bakar feared the loss of his concessions in Pahang if Wan Ahmad was victorious. This energetic contender could also become a serious political rival and he would certainly block Abu Bakar's great influence in the Pahang court.

> On the other hand Abu-Bakar's brother-in-law, Bendahara Tun Koris, was a puppet. He smoked opium: he refused audience. Abu Bakar wrote to him to consult the old men and the Hajis and not to lend his seal! He advised him to levy the old taxes on opium, tobacco and salt and not to introduce new taxes on boats and rice. He wrote as to a child or an inferior. Later he wrote to one of his own captains that rulers ought to have brains but Koris was a fool. Before the end Pahang chiefs excused themselves from attacking Wan Ahmad on the ground that the Temenggong was running the war and owned Pahang.[6]

Winstedt's description of the war indicates that Abu Bakar had invested heavily in the conflict. He financed two chiefs from Negri Sembilan to attack Pahang from across the mountains. He also outfitted his cousin, Raja Kechil, the Resident of Tanjong Putri, and sent him with an expedition along the coast to attack up-river. A $500 reward was offered for the head of Wan Ahmad.[7] Abu Bakar had even managed to get the British, ever fearful of Siamese designs, to bombard Trengganu in November 1862.[8] In May 1863, Abu Bakar, from Winstedt's report, appears to have been running the entire war, and he may have had as many as 3,000 men in the field, not to mention boats, food, medical supplies, and ordnance.

However, it was all to no avail. In May 1863, Bendahara Tun Tahir and Tun Koris fled to Johor and both died shortly thereafter. The remaining Pahang chiefs quickly acknowledged Wan Ahmad and the war was over. Abu Bakar had overreached himself. The best he could do at this point was to cut his losses. By 1864, he had convinced Governor Cavenagh of Singapore of his good intentions. The latter wrote on his behalf to the India Office stressing the fact that Abu Bakar had disengaged himself from Pahang's affairs and even made overtures of friendship toward Wan Ahmad.[9]

So ended Abu Bakar's first offensive. However, the Pahang war appears to have lent impetus to his next move; this time a purely economic one. The war

TABLE 7
Surat Sungai Issued 1863–1866

Year	*No. of Grants*
1863	15
1864	16
1865	5
1866	11
	47

had emptied Abu Bakar's treasury. Even during the war he was in need of money. Winstedt reports that he wrote to the Bendahara "saying that till letters of administration had been granted he had much property but no cash" and asking Tun Koris to "send four or five fishing boats to bring his tin ore to Singapore".[10] After the war, his funds were so low that he tried (unsuccessfully) to sell the family's fifty-acre Tyersall estate in Singapore to the British for $20,000.[11] However, the answer to his money problems was the issuance of the "letters of administration" mentioned above. Presumably these were the Kangchu grants that he began to authorize in large numbers after May 1863.

Freed from his obligations and ambitions regarding Pahang, Abu Bakar turned his energies to the development of his own state. In mid-1863, we note the beginnings of a reorganization of the state administration and an exceptional expansion of planting. The Kangchu records show that an unprecedented number of *surat sungai* were issued between June 1863 and December 1866 (Table 7).[12]

These three-and-a-half years were the peak period for such activity during the entire nineteenth century. This does not mean that forty-seven new rivers were opened. A reorganization was in progress and many of these documents dealt with the revision of earlier grants. However, about half of the *surat sungai* from these years were for entirely new areas. By the end of 1866, planting had been extended far beyond the small core-area on Johor's south coast and a few tributaries of the Johor River. Authorizations had been made to begin planting on most of the major tributaries of the Johor River; some start had been made on the east coast of Johor, and all the rivers of the west coast as far north as the Batu Pahat had been opened.

The reorganization showed that Abu Bakar had also made a major shift in the policy which his father had followed regarding the Chinese. If Kapitan Tan Kye Soon was typical, then the pioneer generation of Johor Kangchu were most likely all Ngee Heng Society headmen. They were primarily soldiers and not merchants. The problem of this period was the ruler's need for cash and not the physical security of the plantations.

Abu Bakar thus formed close relationships with a different strata of Chinese society. He decreased the power of the Ngee Heng headmen and elevated the merchant or *taukeh* class. After 1860, it appears that *surat sungai* were increasingly issued to merchants. These individuals, according to Coope's description of the change, were known as *tuan sungai*, and the Kangchu, who resided at the *kangkar*, was more often than not merely the deputy or manager for the owner. A new form letter was introduced, distinct from the *surat sungai*, which simply granted Kangchu authority to the *kangkar* headmen. This was called the *surat tauliah*, or letter of authority.

> It should be noted, however, that with the introduction of this new system, the meaning of the word Kangchu underwent some modification. For the Kangchu who received the letter of authority *surat tauliah* was not necessarily the *tuan sungai* (owner of the river). The owner might well live in Singapore or, sometimes, own more than one Kangkar. A (Government) Kangchu naturally had to reside in the Kangkar and so in many cases the (Government) Kangchu was really the owner's manager. Actually of course he would invariably be the nominee of the owner of the river and be responsible to him as well as to the government.[13]

The *taukeh* who appears to have been the primary beneficiary of this change was Tan Hiok Nee. In 1863, he emerged as the most important Chinese in Johor. The collection of *surat sungai* makes it possible to fix with some accuracy the date of his seemingly sudden rise. By 1870 he had been named *Major China* of Johor, and he was recognized as the principal Chinese official in the Temenggong's government.[14]

Tan Hiok Nee made his first appearance in Johor in the 1850s. In 1853, he formed a partnership with one Tan Ban Tye and obtained a *surat sungai* for the Bukit Berangan, a tributary of the Johor River.[15] In the following year, he was a shareholder in another partnership, or Kongsi, for what seems to have been a stretch of the left bank of the Johor River between Bukit Berangan and the Kong Kong River.[16]

However, it was not until September 1863 that he became conspicuously prominent. In a one-week period, 5–11 September, Tan Hiok Nee obtained four additional concessions in Johor. On 5 September he received a *surat sungai* granting him the rights over three adjacent rivers: Keringkim (or Kim Kim), Kong Kong, and Tukang.[17] This concession gave Tan control over a fairly big slice of Johor's coastline. On the same day, another *surat sungai* made out to Tan Hiok Nee and his partner in Bukit Berangan clarified their 1853 grant and noted that Tan Hiok Nee's holdings were now contiguous with the new territory.[18] Tan Hiok Nee had gained the Kangchu rights for the entire left bank of the Johor River from slightly south of Kota Tinggi to the western watershed of Sungai Tukang, opposite Pulau Ubin. However, Tan himself was never the actual Kangchu for any of these rivers.

Then, on 8 September, another *surat sungai* was granted, giving Tan Hiok Nee and two others (one of whom was the Malay Resident of Tanjong Surat, Nong Yahya) control of the Santi River, a large estuary on the right bank of the Johor River.[19]

With such extensive Kangchu rights (see Map 4), Tan Hiok Nee became the biggest *taukeh* in Johor. It appears that he was the only one who was authorized to hold multiple grants such as these at this time. It is thus not surprising that on 11 September he also received sole control of the revenue rights for the town of Iskandar Putri.[20]

Relatively little is known about this individual who became so powerful in Johor and also in Singapore. However, thanks to Song Ong Siang, we know more about him than most of the Johor Chinese.

> At an early age Tan Yeok Nee left his native town "Sa-Ling, in Teochew prefecture, China" and came to Singapore. He began his career as a cloth pedlar, making daily visits to Telok Blangah, where the Temenggong's family became his customers, and he struck up a friendship with the Temenggong Abubakar ... By 1866, Tan Yeok Nee had already established himself as a prosperous gambier and pepper trader at Boat Quay under the chop of Kwang Hong, and obtained extensive *kangchu* rights in Johore territory. He was made Major China of Johore by the Maharajah in or about 1870, and went into partnership with Cheang Hong Lim and Tan Seng Poh in the Singapore and Johore Opium and Spirit Farms. He amassed a large fortune which was judiciously invested in the purchase of house property situated in what are today the busy parts of Singapore. He was in his time a prominent Teochew towkay, both here and in Johore.[21]

Tan's rise coincided with the expansion of the Kangchu system which followed the conclusion of the Pahang war. It is highly probable then that he was primarily responsible for refinancing the state of Johor for Abu Bakar. It is rather difficult to get any definite idea of the size of his investment in Johor, but an estimate of the 1863 concessions alone would have to be in excess of $10,000 and might easily have been as high as $50,000.[22]

Another *surat sungai*, dated 1864, suggests that the former Chinese headman of Johor, Kapitan Tan Cheng Hung, had suffered some loss in status.

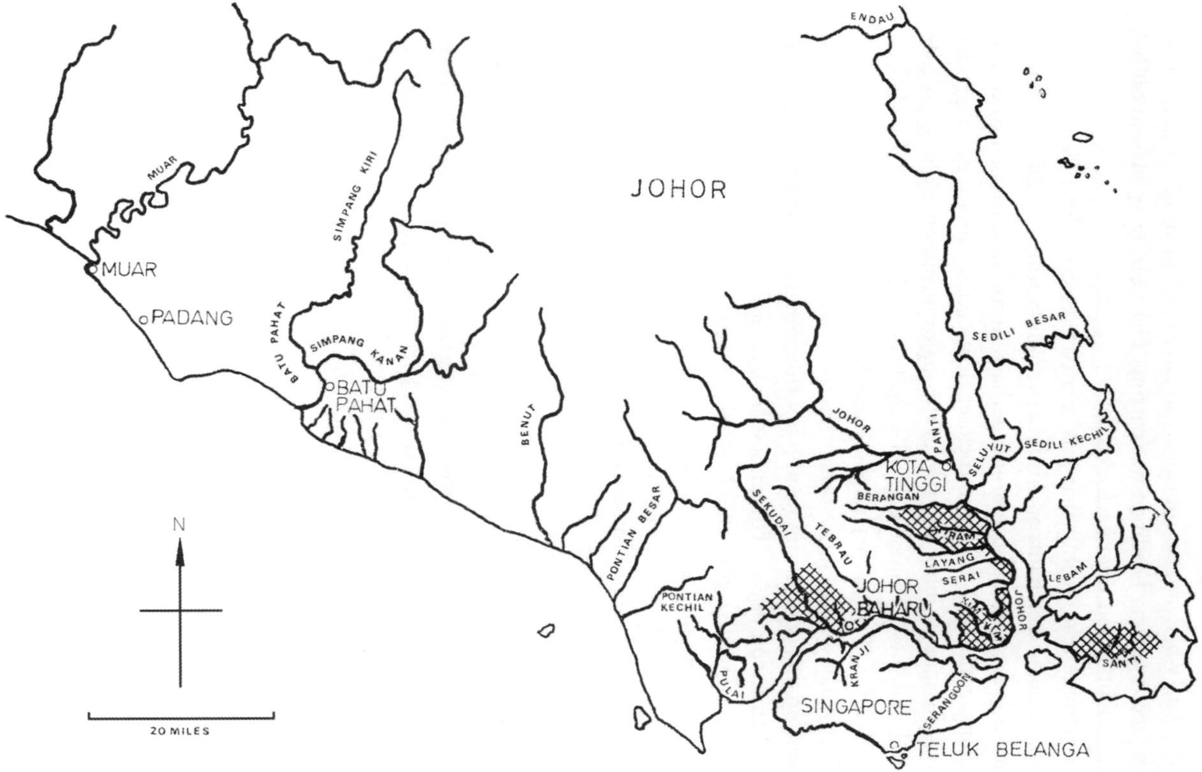

MAP 4

Tan Hiok Nee's Holdings in 1874

He was sued by Tan Teng Lok and Tan Teng Huat who also claimed to be adopted sons of Tan Kye Soon. Cheng Hung was not demoted; he retained the titles of Kapitan and Kangchu. But, he did have to give up forty plantations on Sungai Pandan, which appear previously to have been a part of Tebrau.[23] The day of the secret society headmen was passing. Five years later, he sold off his holdings in Tebrau and went back to China.[24]

The intimate relationship that was created between Abu Bakar and the Singapore gambier merchants at this time is an indication of Johor's progress. The shift, however, brought new and perhaps unforeseen problems for the Temenggong. Johor was now bound closer than ever before to the Singapore economy. The state of Johor was one of the major businesses of Singapore. It is doubtful that these Chinese *taukehs* actually considered Johor an independent country, for as far as they were concerned, it was under the same law as Singapore. Malay sources suggest that the rulers had designed the law to give the impression that people coming to Johor from Singapore "felt as if they were still in the same country".[25] The earliest *surat sungai* show that the holder of the river was subject to the same laws which were practised in Singapore.[26] Although the documents of the 1860s no longer carried this phrase, the Malays went out of their way to make these Chinese feel welcome. One young Malay official, the future Dato Bentara Luar, undertook the study of Teochew and written Chinese in 1861. By his own statement, he knew enough in two years' time to conduct government business with Chinese petitioners without the need of a translator.[27]

Thus, in the latter part of 1863, thousands of new Chinese began moving into Johor. By May 1864, twenty-five new *surat sungai* had been issued. About fifteen of them were for entirely new rivers. This sudden expansion appears to have had a dislocating effect on the Singapore economy. All the capital needed to finance the opening of these new *kangkar* and plantations, like the men who worked them, came from Singapore. This rush of capital was quickly followed by a financial crisis in Singapore. May and June of 1864 were difficult months for the Singapore merchants. Two of the major European merchant firms had failed, their liabilities amounting to over a million dollars. At the same time, a large number of Chinese merchants who were indebted to them were also discovered to be operating with insufficient capital.

If the Johor investment had not caused their troubles, it certainly must have contributed to them. Europeans were in constant competition for the business of the Chinese merchants, and it was often said that a Chinese coolie had only to put on a clean shirt and go to the European godowns to be able to obtain on credit as much as he wished. So long as there were no disturbances of the trade these small traders managed to keep afloat, but if any pressures arose they would collapse and often be found to have been operating on no capital at all. The Singapore economy was thus plagued by what one reporter described as "these periodical *smashes* in the native trade".[28]

Buckley's report of this event shows that June 1864 was the high point of the crisis.

> Trade in Singapore had never had such a shock and there was almost a stagnation in the market as far as selling manufactured goods was concerned. Very heavy failures among the Chinese firms occurred in June, and in that month there was a foolish panic among the natives about the security of the bank notes, and there was a run upon the banks for silver in place of them.[29]

The financial panic also affected Johor. A stray piece of correspondence reports that at least two small pepper and gambier traders went under in this crisis. The planters' debts which they held were transferred to Seah Eu Chin by a *surat kuasa* or power of attorney.[30] Unfortunately, no other correspondence similar to these documents seem to have been preserved; thus no definite statement can be made about the magnitude of the crash as far as the pepper and gambier economy was concerned.[31] It is quite probable that there were many more who went under.

We are also on very speculative ground in estimating the overall amount of capital invested in Johor during the months preceding the crash. From the large number of new rivers opened and old ones reorganized, one gets the idea that Abu Bakar was attempting to double the area under cultivation in a few years' time. By late 1864, there were at least thirty-four rivers opened for cultivation;[32] about 1,000 plantations were in operation and the total Singapore investment in Johor amounted to about $1,000,000.[33] If, as the *surat sungai* suggest, half of these were newly opened, then the total investment in Johor for this one-year period (June 1863 to May 1864) may have been close to $500,000.

The crash that followed this boom must have seemed like a direct threat to everything Abu Bakar was building. Hundreds of small speculators were panicking in Singapore. They no doubt placed excessive demands for repayment of debts on the newly established Johor planters. Had they been allowed to retrieve some of their capital, Johor could have gone under with them. The entire hastily constructed development programme could have been wiped out in a month or two.

It was at this point that Abu Bakar announced a new policy which was, in effect, a declaration of economic independence. He took steps to regulate the flow of trade between Singapore and Johor. He announced new regulations which became the issue of a political and economic dispute between the governments of Johor and Singapore. The so-called Tanjong Putri Controversy has been the subject of an article by C. M. Turnbull.[34]

In a letter to the Singapore government, Abu Bakar explained his new regulations. The first and most controversial of these was that all boats transporting gambier and pepper from Johor and all those bringing goods from Singapore should stop at Tanjong Putri for a pass, at the same time making a statement of their cargoes. No charge was made for this. The stated purpose was that such a measure would allow the government to obtain an accurate record of the state's imports and exports and at the same time help to prevent smuggling of such commodities as opium, liquor, and firearms. It would also prevent the boat people from disposing of the cargoes on their own.

Other regulations involved the issuance of grants or leases for individual plantations, a register of sales of plantations, and a register of mortgages of plantations. These, explained Abu Bakar in his letter to the Singapore government, would provide better security for the shopkeepers who had advanced money to the planters.[35]

The merchants' reaction came in October 1864 with a petition to the Singapore Chamber of Commerce. One hundred and one pepper and gambier traders signed the petition objecting to Abu Bakar's regulation requiring all boats trading between Johor and Singapore to stop at Tanjong Putri. They viewed the measure as an attempt to force the Singapore traders to relocate in Johor or else forfeit repayment of the debts owed them by Johor planters. The petition indicates that twenty Singapore traders had already taken leases on buildings at Tanjong Putri and had resolved to move their business from Singapore to Johor.[36]

The Singapore government took up the cause of the merchants and protested to Abu Bakar. His refusal to repeal the policy caused the dispute to become an international incident. In May 1865, the Singapore government wrote to India: "on the subject of an order recently issued by His Highness the Tumongong requiring all boats laden with the produce of Johore to proceed to the village of Tanjong Putri for the ostensible purpose of allowing their cargoes to be registered, but, doubtless, with the real object of securing either for himself or his advisers and their friends a monopoly of the trade".

The writer quoted the 1824 treaty which Temenggong Abdul Rahman had signed with Crawfurd noting that "His highness is bound to maintain a free and unshackled trade everywhere within his dominions …" In addition to violating this agreement, it was also noted that the trip to Tanjong Putri would require a detour for most of the boats plying between Singapore and the plantations which could "only be considered as a vexatious interference with trade".[37]

In an attempt to force the Temenggong to retreat from his independent stance, the Singapore authorities seized upon an ambiguous clause in the 1824 Treaty and denied that Johor had any authority whatsoever in the Straits:

> Under Article 2 of the Treaty of 1824, the Island of Singapore, together with the adjacent seas, straits, and islets, to the extent 10 geographical miles from the coast of the said main island, was ceded by the Sultan and our friend's ancestors the British Government; whilst, under the ordinary law of nations, a State exercises jurisdiction over all waters within three miles of its own coasts: hence, our friend's rights having been specially transferred to the British Government and the old straits being in no part more than three miles in breadth, that Government exercises jurisdiction over the whole of waters between Johore and Singapore.[38]

In essence it was a threat to annex the entire south coast of Johor.

In order to support his case, Abu Bakar presented two petitions to counter the charges made by the Singapore merchants. One was from twenty-two pepper and gambier dealers in Singapore and the other was from thirty-four Kangchus. Both petitions supported the policy of requiring vessels to stop at Tanjong Putri, but each gave different reasons. The pepper and gambier dealers, like those who had petitioned the Governor, complained that the boatmen and planters conspired to escape repayment of debts. They requested that the Temenggong police the traffic at Tanjong Putri to prevent the illegal sale of produce. They also requested that the Temenggong issue land grants to the planters which the *taukeh* could hold as security for debts. They also asked the Temenggong to give the merchants land at Tanjong Putri so that they could build godowns there.[39]

The Kangchus, styling themselves planters, complained of the treatment that they had received from their Singapore creditors. They said that the Singapore *taukehs* cheated them by using false weights, and requested that the traffic be centralized at Tanjong Putri where weights approved by the Temenggong would be used and where they would, presumably, be free from violent treatment.

> ... should any differences or disputes arise between us, your servants, or between others residing under the Government of Johore, or between those in Singapore who come to Johore to create disturbance, they never cease to show malice towards us when we go over to Singapore, and would often jeer us and speak against those who reside in Johore; even in the public streets and lanes they maltreat us and pull us ruffly [*sic*] about till our bones ache.[40]

Abu Bakar countered the Singapore government's claim to jurisdiction in the Straits with an appeal to traditional usage, noting that the question had not been raised earlier.

> In order that the seat of Government might be as centrical [*sic*] as possible, our father, a number of years ago fixed upon Tanjong Putri for the capital of Johore. No objection was made to this or to the resort of native craft to the place, or to our exercising jurisdiction over them; and not only were extensive steam saw-mills erected there several years ago, but a considerable population has naturally gathered together, the trade of which must be principally carried on by sea. Had the British Government looked upon the whole of the waters of the old strait from bank to bank as under its exclusive dominion, it would surely have been a friendly act to have warned our father or ourselves of the complication which might be expected to arise from this state of things; but it is only now, after much money has been spent in undertakings for the improvement of this part of our territory, that we are virtually told by the British Government that it is forbidden to ship the produce of Johor direct from its shores, and that it must all be brought to Singapore.[41]

The dispute continued until January 1866, when matters came to a head. In a letter to Abu Bakar, the Secretary of Government complained of the arrest of two Chinese in Johor for having violated the Temenggong's regulation. Orders for the arrest were said to have been issued by Tan Hiok Nee on the grounds that the two had failed to stop at Tanjong Putri to obtain their passes.[42] Macpherson, the Secretary of Government, suggested that this arrest had been made on the initiative of Tan Hiok Nee alone and that the Temenggong, on learning of it, would release the two men. Before Abu Bakar could reply, the government received a report from W. H. Read, Chairman of the Chamber of Commerce, that Abu Bakar himself had gone to Johor and punished the two Chinese. One was given a fine of $150, and the other, having no funds, was beaten and again thrown into prison.[43]

Abu Bakar, however, denied the entire charge, claiming that the complaints raised by Read were "wholly without foundation". He continued with an accusation which perhaps gives some clue to his motivation in maintaining his policy: "We have little doubt that the report has originated with some of those Chinese residing in Singapore who have an ill will towards us, because they find that, from the measures we have taken and propose to take for the regulation of the Gambier and Pepper plantations in Johore, a check will be interposed to the uncontrolled influence which they have hitherto exercised over the planters and which has contributed to keep these planters in state of dependence and poverty."[44]

While this letter, dated 17 January 1866, took the hardest line of all, it heralded Abu Bakar's capitulation. On 26 January, he issued a proclamation which designated five more alternative registration stations.[45] In addition to Tanjong Putri, whose name had been changed to Johor Baharu on 1 January 1866,[46] stations were to be set up at Pendas, Kukub, Batu Pahat, Tanjong Surat, and Pengerang. Since vessels were no longer required to go to Johor Baharu, which was the only one of these stations where shops, godowns, merchants, and other port facilities were located, there was less concern that the cargoes would be sold off illegally. This solution satisfied the Singapore government and the merchants. The matter of Johor's sovereignty in the straits also ceased to be an issue. It was formally settled a few years later, together with another jurisdictional question regarding Tanjong Surat, in Johor's favour.[47]

At the same time, Abu Bakar took the opportunity to institute reforms regarding land registration which he had hinted at as early as October 1864. The Singapore government had never objected to these measures; and the Chamber of Commerce, in fact, had given him some encouragement on these points while asking that he repeal the Tanjong Putri regulation. The arrangements for issuing grants or leases and the establishment of registers of sales and mortgages were thought to be useful measures, and likely to be of much benefit to the parties interested in the gambier and pepper plantations.[48] Governor Cavenagh himself also appears to have spoken to Abu Bakar regarding this matter, and he claims some credit for having brought about the ruler's change of heart. On 24 January 1866, he wrote that he had been consulted by Abu Bakar on the question of levying duties in Johor.

> I pointed out that it would be out of my power to sanction any duties being levied upon produce exported, as that would be a breach of the treaty, and if once we consented to its violation in any one respect, it would be difficult to require due adherence to its provisions in others, as His Highness might fairly claim freedom from its obligations on the ground that they had never been strictly enforced. As it was then represented that the Temenggong from 1,200 bamboo [gambier?] plantations did not receive more than $1,000 a month, I stated that, from what I had heard, I believed the Chinese would willingly pay a higher land revenue, provided that they could obtain some document in the way of a title-deed that might be transferable and of which the validity could not be disputed; that what they complained of at present was the want of security for any capital they might expend. I therefore recommended that such title-deeds should be issued.[49]

Winstedt, who has also quoted these lines, then remarks: "With the help of the Singapore government Abu Bakar now drew up Johor land laws."[50]

Two letters written in the latter part of 1866, discussing new measures instituted by the Johor government, suggest that some system of land tenure was being planned.[51]

It is of interest, however, that the purpose of the regulations, which were later embodied in the Kanun Kangchu of 1873, was the safeguarding of investments and not of planters. All plantations were registered by the Kangchu, according to Article 10 of the Kanun Kangchu. Article 14 noted that contracts covering advances made to planters and mortgages of plantations were to be registered with the State Police. Likewise, Article 44 stated that all transfers or sales of plantations had to be similarly registered. It was the Kangchu's duty to see that the contracting parties did this. In addition, Article 47 stated that all foreclosures of plantations had to be investigated by the Kangchu before they could be registered.

The most significant aspect of these regulations was that they also attempted to govern financial arrangements between cultivators and *taukehs*. The system whereby planters were required to sell their produce only to their creditors was to be regulated by a system of account books. Under Article 42, it was the Kangchu's responsibility to see that the planters in his districts kept these books up to date. The government also fixed the amount of commissions which the creditors could charge the planters. Under Article 41, they could charge planters a commission of 30 cents per pikul of rice and also collect 5 katis on each pikul of gambier or pepper.[52]

The object of these regulations did nothing to improve the lot of the exploited planters. In fact, it became more difficult for them to escape their disadvantageous economic situation. The Kanun Kangchu appears to have institutionalized the economic system which had characterized the pepper and gambier agriculture since at least 1835, if not earlier. The issuing of title-deeds simply provided one more guarantee of the planters' continued dependence. As the twenty-two pepper and gambier dealers pointed out in their petition to Abu Bakar, the title-deeds gave them a hold on the planters:

> Whereas we, your servants, would beg, should your Highness approve of it, to give a written grant to every owner of the plantations in Johor according to the size of their land. We, your servants, will then be able to reach the owners of the plantations, and order every one to take out a grant; and if they have no funds, we can assist them: but we shall be obliged, of course, to ask them to let us hold their grants as security so long as their debts are due.[53]

The initiation of a similar practice by the Singapore government in the 1840s had given rise to the exodus of planters from Singapore to Johor.

The tenor of these new regulations, together with the fact that the scheme for alternative registration centres was never put into practice, has influenced the conclusions drawn by C. M. Turnbull. In evaluating Abu Bakar's Tanjong Putri policy, she concurs with the Singapore official point of view that the Temenggong's aim was a monopoly of the trade, which was quashed by official intervention on behalf of the Chinese and English merchants.

In attempting to analyse Abu Bakar's motives, she finds them "obscure". Abu Bakar, she notes, was a "wily young ruler" who was sensitive to British opinions. She finds it difficult to believe that he was moved by altruism to protect his subjects, the Kangchus, from exploitation by their Singapore creditors. The British, she notes, wanted to see progress and prosperity in the Malay states, but in the early days of his rule, Abu Bakar had done little to promote the welfare of even his Malay subjects. Thus, she cannot accept his arguments about "protecting" the Johor Chinese by the Tanjong Putri regulations. She sees his later schemes for registration then as simply a graceful retreat before inflexible British demands: "His apparent compromise in permitting the opening of alternative registration centres was undoubtedly a face-saving capitulation, and the fact that his system of registration was completely abandoned within a few years indicates that the Temenggong's original aim was not registration but monopoly."[54]

There are a number of problems in Turnbull's interpretation. It is quite clear from the evidence given thus far that Abu Bakar was indeed ambitious. Since succeeding to office, he had shown remarkable energy in building up the state, expanding the area under cultivation, and in organizing and centralizing the powers of government.[55] Johor was indeed the economic step-child of Singapore, but the Temenggong had been recognized as an independent ruler by the British government. However, the fact that Johor's status was by no means clearly defined is shown by the manner in which both Abu Bakar and the Singapore authorities sought to exploit the ambiguities of the treaties.

It was inevitable that some attempt would eventually be made to clarify the situation. Such clarification, however, never comes about until some controversy arises to turn ambiguities into issues. Turnbull states that Abu Bakar's motives are "obscure". It is very possible that she has overlooked the significance of the financial panic of 1864 in reaching her decision on this point. It is impossible to say conclusively whether or not Abu Bakar and Tan Hiok Nee (who was obviously associated with the Temenggong in this matter) had planned to centralize the trade at Tanjong Putri from the beginning. It certainly is a possibility.

On the other hand, it is also possible, and perhaps more probable, that the new regulations were an emergency measure precipitated by the crash of 1864.

Abu Bakar was in the midst of promoting a vigorous expansion of cultivation in Johor. He was also hard-pressed for cash. The panic came at what appears to have been the high point of the expansion and it certainly slowed further growth of the state's agriculture. In addition, the panic could have had a positively destructive effect on the plantations which had just been established.

For the Temenggong, this was a major crisis and one which determined the state's future. Overextended merchants were swooping down on the newly established plantations and Kangchu and demanding immediate repayment of debts. These pressures could have easily forced the planters and Kangchu themselves into bankruptcy. They had to be blocked. The effect would ultimately have been the total ruination of the state. We cannot agree with Turnbull that, since Abu Bakar's policy was not "altruistic", it was therefore monopolistic. The Johor planters and Kangchu were engaged in a desperate struggle for economic survival. The Singapore merchants, we must assume, would gladly have bankrupted the entire state in order to keep themselves out of the debtor's prison. In fact, many of them did end up there.

The seriousness of the crisis, however, does not mean that Abu Bakar misrepresented the facts to the Singapore authorities, nor does it necessarily mean that his premeditated motive was to monopolize the trade. As an alternative suggestion, it seems that at first the policy was intended to prevent a vast exodus of capital from Johor, thus protecting the plantations from the depredations of panicking *taukehs*. This could easily have happened. Singapore was a totally "free" economy. Like the rest of Singapore's economy, the entire structure and operation of the gambier economy was self-regulated.[56] All credit arrangements appear to have been based on word-of-mouth contracts between planters and creditors, and the security of the rights of both parties depended entirely on the balance of coercive force. Absconding planters and oppressive *taukehs* were nothing new. As we have seen, very similar circumstances (poor economic conditions and disputes between planters and *taukehs*) had been at the root of the secret society fights in Singapore during the 1840s and 1850s.

Abu Bakar's concern for the welfare of his subjects may not have been entirely altruistic but, when their financial security determined the prosperity of the state, he had every reason to identify with them. Abu Bakar had begun the expansion in 1863 because he had no money. In issuing "letters of administration", that is, the *surat sungai*, he had borrowed heavily against the future of the agriculture. If he had not done *something* in 1864, the *taukehs* probably would have foreclosed Johor. The fact that hundreds of Johor planters were caught in the financial crisis is not mentioned as a major issue in any of the sources, but it does provide us with the major background against which all of these events were taking place. We conclude, therefore, that it was one of the primary causes of the entire controversy.

Everyone was suffering from the financial crisis.[57] The support that the Chamber of Commerce and the Singapore government gave to the cause of the merchants was equally guided by self-interest. After all, most of the European merchants who made up the Chamber were creditors of the Chinese who were being wiped out. The fact that two of the oldest European firms in Singapore had gone under must have given them all cause for concern. Both sides appear to have been primarily motivated by economic considerations. The political and legalistic terms in which the controversy was debated were mostly empty rhetoric. It is noteworthy that the British dropped their claim to absolute jurisdiction in the straits just as quickly as Abu Bakar forgot his alternative scheme for registration. I suggest that the Temenggong had no long-term plan behind his policy; rather, it should be seen as an "emergency" measure.

The merchants had brought other pressures to bear on Abu Bakar besides the harassment of the Singapore authorities. The dramatic drop in the number of *surat sungai* issued after October 1864 indicates that the merchants had cut off funds for further investment in Johor. Once the Tanjong Putri policy had been repealed, however, credit was loosened and the growth of Johor resumed. This circumstance, too, lends support to the theory that Abu Bakar's policy was somewhat hasty and perhaps unpremeditated. If he had been serious about monopolizing the trade, would it not have been wise to wait until the expansion had been completed before attempting to put pressure on the merchants? The policy was not in his best long-term interest and was therefore probably a stopgap measure, which was maintained only so long as it was necessary to wait for the panic to be over and to allow the new plantations to get started.

In later years, we are on firmer ground regarding Abu Bakar's motivation. His subsequent policies show that he did indeed move to exercise control over revenue through the agency of his Kangchu. Turnbull's statement that Abu Bakar "sacrificed any attempts to better the position of his Kangchus in favour of protecting the interests of their Singapore creditors" is inaccurate. What she means is that he sacrificed the planters. There is some confusion in her paper regarding the terms *Kangchu* and *planter*. A part of the confusion appears to be rooted in the correspondence. The petition from the Kangchus is signed "by 34 Chinese planters, residents in Johore (heads of rivers)". A distinction should be made between planters and heads of rivers. The planters or "estate owners" as they are styled in the Kanun Kangchu, were the actual tillers of the soil. They were granted a piece of land, cleared it, and planted it. They had no capital other than their plantation. They were responsible to Singapore *taukehs* for advances and provisions and were required to sell their produce to them at fixed prices. There were between 1,000 and 1,200 planters in Johor at this time.

The Kangchus, while they too may have owned plantations, were far more affluent individuals. They controlled entire river valleys and received authority directly from the Johor government. They were leaders of the planters on their rivers and also controlled the revenue concessions. These individuals had always been of crucial importance for the welfare of the agriculture and the ruler's revenues. From this time on, their position was reinforced and further legitimized. They were not only legally recognized as the principal agents of the government on the plantations, but they also became the primary instruments by which the ruler kept some control over the *taukehs* of Singapore.

The question of revenue farms raises another point which can be related to the Tanjong Putri controversy. The opium and spirit farms were Abu Bakar's major source of revenue. Before 1863, the Temenggong must have been almost totally dependent on one or two Chinese *taukehs* for his entire income. These *taukehs* were the Singapore opium and spirit farmers. Until Tan Hiok Nee was appointed as the revenue farmer for Johor Baharu, Cheang Hong Lim and Tan Seng Poh were the major farmers for both Johor and Singapore.[58]

While the Singapore and Johor farms were let separately after 1862, it is probable that they were both still controlled by the same syndicate. W. G. Gulland has pointed out that all the potential farmers combined into one Kongsi to manage these valuable concessions.

> If the government can get two or three syndicates in the field anxious to secure the Farm, then the letting is a comparatively easy matter, but on the principle that half a loaf is better than no bread these different factions sometimes combine and work together against the Government. It is the duty of the head of the Farm to judge of the means and position of any probable opposition and to decide whether the new concern should be fought, squared or to what extent taken into partnership.[59]

He also reported an incident which may have some bearing on the rise of Tan Hiok Nee in 1863. Writing of Tan Seng Poh, who was both a chief revenue farmer and a major pepper and gambier merchant at this time, he tells of one of his dealings with Abu Bakar:

> Sometimes Seng Poh was not above trying on some excuse or other to get a reduction on the rent during the term of the agreement. One time he tried his little game on with the late Sultan of Johore but came off second best. He was told that the request would be considered and in a few days he was sent for, when His Highness addressing him said: "Seng Poh, you know I have always been your friend and nothing is further from my wish than that you or anyone should lose money in Johore, so as (naming some Johore Chinaman) is willing

> to pay me more than you do, although he may not be so rich or so able as you, still, I have decided to set you free and accept his offer." This was the last thing that Seng Poh had bargained for, as His Highness very well knew, and he expressed himself as hurt that mention should have been made of the matter to any third party and ended by begging that His Highness would say nothing more on the subject to anyone, as he would keep the Farm on.[60]

Tan Hiok Nee had a dual purpose as far as the Temenggong was concerned. During the period between 1863 and 1866, his function was to police the flow of gambier and pepper out of the country and the flow of opium into the country. When the ruler was forced to repudiate the policy of registering and controlling the state's exports, greater emphasis was placed on the latter function. Tan Hiok Nee became the lever through which the ruler increased his bargaining power with the Singapore opium and spirit farmers.

This position, of course, was to Tan Hiok Nee's advantage as well. In 1871, he was taken into partnership with the Singapore farmers. "The *Daily Times* reports the amalgamation of the Singapore, Malacca, Rhio and Johore Opium Farms in November 1871, whereby the Syndicate was able to establish a uniform price for chandu at the four Settlements. The co-operation of Mr. Tan Seng Poh, the Rhio Opium Farmer at the time, afforded valuable assistance to the Syndicate in crushing out the organized system of smuggling which had for some time robbed the farmers of a large portion of the lawful fruits of their monopoly."[61]

Although Tan Hiok Nee was a great aid to the ruler at this time, it may be that he later became too independent or too closely associated with his Singapore partners. He apparently remained a partner in the opium syndicate through 1875.[62] In that year he left Johor. It is impossible to shed any light on the circumstances of his departure from Johor as none of the records pertaining to the sale of his many concessions have been preserved. They may not have been disposed of through the normal channels. He did not suffer, however, and retired a wealthy and influential man.[63]

Abu Bakar, even during the 1860s, did not place his faith in this one individual. There is ample evidence that wide-ranging measures were taken to tighten up the entire system. The *surat sungai* began to undergo modification both in form and, it seems, in function. As was noted above, these were held increasingly by merchants rather than by Kangchus. The Kongsi or partnership which held the *surat sungai* was thus a small-scale corporation formed only for the purpose of controlling the revenue concessions. The *surat tauliah* was the authority for the Kangchu only. This separation of functions made it easier for the government to impose controls on both parties.

The first modifications in the form of the *surat sungai* appeared in about 1860, when Abu Bakar and his brother Ungku Abdul Rahman began to take full control over Johor's affairs. Until this time, the *surat sungai* were very rudimentary documents. They originally gave very little information other than names, dates, and a vague statement of taxation conditions. Sometimes the Kangchu was designated, and sometimes he was not. For these early grants, it is impossible to say whether or not this was an oversight or whether it meant that the Kangchu was not among the owners of the river.[64]

From the 1860s, the basic form of the *surat sungai* began to undergo a gradual process of modification. By about 1873, the model *surat sungai*, which remained unchanged for the remainder of the century, had come into use. The first significant change came in 1860 when a *surat sungai* for Sungai Santi gave the earliest notation of share distribution and showed how many shares were held by each partner in the Kongsi.[65] This information soon became a regular feature of all later *surat sungai*. A second innovation was the regular designation of the Kangchu, if he was a member of the Kongsi. This practice may mark the first attempts to separate the Kangchu authority from the *surat sungai*.

Following these changes, a paragraph was added relating to the disposition of timber in the neighbouring jungles. The first known example of this ran as follows: "And furthermore, these Chinese may not take timbers used for the construction of *wankang* [lighters used for the shipping of pepper and gambier to Singapore]. If they wish to sell [these timbers] they must apply for a licence. Once they get the licence, no one can forbid them, for we have ruled it, and so if it is cut, it will not be illegal."[66] This innovation obviously heralded the institution of a separate licence for timber at about this time. The inclusion of such clauses had become a standard practice by 1865.

It was in 1865 that the first samples of a thoroughly revised and expanded *surat sungai* began to appear. These closely resembled the *surat sungai* of later years. A few minor changes were added between this date and 1873 when the form of the document appears to have become stabilized and fixed. Hereafter, the only major innovation came in 1881 when the Johor government began having the documents in print rather than in handwriting. In 1873, the *surat sungai* contained the following features:

(1) the name of the Kangchu, if he was a member of the Kongsi;
(2) a statement of the share distribution;
(3) a more specific description of the area covered by the grant;
(4) a requirement that Kongsi members inform the government when appointing a successor or deputy;

(5) an injunction forbidding the cutting of valuable timbers and the collection of jungle produce — the types of trees and produce were listed by name;
(6) a direction that Chinese should not interfere with Malays, their settlements, movements, or livelihood within the granted area;
(7) a requirement that planting should begin within one year of the date of the grant;
(8) a direction that shareholders should sell their shares within the Kongsi rather than to outsiders; and
(9) a requirement to open a fixed number of plantations, usually 100.[67]

A final feature of this reorganization of the *surat sungai* was the practice of regularly referring to previous grants when a river was resold. These references always state the type of document the river was originally held under, the date of its issue, and the individuals and actions involved.[68] It has been possible to "restore" a number of lost *surat sungai* as a result of these references.

After 1866, apparently in an effort to bring the Kongsi under more strict control following the Tanjong Putri crisis, a new form of document was introduced. This was the *surat jual-beli* or bill of sale, the first of which was issued in 1867.[69] These documents recorded the buying and selling of some or all of the shares or various concessions or property that the seller held under a *surat sungai*. The *surat jual-beli* invariably included the following information:

(1) name of buyer(s) and seller(s);
(2) price;
(3) description of what was purchased;
(4) authority by which the seller held the property (for example, *surat sungai*, *surat jual-beli*).

The *surat jual-beli* was used to record the purchase of entire *surat sungai* grants, as well as for smaller portions of such grants including a fixed number of plantations, equipment such as *kangkar* houses and boats, and one or more shares in the Kongsi.[70]

The *surat jual-beli* appears to have stood in place of the *surat sungai*. Before 1867, whenever a river was sold or shares changed hands it was necessary to issue a new *surat sungai*. We have already noted that a large number of such reorganizational grants were issued between 1863 and 1867. After the appearance of the *surat jual-beli*, no new *surat sungai* were issued when an area was sold. In subsequent sales, the authority quoted in the next *surat jual-beli* was the former *surat jual-beli* together with the original *surat sungai*.

One assumes that shares and property held under *surat sungai* were being bought and sold on an informal basis right from the beginning. There was always a tendency towards the consolidation of the shares. With the introduction of the *surat jual-beli*, this aspect of Chinese economic activity became visible and more subject to government controls. The new documents allowed for greater flexibility within the system and also stood as a record of the current value of any given revenue concession.

Additional innovations in the administration began during these years. These included the *surat tauliah* or letter of Kangchu authority. Other forms, such as the *surat kuasa* (power of attorney), *surat perjanjian* (contract), and *surat concession*, also came into use but have not been preserved in any organized files or letter-books, as have the *surat sungai* and *surat jual-beli*. There are a few of these uncollected documents in the miscellaneous collection *Kumpulan Surat di-Simpan oleh Setia Usaha* (Collection of Correspondence of the State Secretary),[71] and many more are referred to in extant correspondence. No copies of the *surat tauliah* have survived to the present day, and it is fortunate that Coope has left us at least one example of this.

All this shows that there was a substantial expansion of the Malay administrative apparatus during these years. As we have seen, the task of organizing a bureaucracy had been started in the late 1850s when the first moves to settle Tanjong Putri were undertaken. Johor's administration was staffed by such individuals as Mohamed Salleh bin Perang and Enche Long. The most important figure, however, was Abu Bakar's brother, Ungku Abdul Rahman.

In 1863, he appears to have been given sole responsibility for the issuing of *surat sungai*.[72] Hereafter until his death, sometime after 1876, he signed all *surat sungai*. We are probably correct in assuming that much of the reorganization and expansion of the Kangchu system and the cultivation was under his direct charge. He was, in fact, second in command of the state. In Abu Bakar's absence, as when he left the country in 1866, Ungku Abdul Rahman served as the Regent. The fact that he himself was a member of several of the Kongsi which were granted *surat sungai* for west coast rivers, particularly, the Batu Pahat, suggests his close involvement with this aspect of the expansion of the 1860s.[73]

In addition to the expansion of pepper and gambier cultivation, other forms of agricultural enterprise were undertaken at this time. Under the direction of Ungku Abdul Rahman, police stations and coconut plantations were established at Tanjong Kupang, Batu Pahat, and Padang. Hundreds of Javanese labourers were brought into these places. *Parit* or canals were dug to drain the land, coconuts planted, and roads built in these settlements.[74] These were outside the Kangchu system and there is no government correspondence relating to them. Except for tin mines opened near Padang in 1871, these were areas of Malaysian settlement rather than Chinese. In addition to the Javanese coolies, it is reported that there was one long-established Malay village at Padang. To oversee the plantations and police stations, Abdul Rahman had Malays brought in from Teluk Belanga. Thus, the "Malay" population of the state was being increased — Abdul Rahman was subsidizing it.

With such an able individual in charge of Johor's development, Abu Bakar began seeking other means of ensuring and enhancing his position. In 1866, as soon as the Tanjong Putri controversy had been settled, the Temenggong travelled to England. Rupert Emerson has noted the significance of this visit: "Recognizing that Singapore was not the center of the Empire, [the Johor rulers] have made themselves at home in London and discreetly thrown their influence there into the balance against the local officialdom of Malaya."[75] Henceforth, it became possible for Johor rulers to bypass the British officials of Singapore and take their case directly to the seat of the Empire. In characterizing Abu Bakar's catholicity, Winstedt has noted: "He lived as a young man half in the traditional Malay world and half in the world of a cosmopolitan British port."[76] Emerson has further commented that "this division of his time and personality continued, with the addition of Europe, throughout his life to his great benefit and profit."[77] Abu Bakar's visit laid the foundation for his diplomatic offensive which helped to make him the most formidable ruler in the entire Malay world. The *Hikayat Johor* has given an account of this visit. He was accompanied by his chief minister, Ja'afar bin Haji Mohamed. In England he was received by Queen Victoria and became a "close friend" of the Prince of Wales, later King Edward VII. He also received various awards and citations and was well received in the courts of other European countries.[78]

One significant result of this trip sent him back to the most traditional part of the Malay world, Riau. Winstedt writes:

> Perhaps that visit had taught him that the title Temenggong was unknown in Europe. Perhaps his gracious reception by royalty set him thinking ... Why should he not assume a title more in accord with his birth, his power and his place? Accordingly on 18 April 1868, Abu-Bakar sent his cousin Engku Haji Muhammad and his Dato' Bentara (Ja'far bin Haji Muhammad) to Riau to that genealogist and prolific historian Raja Haji Ali [the author of the *Tufhat al-Nafis*] (his deceased uncle's brother-in-law) to needle the way to the Yamtuan Muda and enquire if the Temenggongs could now assume "sovereign power", — which in fact they had assumed already, but at Riau it was a euphemism for "a royal title".[79]

Thus, with the approval of both the Governor of the Straits Settlements and the Sultan of Lingga, Abu Bakar assumed the title of Maharaja of Johor on 30 June 1868. Although once the most prestigious of titles in the Malay world, it had long since fallen out of use among Malays.[80] In the nineteenth century, Sri Maharaja was but an appendage to the title of Temenggong.[81] However, Maharaja was then the title of the highest-ranking Indian princes and was recognized throughout the world.

The trip to Riau was an important piece of symbolism. Riau, even though only a quiet backwater by 1868, was still the spiritual centre of the Malay world. Abu Bakar's envoy was proof of his acknowledgement of the power of tradition among Malay rulers. Legitimacy, as far as they were concerned, came from two sources: the British and tradition. It was as necessary for Abu Bakar to verify his genealogy and obtain the approval of the Sultan as it was for him to visit the Queen. Abu Bakar had been on friendly terms with the Riau court for some years. Examination of the genealogies must have been largely a matter of form. It could have been no surprise when Sultan Sulaiman told Enche Haji Muhammad that he and the Yamtuan would like Abu Bakar to "become a Raja".[82]

Since he could not be called Sultan or Yamtuan, the compromise title of Maharaja was decided on. Abu Bakar had to wait another seventeen years before he could assume the title of Sultan. In the meantime, however, the new title set him off from the other Malay rulers of the Peninsula and gave him a more universally recognized claim to princely status than did that of Temenggong. Actually, Abu Bakar appears to have expropriated the title on his own for this very reason. During his trip to England in 1866, he had already begun to style himself as Maharaja.[83]

Abu Bakar's trip to England was particularly well-timed. It allowed the Maharaja the opportunity to establish his name there and to form connections just prior to the long-awaited transfer of the Straits Settlements from the East India Company to the Colonial Office.[84] When Sir Harry St. George Ord was installed as the first British Governor, Abu Bakar took steps to continue the intimate relationship which the Johor rulers had always maintained with the Singapore governors. The *Hikayat Johor* reports: "Only a short while after His Honour had arrived in Singapore, he had already become a good friend of His Highness".[85] Ord played an important role in settling the still outstanding problem of Abu Bakar's war with Pahang:

> ... one of Ord's first undertakings was the settlement of the outstanding boundary dispute. Just before his arrival the Temenggong offered to cede the islands north of 2°40′ to the Pahang chief. This broke the deadlock, and Ord was able to take up the negotiations. In August, 1868 he visited the east coast in the steam yacht *Peiho*. At Pahang, he arranged a settlement between

> Abu-Bakar and Ahmad, with the Endau river as the dividing line on land, and its latitude as the dividing line through the islands. Ahmad was thus recognized in Pahang. But the Temenggong remained the doyen of the native chiefs …[86]

By 1873, Abu Bakar had been successful in consolidating his position. The boundaries of his state were fixed as were the limits of his sovereignty. Johor's status as an economic dependency of Singapore had been reluctantly acknowledged, but the ruler's administrative controls gave him adequate leverage within the system. If he had not been successful in expanding the boundaries of his state and in realizing its independence, he had not come away empty-handed. He still retained great power to interfere in the other states. By yielding when necessary and by adopting the trappings of the British, he had risen in status both with Europeans and with Malays. He was "civilized". According to Governor Ord:

> The present Maharaja of Johore … was born in his father's house at Singapore where by Treaty the family have considerable landed property adjoining the town and was educated by an English Clergyman … In his tastes and habits he is an English Gentleman. As a Ruler, he is anxious to promote in everything the advancement and civilization of his people and is the only Rajah in the whole Peninsula or the adjoining states who rules in accordance with the practice of civilized nations.
>
> He is deeply attached to the British Government and, feeling that with their support and encouragement he is most likely to benefit his country, he takes no step of importance in administration without the advice of the local Government, whilst he is ready at all times to place the whole resources of his country at our disposal.[87]

NOTES

1. Mohamad Said, *Hikayat Johor*, pp. 12–13.
2. John Cameron, *Our Tropical Possessions in Malayan India* (London, 1865). Reprinted in 1965 by Oxford University Press, Kuala Lumpur, pp. 137–38.
3. C. M. Turnbull, "The Origins of British Control in the Malay States before Colonial Rule", in *Malayan and Indonesian Studies*, ed. Bastin and Roolvink, p. 174.
4. Winstedt, "A History of Johor", pp. 99–100.
5. Tarling, *British Policy*, pp. 65–74.
6. Winstedt, "A History of Johor", p. 102.
7. Ibid., p. 103.
8. Tarling, *British Policy*, pp. 72–73.

9. Winstedt, "A History of Johor", p. 106.
10. Ibid., pp. 99–100.
11. Ibid., p. 107.
12. *SKMK-I*, Nos. 37–85. For a chronological list of *surat sungai*, see Trocki, "The Johor Archives", pp. 20–35.
13. Coope, "The Kangchu System", pp. 249–51. Coope gives a translation of "a somewhat late example, as the Ruler is referred to as 'Sultan' ".
14. Song Ong Siang, *One Hundred Years' History*, p. 335. Judging from the amount of power that Tan Hiok Nee exercised in Johor in 1866, it is possible that he received the title much earlier than 1870. However, the first use of the title in the correspondence of the Johor Archives is found on a *SJB*, 1 November 1872, No. 14.
15. *SKMK-I*, No. 80, 25 December 1853.
16. *SKMK-I*, No. 20, 27 November 1854.
17. *SKMK-I*, No. 45, 5 September 1863.
18. *SKMK-I*, No. 46, 5 September 1863.
19. *SKMK-I*, No. 44, 8 September 1863.
20. *SKMK-I*, No. 59, 11 September 1863.
21. Song Ong Siang, *One Hundred Years' History*, p. 335.
22. This is a rather speculative (but conservative) estimate. The *surat jual-beli* suggest that the initial investment in a river was about $1,000. For instance, when Sungai Santi was reorganized in 1860 (*SKMK-I*, No. 26, 8 September 1860), one share seemed to be worth $290. There were four shares. However, they could increase considerably in value. In 1871 (*SJB*, No. 7, 5 March 1871), when a share of this river was sold, it brought $2,600. Thus the total value was about $10,000 for this one river. Most of the concessions that Tan Hiok Nee bought at this time were, or seemed to be, established areas rather than new ones, thus they would have been more valuable.
23. *SKMK-I*, No. 60, 12 August 1864.
24. *SJB*, No. 11, 2 October 1872, refers to this sale and *SJB*, No. 74, 8 May 1883, dates the sale as 24 June 1869. Kapitan Tan Cheng Hung received $6,000 for his concessions in Tebrau, but held on to one share which he gave Ja'afar bin Haji Muhamad under a power of attorney. This was later sold for $4,000. Dato Ja'afar, who had purchased the other shares in the river, sold them all to a Kongsi made up of four Arabs in 1872 for $12,000.
25. *Johor Baharu Saratus Tahun* (Johor Baharu, 1955), p. 14. Also Mohamad bin Haji Ilyas, comp., *Tawarikh*, p. 77.
26. Most of the *surat sungai* issued between 1844 and 1853 contained the following clause: "The agreement of His Highness the Temenggong with this Chinese is that for three years he will collect no taxes. After three years, the Chinese must pay them without fail in accordance with the laws of Singapore which are followed by us in regard to the Chinese planters in Johor." See Trocki, "The Johor Archives", pp. 11–12, for a transcription of the entire document in Malay

and the English translation. However, after 1853 this clause was altered to read "After three years, the Chinese must pay them without fail according to the laws which we have made." (See *SKMK-I*, No. 20, 27 November 1854, in Trocki, "The Johor Archives", pp. 12–13.)

27. Mohamad bin Haji Ilyas, comp., *Tawarikh*, p. 80. "With the help of God, after about two years I was able to read quite a bit and write in Teochew. I was able to read all of the account books and no longer needed a Chinese translator. Thus I was able to speak, read short letters and write. I no longer needed a Chinese scribe."
28. *SPP*, 21 May 1864.
29. Buckley, *An Anecdotal History*, p. 711.
30. *SSSU*, No. 9, 10 November 1863, (17 Jemadil 'awal 1280), *Surat Kuasa Kapada Seah En Chin atas harta Lee Kai Tai dan Lee Chang Wat.*
31. The *SSSU* contains about two or three more *surat kuasa*, but numerous others are referred to in other pieces of correspondence, particularly the *surat jual-beli, surat pajak*, and *surat gadai dan hutang*. However, there does not appear to have been a separate register for these documents, or, if there was, it has not been preserved. It is a characteristic of the available documents that they pertain mainly to the Kangchu and the river-holding Kongsi; correspondence relating to individual planters and plantations is very rare and incidental.
32. CO 273/16, "Petition from 34 Chinese Planters, residents in Johore (heads of rivers)", 22 May 1864 (15 Zulhaji 1280), which is enclosed with Abu Bakar to Secretary of Government, 20 October 1864. See below pp. 133–34, fn. 39, 40.
33. CO 273/16, "Petition from the Chinese merchants resident in Singapore to the Honourable Colonel Orfeur Cavenagh, Governor of Prince of Wales Island, Singapore and Malacca." Enclosed with Logan to Secretary of Government, 3 October 1864.
34. Turnbull, "The Johore Gambier and Pepper Trade", pp. 43–55.
35. CO 273/16, Abu Bakar to Secretary of Government, 20 October 1864.
36. CO 273/16, Logan to Secretary of Government, 20 October 1864, Enclosure.
37. CO 273/16, Secretary of Government, Straits Settlements to Secretary of Government, India, 27 May 1865.
38. CO 273/16, Secretary of Government, Straits Settlements, to Abu Bakar, 12 January 1865.
39. CO 273/16, Abu Bakar to Secretary of Government, 20 October 1864, Enclosure.
40. Ibid.
41. CO 273/16, Abu Bakar to Secretary of Government, Straits Settlements, 7 April 1865.
42. One reason why there was such concern over this point was that Abu Bakar had stated he would impose no penalty for non-compliance with his regulation that boats should stop at Tanjong Putri. See CO 273/16, Abu Bakar to Secretary of Government, Straits Settlements, 3 December 1864 and *SSR*, v. 41, p. 375, Secretary of Government, Straits Settlements to Abu Bakar, 24 January 1866.

43. *SSR*, W. 56, Item 25, Read to Secretary of Government, 17 January 1866, p. 162.
44. *SSR*, W. 56, Abu Bakar to Secretary of Government, 17 January 1866.
45. *SSR*, W. 56, Item 44, Abu Bakar to Secretary of Government, 26 January 1866.
46. Mohamad Said, *Hikayat Johor*, p. 12. He reports the change but gives no reason for it. Winstedt, in "A History of Johor", p. 108, notes: "His business and political sense led him to change the fanciful name Iskandar Putri of his new capital to one that all races could remember and all Malays associate with the old-time history of the State."
47. The British government had earlier laid claim to Tanjong Surat, also under Article 2 of the 1824 Treaty. The low-lying ground is technically an island being cut off from the mainland by a swamp. Correspondence relating to this dispute is also to be found in CO 273/16.
48. CO 273/16, Logan to Secretary of Government, 21 November 1864.
49. Orfeur Cavenagh, *Reminiscences of an Indian Official* (London, 1884), p. 361.
50. Winstedt, "A History of Johor", p. 108.
51. *SSR*, v. 45, p. 46, Governor to Regent of Johore, 7 August 1866. *SSR*, v. 45, p. 60, Governor to Regent of Johore, 29 September 1866. At this time Abu Bakar was away in England and his brother, Ungku Abdul Rahman, was Regent in his place.
52. Coope, "The Kangchu System", pp. 253–57.
53. CO 273/16, Petition "Signed by 22 dealers in gambier and pepper, residents in Singapore, 1st month Zool Hadjee 1280" (8 May 1864), Enclosed with Abu Bakar to Secretary of Government, 20 October 1864.
54. Turnbull, "The Johore Gambier and Pepper Trade", p. 53. Actually the new regulations suggest that the business of registration of cargoes was taken over by the Kangchus themselves. This would have made the alternative centres redundant.
55. Mohamad Said, *Hikayat Johor*, p. 12. He reports Abu Bakar's measures to expand Tanjong Putri at this time: "Then the place opened by His Highness at Tanjong Putri became large and many merchants came there to trade. His Highness returned there often and issued commands for the construction of government buildings to become customs' station, police station, courthouse and other offices. He also placed officials in charge of these offices. Then he built a palace and a mosque. People built roads and houses and the place was set in order."
56. As far as can be determined, the British government did nothing to regulate the pepper and gambier economy as such. They established a system of land registration and collected a quit rent. It is probable that most title-deeds in Singapore were held by *taukehs* against the planters' debts. However, the system of compulsory deliveries of produce and compulsory purchases of provisions could not have been recognized as such under British law. The real difference between the Singapore and Johor laws is that in Johor under the Kanun Kangchu of 1873 the basic features of the Chinese system were institutionalized, codified, and given legitimacy by the state.

57. Turnbull, "The Origins", pp. 176, 178, and 180, indicates that Singapore merchants, particularly Paterson & Simons, had invested heavily in the Pahang war, partly by making loans to the Bendahara and partly through their investment in the tin mines at Kuantan. Paterson had lent $12,000 to the Bendahara and he lost heavily on the tin mines following Wan Ahmad's victory. "His victory brought tranquility to Pahang but did not restore prosperity to the Singapore miners and traders. During the 1863 campaign Wan Ahmad's men looted Paterson & Simons' warehouses in Kuantan, and after his triumph the new Bendahara repudiated their claim for nearly $50,000 Spanish dollars compensation for damage to property and loss of mining rights. He confiscated the tin himself and shipped it for sale in Singapore with a rival mercantile firm."
58. The value of opium farms is perhaps the best gauge of Johor's expansion. In 1846, the Johor portion of the farm brought the ruler $300 per month. In 1855, the value of the farms had risen to $3,500 per month. By 1860, the Johor and Singapore farms were still being let out jointly. The Johor ruler received 22.5 per cent which included $8,025 and $1,025 monthly for the opium and spirit farms respectively. However, in 1861, according to the findings of Tan Soo Chye in his academic exercise ("British Relations with Johore 1855–1869"; University of Malaya, Singapore, 1951), "it was discovered that the Temenggong was receiving through the Singapore treasury a sum considerably more than the gross sale of excisable articles in Johore amounted to." (pp. 3, 24) After 1861, the Singapore and Johor Farms were let separately. See also, Trocki, *Opium and Empire*, Ch. 5.
59. Quoted by Song Ong Siang, in *One Hundred Years' History*, p. 131.
60. Ibid., p. 132.
61. Ibid., p. 159.
62. *Singapore and Straits Directory*, 1874 "Johore", p. 4. The Johor opium and spirit farmers for 1874–76 were Cheang Hong Lim, Tan Hiok Nee, and Tan Seng Poh.
63. Song Ong Siang, *One Hundred Years' History*, p. 335.
64. Trocki, "The Johor Archives", pp. 2–3 and 11–14.
65. *SKMK-I*, No. 26, 7 September 1860.
66. *SKMK-I*, No. 29, 19 October 1860.
67. Trocki, "The Johor Archives", pp. 12–14.
68. *SKMK-I*, No. 36, 25 December 1862, is the first grant in which such reference to an earlier grant was made. However, it was not the first time successive *surat sungai* had been written for the same area.
69. The Johor Archives' Register entitled *Buku Daftar Surat*^{2} *Jual dan Beli, Pajak dan Gadai dan Hutan 1284–1301*, A.D. 1867–1883, contains eighty-seven such documents.
70. Trocki, "The Johor Archives", pp. 14–15.
71. This collection contains about fifty items, all original documents, collected in separate envelopes. Most of them are licences, contracts, and promissory notes. The earliest entry dates from 1843.
72. The first *surat sungai* to bear his, or any, signature was *SKMK-I*, No. 37, 5 June 1863.

73. He was listed as a shareholder in three different Kongsi on Batu Pahat. *SKMK-I*, Nos. 63, 65, and 87, dated 5 December 1864, 29 March 1865, and 17 July 1868.
74. Mohamed Ibrahim Munshi, *The Voyages of Mohamed Ibrahim Munshi*, trans. Amin Sweeney and Nigel Phillips (Kuala Lumpur, 1975), pp. 3–4.
75. Rupert Emerson, *Malaysia: A Study in Direct und Indirect Rule* (Kuala Lumpur, 1964), p. 198.
76. Winstedt, "A History of Johor", p. 109.
77. Emerson, *Malaysia*, p. 199.
78. Mohamad Said, *Hikayat Johor*, pp. 12–13.
79. Winstedt, "A History of Johor", p. 109. Winstedt's account of this trip appears to come from a Johor manuscript. A copy of this is on microfilm in the University of Singapore Library, together with a number of other miscellaneous Johor documents including genealogies. I could find no copies of these documents in Johor and the microfilms seem to be the only available copies. The documents on microfilm are apparently Winstedt's working copies and contain notations scribbled in the margins. This particular one marked "The Trip to Riau" is twelve pages long and printed in *jawi*.
80. The rulers of Srivijaya and the first rulers of Malacca had the title of Maharaja. However, this practice had disappeared from Malay usage by the nineteenth century.
81. Mohamad Said, *Hikayat Johor*, p. 13. This simply notes that the change involved shortening of the title Temenggong Sri Maharaja: "… *dengan kesuka'an dan persetujuan orang negeri di-adakan suatu istia'adat mengubah akan gelaran Raja Temenggong Tun Abu Bakar diringkaskan jadi Maharaja Johor*."
82. Winstedt, "A History of Johor", p. 109.
83. Tarling, *British Policy*, p. 81, fn. 326, citing Kaye's Mem. of 10 May 1866. CO 273/15 (6997) notes that "In England he was styled not Temenggong Sri Maharaja but Maharaja …"
84. C. N. Parkinson, *British Intervention in Malaya, 1867–1877* (Singapore, 1960), p. 1. The Straits Settlements were officially transferred to the Colonial Office on 1 April 1867 and the new Governor, Harry St. George Ord, was sworn in at the same time. Full accounts of the transfer and events leading up to it are given in the Parliamentary Papers and also Buckley, *An Anecdotal History*, pp. 754–80, and L. A. Mills, *British Malaya*, pp. 263–75.
85. Mohamad Said, *Hikayat Johor*, p. 13.
86. Tarling, *British Policy*, p. 81.
87. Quoted in Parkinson, *British Intervention*, p. 41.

6

Johor and the Maharaja

1873–1884

The 1870s and 1880s were turbulent years in the Malay world. Johor, no less than any other state, was deeply affected. Starting in 1874, the government of the Straits Settlements began its "forward movement". A decade later, the entire group of southern Malay states had been taken under some type of formal British protection. The states of Perak, Selangor, and Negri Sembilan had British Residents installed in their courts. Even though Johor possessed a greater measure of political independence, it was even more intimately linked with British Singapore by economic ties than the other states. In 1885, Johor too agreed in principle to accept an "adviser", though none was appointed until 1914.

Between 1874 and 1885, Johor was at the peak of its wealth and power. It was seen as an exemplary Malay state. Both the British and the Maharaja were proud of it. Malays of other states admired and envied Johor's position, and many of the other Malay chiefs sought to emulate Abu Bakar. The English voiced the hope that the others would indeed follow in his footsteps. But, for a variety of reasons, no one managed to duplicate Johor.

There were several factors that made Johor seem attractive and progressive. First of all, Abu Bakar himself was the state's best advertisement. His reception by Queen Victoria gave him the opportunity to present himself as a civilized and cultured gentleman, which indeed he must have been. He gained entry to the world of the British aristocracy which at the time was a major centre of international power. According to Parkinson, the British aristocracy was mainly characterized by its peculiar coordination of commercial, maritime, naval, military, and colonial policy, which was "achieved to some extent through such institutions as Parliament, the Stock Exchange, Lloyds, and the Baltic, but more through social relationships and a pattern of life created and strengthened in public schools, universities, clubs, race-courses, and the hunting field".[1] As an accepted member of this society, Abu Bakar was able to put forward the interests of his state and further his own ambitions at the highest levels, both in Malaya and in Britain.

More important than the ruler's social status, however, was the state. Johor offered a striking contrast to the other states of the Peninsula. In 1874, it had a population of resident Chinese numbering close to 100,000. These planters were, on the whole, peaceful, orderly, and productive. The government consisted of a small and tightly-knit group of Malay administrators and Chinese businessmen. In general, an acceptable form of law and justice had been instituted. Moreover, the ruler's word was respected by all his subjects.

In the states of Perak, Selangor, and Negri Sembilan, there were also thousands of Chinese engaged in productive activity. However, their wealth was often squandered in warfare as rival secret societies and dialect groups competed for domination of the tin-fields. The Malays in these states seemed incapable of controlling the Chinese. The Sultans of Perak and Selangor had little authority over their own officials and minor chiefs, and in Negri Sembilan there was no agency of central government at all. Local chiefs such as the Mentri of Larut, Nga Ibrahim, and the "Viceroy" of Selangor, Tungku Kudin, were wealthier than their Sultans. The combination of administrative disorganization and Chinese factional fighting created a situation of almost continual warfare in all these states.[2] By comparison, Johor was a "Garden of Eden".

In Pahang, the ruler was a formidable individual. Bendahara Wan Ahmad had countered Abu Bakar's attempt to dominate Pahang in 1863 and had then secured his own position *vis-a-vis* the minor chiefs. However, the state had little tin and was not yet open to European capital. Though usually orderly, the government was disturbed by sporadic conflicts between the ruler and some up-river chiefs and thus offered no secure field for large-scale investment. It remained poor and followed a much more traditional course. Again, Johor's wealth and relative degree of progress put Pahang in a generally unfavourable light.[3]

This chapter will attempt to describe the rather unique system of government that had evolved in Johor at the high point of its prosperity under the pepper and gambier regime. In 1874, the *Singapore and Straits Directory (SSD)* contained a seven-page section on Johor.[4] This appears to be the earliest published statement of the structure and composition of Abu Bakar's government. It provides enough information to enable the historian to reconstruct the basic features of the state as it was at that time. One striking detail is the relatively small number of officials actually employed in the administration. Another remarkable feature is that the "government" is shown to have been composed of an almost equal number of Chinese and Malays.

The Malay side of the government included a Council, a Treasury Department, a Police Court, a jail, a Public Works and Land Department, and a Commissariat. A railway was under construction, and the Johor Free School had been established since 1864. These latter, together with the Arsenal, the Marine and its three steamboats, and the Medical Department were under the direction of privately hired European officials.

Nothing certain can be said of the functions of any of these bodies. At this time, the state had no written constitution. The Council seemed the most important. Its composition was as follows: There were twenty-four members, including two Chinese, Major Tan Hiok Nee and "Captain Tye Hiang" (Seah Tee Heng); the rest were Malays. Six of them were close relatives of the ruler, either brothers, cousins, or uncles. Most of them bore the title of either *ungku* or *raja*. Ungku Abdul Rahman, the ruler's brother, appears to have been the ranking member of the Council. There were also three Hajis and three others, presumably of Arabian descent, who were called "Syed". Ja'afar bin Haji Mohamed, the Dato Bentara, and Mohamed Salleh bin Perang were also listed as members. Very little can be said of the identity of the other members of the Council. If Dato Ja'afar and Mohamed Salleh are at all typical, perhaps all the rest were likewise either related by blood in some fashion to the ruling family or were the descendants of the principal followers of earlier Temenggongs.[5]

The Council appears to have formed the core of the Maharaja's government. We are probably correct in assuming that all the Malays on it were Teluk Belanga people and represented the principal following of the ruler. One assumes that the composition of the group was essentially the same as the followings of Temenggongs Ibrahim and Abdul Rahman. In other words, it was a larger and latter-day version of the traditional group of kin, supporters, and advisers which surrounded almost all the major Malay chiefs. In this case, however, the following was given a more formal status within the state and dignified with the title of "Council".

Since the only source of information regarding the composition of the government at this time is the Directory which is in English, it is impossible to give the Malay name for this body or for the other departments. It appears that Abu Bakar had followed contemporary British colonial models in organizing the state at this time. This may have been only a matter of form rather than substance. The local administrative set-up bears a strong resemblance to traditional Malay governments with the exception of the titles.

When one looks at the apparatus of local administration, a dualism in the government is obvious. On the local level, there were two seemingly separate groups of government servants, one Malay and the other Chinese. The Malay administration appears to have been a slight variation on the earlier *pengulu*-system which had been set up by Temenggong Ibrahim around 1848.

In 1874, there were two "Commissioners". Endau and the east coast of Johor were under Ungku Abdullah. Muar, which at this time was the northern border of the state, and the west coast were under Ungku Abdul Majid. The state was further broken up into thirteen smaller administrative divisions which were called "Residencies". Two of the Residents actually held the title of *pengulu* and another was an *orang kaya*. The use of these traditional titles suggests that the Residents were, in fact, *pengulu* or river chiefs.

The Residencies were (from east to west) Endau, Sedili, Pengarang, Tanjong Surat, Johor Lama, Lenggui, Pasir Godung, Tanjong Kupang, Tanjong Bulas, Senggarang, Batu Pahat, Padang, and Muar (see Map 5). There were also two "Dependencies" which appear to have had roughly the same status as the Residencies. These two were for the administration of the islands off the Johor coast. One chief, Enche Mahmud, stationed at Pulau Tinggi, was in charge of all the islands in the South China Sea. The other, Pengulu Mirdang, ruled the islands in the Straits of Malacca from Pulau Pisang.

In addition to the Residencies and Dependencies, there were also thirteen police stations. Most of these were located at the Residencies and were under police officers with the rank of "Constable" or "Duffadar". The Directory also notes: "To each station is attached one or two Malay Sampans manned by Police Peons."[6] Police stations were located at Tanjong Kupang, Tanjong Kukub, Satengah Lahu, Batu Pahat, Padang, Muar, Pulau Tinggi, and Endau.[7] This whole "branch" of government (that is, police, Residencies, and Dependencies) must have represented what remained of the Temenggongs' sea peoples.

There was a certain amount of duplication of personnel. Allowing for spelling irregularities, about five Residents (or Assistant Residents) also doubled as police constables. It is also worth noting that about four of the Residents appear to have also been members of the Council (that is, Syed Abdullah, Nong Yahya, Enche Ali? and Enche Hoosman?).

In the "central" government, departments under Malay charge were generally headed by members of the Council. The Treasury was under Ungku Haji Mohamed. Enche Mohamed Salleh bin Perang was Commissioner of Police. Enche Yahya Awal was the Chief of Public Works Department.

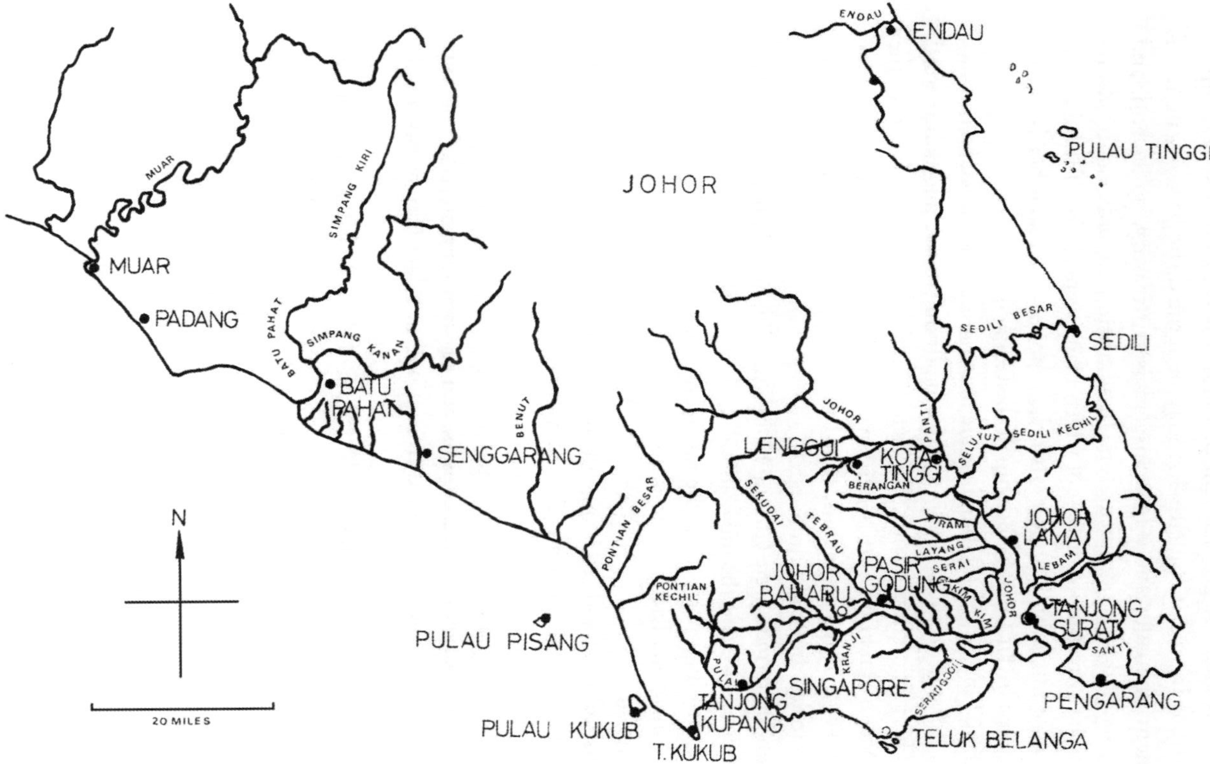

MAP 5
Administrative Divisions of Johor, 1874

While the latter was not named to the Council, it appears that his father, Enche Awal, was.

On the whole, the government of Johor was thus not a very complex organization. It only included what may be termed the bare essentials of government: the ruler and a few close advisers; treasury, police and land departments; and local administrators. In all, there were only eighty Malays named in the Directory for 1874, of which many were clerks. If the duplications are accounted for, it appears that the number of actual officials cannot have exceeded by far the membership of the Council.

On the Chinese side, the numbers are much more impressive. Here, however, it is difficult to draw the line between administrative and commercial listings. This section of the Directory includes the spirit and opium farms, the office of Major Tan Hiok Nee, twenty-two pepper and gambier shops in Johor Baharu, seventy-three Kangchus, four Indian shopkeepers, a rice mill, two tapioca factories, and eight tin mines.[8]

The opium farmers were Cheang Hong Lim, Tan Seng Poh, and Tan Hiok Nee. Tan Hiok Nee was the only "Johor" Chinese of the three. The other two were the controlling partners in the much larger syndicate which also ran the farms for Singapore, Riau, Malacca, and perhaps for a number of other states on the Peninsula.

The list of seventy-three Kangchus is of great importance, for this is the first listing of all current Kangchus and of the rivers on which cultivation was in progress. It offers an opportunity to verify the information given in the collections of Kangchu records in the Johor Archives. There are a number of interesting discrepancies between this list and the archival materials. The *SSD* list appears to have been compiled from a body of data which was totally distinct from the *surat sungai*.

Among the obvious contrasts is the failure of the *SSD* list to mention the Kongsi — only the Kangchus are named. Frequently, the names of these Kangchus are found nowhere in the archival materials. In many cases, different place names are used for the same *kangkar*. Even where correspondences do exist in the two compilations, spelling differences are often radical. There is no indication that one list or the other is wrong. Rather, each list seems to have been compiled for different reasons. Thus, they represent two different official views of the Kangchu system. These discrepancies make it possible to push our enquiry a few steps further. Ultimately, they lead us to some tentative conclusions about the operation of the Kangchu system, the Johor government, and the relationship between Johor and Singapore.

Mention has already been made of the changing status of the Kangchu in Johor. As early as 1864, there was a tendency for the *surat sungai* to be held by persons other than the Kangchu. In this situation, the Kangchu became the deputy of the *tuan sungai* or "owner of the river", as Coope has termed him. A comparison of the Directory's listing with my own compilation of all current *surat sungai*, together with *surat jual-beli* and *surat pajak*, shows that there was relatively little correspondence between the actual Kangchu and the holders of *surat sungai* (see Appendix B). Out of the seventy-three Kangchus named in the *SSD*, only thirty, or about forty-one per cent, appear as members of the river-holding Kongsi given in the *surat sungai* or *surat jual-beli*, or as leaseholders under *surat pajak*. This would suggest that the other forty-three Kangchus were all deputies or managers employed by the holders of the *surat sungai* or other relevant documents. Almost sixty per cent of the Kangchu rights were held by absentee owners who themselves were not Kangchus.

There is no way of knowing exactly how much of the original government records have been preserved. Obviously, many of them have been lost. The loss includes any collection of *surat tauliah* or register of such Kangchu letters of authority. This register may have been the source from which the *SSD* list for 1874 was compiled. The missing data appear to represent one facet of the government about which nothing can be said other than what is in the Directories. The register was probably the one maintained by the police which is referred to in Article 1 of the Kanun Kangchu: "All persons who have been appointed Kangchus or who wish to become Kangchus or their deputies or attorneys must come forthwith to the State Police and enter their names in the register kept by the Proper Officer."[9] The *surat sungai* and other records that have been preserved were apparently generated by the Council. This conclusion is supported by the fact that Ungku Abdul Rahman, the ranking member of the Council, signed all such documents between 1863 and 1875. In the latter year, he appears to have died or retired from government service. He was replaced by his brother, Ungku Abdul Majid. In 1885, Abdul Majid headed the Council and had been signing *surat sungai* since 1875.

We have noted and discussed some of the descriptions of the Kangchu system offered by writers such as Coope, Tan Tek Soon, Mary Turnbull, and James C. Jackson. Others have been written by J. Elcum, the British administrator who dismantled it,[10] and F. Lees.[11] None of these accounts, however, except for Coope's and Elcum's, discusses the archival documents which we have used to reconstruct the sequence of the settlements. Only Coope and Elcum have had access to them before. So far, no satisfactory description of the relation between the Kangchu system and the Johor government has been offered.

The Kangchu system cannot be treated separately from the Johor government. It was more than a mere system of agricultural pioneering. As revealed by the documents of the Johor Archives, it appears to have been something like a quasi-governmental business. It is best to begin by describing the basic structure of the Kangchu system as it appeared in the 1870s.

The first requirement is a more comprehensive statement of what a *surat sungai* in fact was. In the text of the document, it clearly states it was a licence (*keterangan*) authorizing the opening of gambier and pepper plantations in a given watershed. It also laid down some of the laws applying to the activity of the holders and planters. In this sense it was a kind of contract. For example, it stipulated that 100 plantations should be opened within a year. It was not permitted to take valuable timbers, interfere with Malays, or with miners. The *surat sungai* also stated the membership of the Kongsi and the distribution of shares within it. It was thus also a kind of letter of incorporation.[12]

Although nowhere in the text of any *surat sungai* is there a mention of the revenue farms, the remarks of Coope and other writers indicate that the holder also held the usual monopolies. This aspect of the *surat sungai* is also confirmed in related correspondence, particularly the *surat pajak bahagian sungai* where the farms are often enumerated. They included the right to sell opium, spirits, and pork, together with concessions for gambling, pawnbroking, and prostitution.[13]

The *surat sungai* thus had at least four functions. It was a licence, firstly, for the opening of plantations and, secondly, for the management of revenue farms. Thirdly, it was a contract between the government and the holders. Fourthly, it was a letter of incorporation. In the course of time, the *surat sungai* lost most of these functions except for the revenue-farming licence. It ceased to be an agricultural document once the plantings were established within the given area.

By 1863 there is evidence that, even in the initial stages of opening up a river, the holders of the *surat sungai* were only marginally concerned with agriculture. The multiple acquisitions of Tan Hiok Nee at that time are the best indication that Chinese had come to see the revenue-farming rights of the *surat sungai* as being of major importance. It was not long before the government too began treating them as such in an official manner. This awareness is seen in the development of supplementary documents such as the *surat jual-beli* and the *surat pajak*.

The use of such documents coincided with the entrance of the *taukehs* as primary figures in the Kangchu system. By the 1870s the business of opening up a river valley had developed into a highly elaborate and expensive operation. The stipulation that 100 plantations should be opened can probably be taken as a statement of the optimum minimum in terms of revenue. It would certainly have kept out the small-time operators.

Such an establishment required the mobilization of resources on a large scale. One estimates that the necessary labour force would have numbered about 500. If the average plantation was about 50 acres, a total of some 5,000 acres of virgin jungle would have to be cleared.[14] Tons of equipment and supplies would have had to be transported to make such an undertaking possible. In all, it must have taken about $100,000 to open up a river on this scale. The cooperation of the *taukehs* was vital to the entire operation. In fact, a combine of several pepper and gambier dealers would have had to back the scheme and be willing to wait anywhere from one to three years for a return on their investment.

Although the system by which the cultivation and planters were organized and financed has already been observed, it will be useful here to describe it in more detail. The best and perhaps the only contemporary description of the process by which cultivation was organized is that of Tan Tek Soon in his article "Chinese Local Trade".[15]

He states that first of all the Kangchu, or prospective Kangchu, would secure permission from the government to occupy the region, which cost him $100. Tan is not clear about the nature of this "permission". One assumes he is referring to either a *surat sungai* or a *surat tauliah.*

> The system in vogue is usually somewhat as follows. A Chinese who had previously succeeded in securing the confidence of a number of gambier and pepper traders in town, generally five or six, would first proceed to an unoccupied district in Johore or Muar and select a tract of jungle land for his purposes. This land is usually situated close to the bank of some river or stream navigable for boats ... Latterly his district has been properly surveyed and demarcated, but formerly he usually exercised control only from the river bank to the nearest watershed. For opening up the jungle and planting he arranges with a number of semi-dependent planters, to each of whom is allowed sufficient acreage for present cultivation as well as for future expansion. These planters are induced to undertake the enterprise by an arrangement under which for the first eighteen months or so the kangchu has to supply them with all the necessaries of life, implements of husbandry, seeds and cuttings. The cost of these would be debited to planters' account in the kangchu's books. When the first crop is ready for the market, a settlement would be made all around. The kangchu then distributes the planters' debts to each of his own creditors, the town traders, apportions the plantations among them, and transfers the produce only by legal deed called a "pajak". Henceforth each

> planter would be financed by his own town trader, but must dispose of his product only to his shop until his debt is all paid. The trader supplies him with rice, groceries, and money for further planting, all at stipulated prices, and receives his produce in exchange, with deductions for weight according to a defined scale, and at prices regulated by his guild, the Gambier and Pepper Society, about 30 per cent below the actual market value.[16]

This account gives a clear picture of the Kangchu's role, towards the end of the century, in initiating settlement. According to Tan Tek Soon, the Kangchu was essentially a labour recruiter. He organized the founding of the settlement. From this account, it is easy to see why the Kanun Kangchu gave the Kangchu the duty of overseeing the credit relationship between the *taukeh* and the planters. He had been instrumental in organizing it in the first place. It should also be noted that the *pajak* mentioned in the above account had nothing to do with the archival collection of *Surat Pajak Bahagian Sungai*. These latter documents were solely concerned with the revenue farms and Kangchu rights in general, and had nothing to do with plantations or pepper and gambier. There were thus at least two different types of *pajak*. The one described by Tan may be called the plantation *pajak*, and the one collected in the Johor Archives can be styled the revenue *pajak*. The former was an agreement between a planter and his creditor, while the latter was between a revenue farmer and members of a Kongsi.

The system which Tan Tek Soon has described, however, makes no mention of the Kongsi. In fact, no written description of the Kangchu system or the pepper and gambier cultivation makes any mention of this type of body. The only evidence of its existence is in the collection of *surat sungai* and related documents in the Johor Archives. Since these documents are in no way descriptive, an attempt must be made to identify the Kongsi and its functions as shown in the documents.

In examining written descriptions of the Kangchu system, two possibilities are suggested. One is that the Kongsi was made up of planters; and the other is that they were pepper and gambier traders. It seems possible to discount the first possibility. Since the Kongsi had control of the Kangchu rights and the shares which they held were often quite valuable, it is doubtful that they could have been planters, for these were not very affluent individuals. This conclusion is borne out by the fact that, in the few instances where the names of some planters have been obtained, it has been impossible to find any of their names on the *surat sungai*. This leaves the *taukeh*.

Tan Tek Soon has described one aspect of the system which may be a hint of the existence of the Kongsi:

> For the transportation of the produce from the plantations to town another socialistic combination is effected. The several traders interested in a river or its vicinity and the kangchu would furnish the necessary capital between them to build a gambier tongkang of sufficient capacity to carry off the produce in fortnightly or monthly trips. This boat would then be manned by some half-a-dozen boatmen, one as steersman and the others as assistants generally. The freight of produce is placed at as low a rate as possible, chargeable to the planters. At the end of the month this is divided among the boat-people at a fixed proportion, the kangchu also receiving one share as nominal owner. A deduction is also made monthly until the capital account is paid off ... Owing to its importance and the vested interests which have in time grown around this traffic, no competition is ever permitted. Even when a boat is undergoing repairs, the planters are not allowed to ship their produce by a neighbouring boat. Should the market price of their goods induce them to do this, they quietly submit to double payment, once to their own boat-people and again to the actual carrier.[17]

There are, however, some difficulties in relating this information to that found in the *surat pajak*. The transportation concession is never mentioned as a part of the lease. The stock description of the rights included under the *surat pajak* is as follows: "To sell opium, spirits, pork, gambling, pawn-broking and other such rights which are attached to the above-mentioned river which are held by all Kangchu in the territory of Johor." On rare occasions, a *surat pajak* makes mention of the *kangkar* house and other concessions such as the putting on of a *wayang* or Chinese opera, but there is not a word about boats.

While it would have made sense for the Kangchu and/or the pepper and gambier traders to control the means of transportation to and from the plantations, it seems that this concession was not covered under the relevant documents — unless, of course, it was taken for granted. However, it has proven difficult to identify very many of the shareholders named in the *surat sungai*, *surat jual-beli*, etc., as having been pepper and gambier traders. While allowing for the vagaries of spelling, if pepper and gambier traders were regularly members of Kongsi, then one would expect to find frequent correspondence between the 1874 *SSD*'s list of twenty pepper and gambier dealers located in Johor Baharu and the list of shareholders taken from the *surat sungai*. There is, however, no correspondence at all between these two lists of names. Unfortunately, we have no good listing for the pepper and gambier dealers in Singapore. The *SSD* for the 1880s do have lists; however, they do not give personal names but only the firms' chap, or trade mark.[18] This being the case, one feels justified in concluding that the Kongsi members were

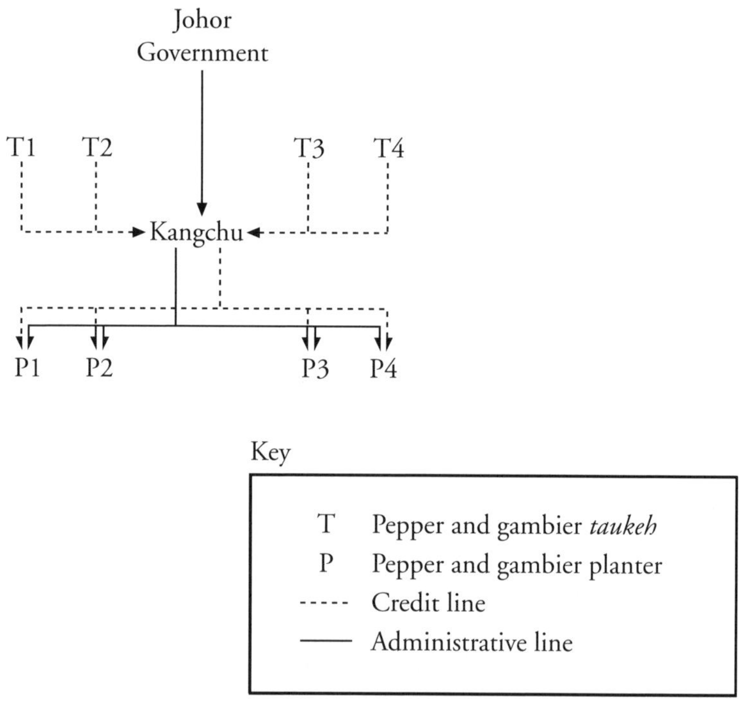

FIGURE 4
Organizational Period: Credit and Administrative Relations

usually not active pepper and gambier traders. And, even if they were, there seems to be no necessary correlation between the group of *taukehs* who supported the planters on a given river and the Kongsi for that river. This circumstance suggests that there was either an additional level to the Kangchu system, which was not recognized by Tan Tek Soon or other writers, or a supplementary hierarchy. Let us try to diagrammatize the system Tan has described.

In the "organizational" period (see Figure 4), the Kangchu was both the administrative and the credit agent. He contracted debts with the various *taukeh* and also contracted with the Johor government. He redistributed the debts among the planters and acted as the government representative and tax monopolist of the district. Thus, for this period, both the administrative and credit lines were channelled through the Kangchu.

Once production began (see Figure 5), the Kangchu reassigned the debts directly to the planters. The exchange of goods and credit for produce was then carried on directly between planters and *taukeh*, with the *taukeh* presumably

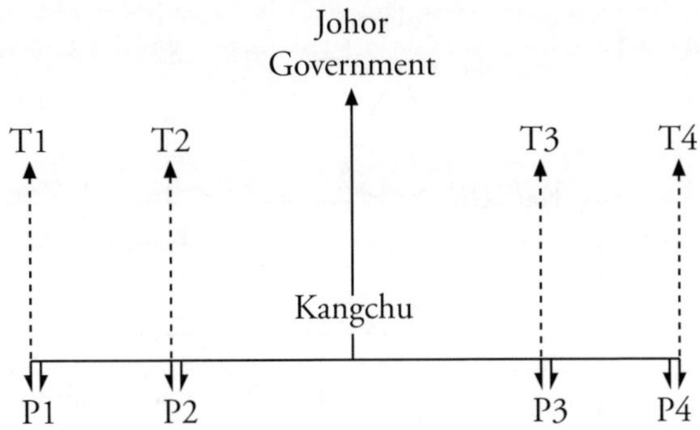

FIGURE 5
Productive Period: Credit and Administrative Relations

holding mortgages on the plantations which they backed. As we know from the Kanun Kangchu, the Kangchu apparently continued to monitor these relationships even though he was now technically outside them.

As we can see, this leaves no place for the Kongsi. One must assume here that the Kongsi should perhaps be understood as a special group of financial backers who were investing not in the cultivation but in the office of the Kangchu and, more specifically, in the opium, spirit, and other revenue farms under his control. This was then an additional and separate level in the system. A possible organization chart which includes the Kongsi might be as shown in Figure 6. The administrative link between the government and the Kongsi is represented by the *surat sungai*, *surat jual-beli*, or *surat pajak*, while that between the government and the Kangchu was the *surat tauliah*. The Kangchu thus received authority both directly from the government and indirectly through the Kongsi. From the latter, he may also have received credit. The *taukeh*-planter relationship appears to have been unaffected by the role of the Kongsi.

In this situation, the Kongsi shareholders would have had no direct interest in the planters, but only in the profits of the revenue farms and in the office of the Kangchu. The Kangchu himself, given the rather inconsistent correspondence between the *surat sungai* and the *SSD* lists, may or may not have been a member of the Kongsi. In a number of cases, the Kangchu held the farms from the Kongsi by means of a *surat pajak*, but this does not seem to have been a consistent practice.

On the whole, the Kanun Kangchu has little to say about such matters and never refers to anything like a Kongsi. Its main concern appears to have been

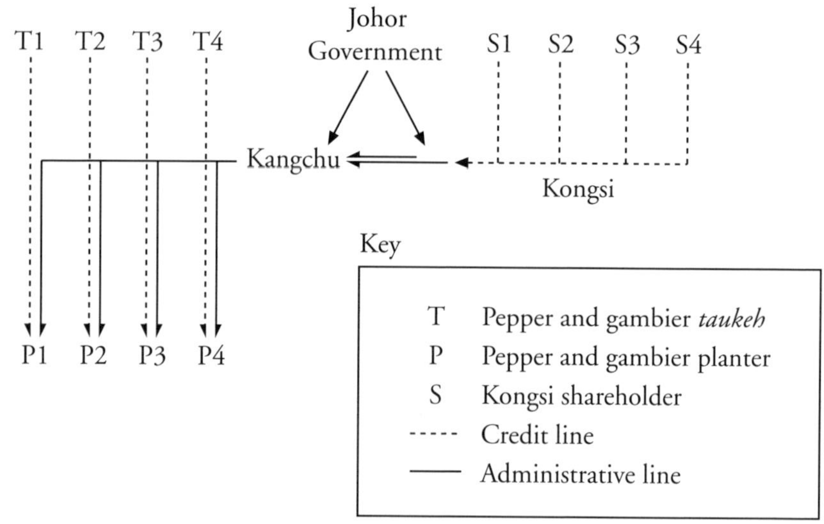

FIGURE 6
Productive Period: Position of Kongsi in the Kangchu System

the regulation of planting and defining the Kangchu's role as an administrator and overseer of the financial arrangements between planters and pepper and gambier dealers. We must look elsewhere for our definition of the Kongsi.

A number of considerations add weight to the hypothesis that the Kongsi were corporate bodies formed to hold only the revenue rights of the river. The first consideration is the Kangchu's own need for capital. In order to assume such an office, an individual had to be able to meet a number of initial expenses which had nothing to do with the agriculture. These included building a *kangkar* house; making initial purchases of taxable commodities (opium, spirits, and pork), and financing the pawnbroking, prostitution, and gambling concessions.

A second factor is the membership of Tan Hiok Nee in a large number of Kongsi between 1863 and 1875. As he was the Major of Johor and held the state revenue farms in 1864, it would have been to his advantage to invest in as many of the Kangchu revenue farms as possible. He invested in the most populous and thus most profitable districts. A third factor which suggests that the Kongsi was a purely financial arrangement was the presence of a small number of Malays and other non-Chinese in some of these Kongsi. These people were not pepper and gambier dealers, and would have had no use whatsoever for direct monopolies over the produce of the plantations.

TABLE 8
List of Malay Shareholders

Names	*No. of Kongsi Joined*
Nong Yahya*	4
Enche Sulong	1
Enche Hitam	1
Ungku Abdul Rahman*	7
Ali bin Abdul Majid	2
Enche Andak*	3
Ungku Osman bin Ungku Abdul Rahman*	1
Tuan Haji Mohamad Salleh*	1
Enche Wan Ibrahim bin Abdul Majid	1
Ungku Abdul Majid*	8
Wan Omar bin Abdul Majid	1
Enche Ja'afar bin Nong Yahya	2
Tuan Haji Osman*	2
Enche Aminah binte Ungku Abdul Majid	1
Ja'afar bin Haji Mohamed*	1

* Council Member

These Malays who held shares in the Kongsi are an interesting phenomenon. As can be seen from the Chronological List, there were relatively few of them.[19] Table 8 gives a list of all Malays who held shares in various rivers between 1860 and 1885 drawn from the *surat sungai* and *surat jual-beli.*

This list is not an exact statement of the number of shares that each held; it is simply a compilation of all the different Kongsi to which these Malays belonged. In a few cases, two of the abovementioned individuals held shares in the same Kongsi. It is also possible that a few have been counted twice because the Kongsi was reorganized. But, at the very least, Malays held shares in thirty different Kongsi. This is a significant number.

Here there is little difficulty in identifying these Kongsi members. All those marked with an asterisk were members of the Council in 1874. All the others shown were the children of these officials. The only doubtful ones are Enche Sulong and Enche Hitam, and probably these two were similarly connected. Not only were all these Malays connected with the Council but most appear to have been blood relatives of the ruler. The practice of holding shares appears to have been initiated in 1860. It was begun not by the government but by two individuals, most significantly Tan Hiok Nee and Nong Yahya, the Resident of Tanjong Surat.[20] After one known objection, the ruler appears to have acquiesced in the arrangement and it soon became a relatively frequent practice. The biggest Malay shareholders were also the biggest government officials. By the 1870s, Malay membership in these Kongsi appears to have been seen as a way in which certain officials could gain direct profits from the revenue farms. It is noteworthy that in addition to other types of Kongsi, Ungku Abdul Rahman became a partner of Tan Hiok Nee when the latter began acquiring concessions in the Sekudai area.[21] Malays, however, also joined less important Kongsi. In these cases, it may be that their presence in the Kongsi was intended to encourage the development of outlying areas. It is also possible that the Malay shares were gifts calculated to win official favour. An example of this type of investment would be the membership of Ungku Abdul Rahman and Ungku Abdul Majid in a number of Batu Pahat Kongsi. The overwhelming number of Malay-held shares were owned by these princes and their children. These two brothers of Abu Bakar were the major officials of the state. Practically all *surat sungai* issued after 1863 were signed by one of them. If the shares held by their children were purchased by one of the two officials on their behalf, this would suggest that Kongsi shares were treated very much as we treat shares of stock today. One could simply hold the shares and collect "royalties", from the Kongsi.

It appears that the Kongsi members as individuals could hold their shares simply as investments and not engage in the day-to-day business of the river. The Chinese themselves often treated shares similarly. In certain Kongsi, only one or two members were the principal investors and/or actual administrators of the concession. The others could easily have been wives, children, or other relatives. This may explain why partners in many Kongsi share the same surname. If we take as an example the Kongsi which received the Kangchu rights to Sedili Besar in 1873, the share distribution was as follows:[22]

Ngiu Lee Chew	1 share (Kangchu)
Ngiu Chang Poh	1 share
Ngiu Chang Hee	1 share
Ngiu Chang Heng	1 share
Ungku Abdul Rahman	1 share

The fact that the second, third, and fourth members of the Kongsi have the same element "Chang" in their given names indicates that they are siblings. It is a traditional Chinese practice for all members of the same generation in a family to share a given name in common. The difference in the first member's given name and the fact that he is also the Kangchu indicate that he is the father. Subsequent documents dealing with this concession further show that the three children were all minors.[23] Thus the picture of this Kongsi is simplified. Ngiu Lee Chew was the principal investor and had put up either all or four-fifths of the capital. If Ngiu put up all of the capital, then the Malay-held share was a gift. Alternately, Ungku Abdul Rahman, perhaps wishing to encourage settlement within this isolated region, put up the other fifth. Then, with the hope of bringing his children into the family business and of giving them some sort of income, the Kangchu gave them three of his shares.

This is an "ideal" type of Kongsi in that it is possible to identify the members. There are no "unknown" partners — the Kongsi was simply the Kangchu, his dependents, and a friendly silent partner. This pattern can probably be said to have held true for many Kongsi, particularly in their initial stages. Of course, the majority of Kongsi are not quite so simple. Frequently, one or two years after the issue of a *surat sungai*, there would be some manipulation of the shares. Partners would sell out; one member might buy up all the other shares; people could die or return to China. Things became more complicated, and the Kongsi had fewer members — this is what happened in the Sedili Kongsi.

In 1874, the year after the concession was granted, Ngiu Lee Chew died and whatever clearing had been done in the district was stopped and the area went back to jungle. In 1886 Ngiu's widow, Chua Chun Kiok, formed a new Kongsi. She appears to have taken over two of the family's original shares. Four other people, all surnamed Ngiu, invested new capital in the venture, and a new attempt was made at opening the river under a new Kangchu.[24] It seems rather strange that the rights to a river could be held for as long as thirteen years without any effort being made to open plantations, or without the government's giving the concession to someone else. This anomaly suggests that Abdul Rahman's share had indeed been a gift. But, the isolation of Sedili in the 1870s and the fact that no settlements on that coast seem to have been successful until the 1890s suggest another reason why no one took an interest. It is doubtful that the government would have allowed such neglect if officials really felt that any other group could be successful.

When one examines other individual Kongsi, the picture becomes increasingly complex. On the west coast, a Kongsi comprising fifteen partners, all surnamed Koh, opened Sungai Benut in 1865.[25] A few years later, the Kongsi went bankrupt and one Tan Nong Kia, a partner in nearby Pontian,[26] began to buy out as many partners as he could. After some litigation, he acquired full rights to the river in 1874.[27] The *SSD* list for 1874 shows that he was also the Kangchu even though he was not named as such in the *surat sungai*. Tan organized no Kongsi other than himself; he was both the sole owner and the Kangchu. A few years later, he opened another concession on

Pinggan, a tributary of Benut.[28] He also sold off his Pontian concession at about the same time.[29] Since there are no further documents regarding his connection with these holdings, it is difficult to say what happened to him. In 1883, he was no longer listed as a Kangchu for any river. It is possible that he hired a deputy to look after his *kangkar* and retired to Singapore. Assuming this was the case, this other "family" Kongsi which had failed was subsequently bought out by a wealthier *taukeh*. After a few years, the successful *taukeh*, in the fashion of Tan Hiok Nee, farmed out his rights to a deputy.

Another pattern, or perhaps exception, was one Kongsi made up entirely of Arabs (or perhaps Malays). It included two brothers, Sayed Jand bin Omar al-Jand and Sayed Abu Bakar bin Omar al-Jand, together with Shaik Abdul Raham bin Mohamad al-Khatib and Shaik Mohamad bin Ali al-Tawi. The last-named individual was also a member of the Council in 1874. Their Kongsi held important concessions on Sekudai and took over the Tebrau rights after they had been purchased from Kapitan Tan Cheng Hung by Ja'afar bin Haji Mohamed.[30] Naturally, they too farmed out the revenue rights to Chinese. If we collate all the available information for Tebrau as of 1874, we find that the Arabs actually held Tebrau through two intermediaries. In 1873, they leased the rights to Tebrau by means of a *pajak* to one Seah Yau Sah.[31] However, the *SSD* for 1874 shows that the Kangchu for Tebrau was Tan May Ah Cha. One assumes he was Seah's deputy. (See Appendix B.)

The name of Seah Yau Sah appears on several other *surat sungai*. He had bought Kapitan Tan Cheng Hung's Telar holding in 1871 and the *SSD* list shows him to have been the Kangchu there in 1874.[32] Thus, he too is one of the few individuals who can be classed as both a *taukeh* and a Kangchu. In 1874 he controlled both the former Kapitan's holdings: one by means of a *surat pajak* and the other through a *surat jual-beli*.

A fourth example is that of the Kongsi which acquired the rights to Rengit, a tributary of the Batu Pahat in 1874. There were three shareholders: the Kangchu, Buku Kia Lee, and Buku Ah Tiam and Lim Ah Sim.[33] The picture is complicated by the fact that the *SSD* gives Buku Tchew Kang as the name of the Kangchu. Regardless of this problem, other evidence shows that the key member of this Kongsi must have been Buku Ah Tiam (or Tian). In the *SSD* for 1883, 1884, and 1885, he is listed as the owner of Chop Seng Heng and was a member of the Kongkek Committee.[34] Obviously, he was a wealthy *taukeh* and a pepper and gambier dealer. In 1881, he held shares in two other rivers, Perah and Bukit Ketam in Muar.[35]

Given these rather diverse examples, it is clear that one cannot draw many firm conclusions about the usual composition of the Kongsi. Sometimes *surat sungai* were held by a single individual who could have been either a wealthy *taukeh* or an indebted Kangchu. Some of the Kongsi included the Kangchu and his family, some the Kangchu and his backers. Others were held by the backers only, and the Kangchu was merely a deputy. Malay membership seems to have been possible in any of the different combinations. Whatever the Malay role, however, most shareholders were Chinese. Some of them may have been pepper and gambier dealers, but as far as can be determined, most were not. It is noteworthy also, that the very biggest pepper and gambier dealers in Singapore, Seah Eu Chin and his children after him, never held any *surat sungai*. In the final analysis, there seem to be so many different types of Kongsi that the search for the typical one may be a pointless task. There appears to be only one real consistency in the Kongsi's function — the concern with the revenue farms.

Because they controlled the revenue farms, the Kongsi were of crucial importance to the state and, of course, to the wealthiest of the *taukeh*. As time passed, affluent Chinese or government agents (the latter could have been either Malay officials or Chinese "semi-officials") tended to take control of the most successful concessions. The first of these Chinese magnates was Tan Hiok Nee. Besides being the Major of Johor, Tan Hiok Nee was the biggest opium farmer, the biggest holder of Kangchu rights, a member of the State Council in 1874, and a pepper and gambier dealer. His many interests were obviously a part of his value to the ruler and made it possible for Abu Bakar to defend Johor's interests during the Tanjong Putri controversy and in the succeeding period. His importance to Johor in the years between 1864 and 1875 cannot be underestimated. It must have been a matter of great significance when he, in the words of Song Ong Siang, "gave up entirely his connection with Johore" and retired to Singapore.[36] The circumstances surrounding his departure and his replacement may give us a clue as to the nature of the relationship between the opium farmers and the group of pepper and gambier *taukehs*.

There are a number of problems connected with Tan Hiok Nee's departure from Johor. First of all, it is interesting that the "Major" was not replaced. Song Ong Siang reports that Abu Bakar asked Tan Seng Poh to take over the job in 1876, but the latter refused.[37] Given the fact that Seng Poh was the leading figure in the Singapore-Johor opium and spirit farms, it is not difficult to see why Abu Bakar offered him the position. Clearly the Maharaja needed an alliance with a powerful Chinese to oversee the revenues of Johor. Since neither Tan Hiok Nee nor Tan Seng Poh wanted the position, Abu Bakar had to look elsewhere.

The second problem with Tan Hiok Nee's departure is that there are no records showing the disposal of his substantial personal holdings (Map 4). There are no *surat jual-beli*, *surat pajak*, or additional *surat sungai* covering the areas which were formerly held by the Major. What happened to them? A few pieces of correspondence from the collection, *Kumpulan Surat² di-Simpan oleh Setia Usaha*, may provide an answer. These show that in 1886, the Johor government, acting through agents, purchased twenty-one shares in the Singapore Opium Syndicate.[38] The Dato Mentri, Ja'afar bin Haji Mohamed, borrowed $21,000 from the government and lent it to two prominent Johor Chinese, Seah Ling Chai and Seah Jim Kui (no relation). Ling Chai owned thirty-two shares in the Syndicate and he sold five of them back to the government. Jim Kui owned twenty-eight shares, sixteen of which he turned over to the government. It appears that shares in the Syndicate at this time cost $1,000 each. Why was the government holding twenty-one shares of its own revenue farms?

The most reasonable explanation seems to be that the government itself had taken over Tan Hiok Nee's former concessions. It may be that it was impossible to find any Chinese who were willing to finance them. Rather than taking one wealthy Chinese into collaboration, the government appears to have joined with two, or perhaps three, of the more prominent Johor *taukehs*, to represent the state's interests in Singapore's financial circles. Of major importance in this group was Seah Ling Chai.

Seah Ling Chai was the son of Johor's second Kapitan, Seah Tee Heng. Both father and son held Kangchu rights in the Sekudai area in the 1880s.[39] Seah Tee Heng also owned a pepper and gambier firm in Johor. The Kapitan died in 1884 and Ling Chai took over his pepper and gambier shop and his Kangchu rights in Sekudai.[40] This acquisition made him, like Tan Hiok Nee before him, the most important *taukeh* in Johor. He was another exceptional individual, being a pepper and gambier dealer, a Kangchu and a major revenue farmer. In addition to his Sekudai holdings, which appear to have been crucial to his position, he also held many other concessions. By the time his father died, he held shares in eight rivers.[41] Seah Ling Chai was neither a Kapitan nor a Major. His official position in Johor was Johor Manager of the Kongkek.[42]

The shopkeepers had banded themselves together into an organization called the Kongkek, or Pepper and Gambier Society. Information regarding the origin of this body is lacking. It is not mentioned in the *SSD* for 1874; however, this should not be taken to mean that it did not exist then. The pepper and gambier dealers had acted in concert to protect their interests in 1864 during the Tanjong Putri controversy in petitioning the Singapore government. This action marked the first known instance of some combination amongst them. It may also mark the foundation of the Kongkek, but on the basis of available evidence, it is impossible to answer this question in any definitive way. Whatever the origins, the group was most active and prominent in the 1870s and 1880s. The Kongkek fixed prices, standardized weights and measures, and in general, looked after the interests of the *taukehs*. It was a kind of prototypical Chinese Chamber of Commerce.[43] The evidence suggests that the Kongsi shareholders, as a group, were outside this organization. Even though individual shareholders may have belonged to it, there is no indication that the latter had a separate formal organization. Shareholders and shopkeepers should be treated as two functionally distinct groups. Song Ong Siang suggests that the Chinese themselves recognized a distinction: "In the 'eighties the 'Kong-kek' Cup was regularly presented by the Gambier and Pepper Society, and the 'Kang-chu' Cup by the Kang-chus of Johore for the Spring and Autumn Race meetings."[44]

It would seem logical that the "Kang-chu" Cup was sponsored by the holders of *surat sungai* in Johor rather than by the actual Kangchu. Most of these shareholders must also have been partners in the Opium Syndicate.[45] Tan Hiok Nee, listed by the *SSD* and mentioned by Song Ong Siang as a partner in the Opium Syndicate, was only the "tip of the iceberg". The various *kangkar* represented small subdivisions of the Syndicate. The shareholders listed on the *surat sungai*, Malays included, were thus all members of the Syndicate. It is clear that the Johor government was closely linked to the Opium Syndicate through its many Kangchu concessions and, ultimately, through the wealthiest Chinese in the state, who were always revenue farmers.

The Kongsi, grouped within the Opium Syndicate, and the *taukeh*, grouped in the Kongkek, merged at the top as a result of a kind of interlocking directorate. In the period of the Tanjong Putri dispute, there appears to have been no Kongkek. But the 101 merchants who signed the petition protesting against the Temenggong's policy were probably dominated by the most affluent dealers in Singapore. Someone like Seah Eu Chin would have been the logical organizer. The fact that later *SSD* show that Seah Leang Seah, his son, was the President of the Kongkek[46] confirms the suggestion that Seah Eu Chin enjoyed a similar status in his day — the 1850s and early 1860s.

The Seah Family was linked by marriage to Tan Seng Poh. When Seah Eu Chin retired from business in 1864, Tan Seng Poh (his brother in-law), who had been an assistant in the firm for some years previously, became manager and carried on the business in conjunction with the two elder sons of the founder until 1876, when he retired.[47] Thus, between 1864 and 1876 at least, Tan Seng Poh was not only one of the major partners in the Opium Syndicate (significantly not representing the Johor branch), but he was also manager of one of the largest pepper and gambier concerns and controlled through indebtedness many of the smaller traders and numerous planters.

He probably was also a controlling member of the Kongkek. There is no available list of the organization's membership in the 1870s. However, it seems certain that either Tan Seng Poh or one of Seah Eu Chin's other sons was on the Committee of the Kongkek in these years. Song notes that Seah Song Seah, another of Eu Chin's sons, was at one time a partner in the Opium and Spirit Farm.[48] It thus seems that both the pepper and gambier industry and the opium-farming business were dominated by the Seah-Tan clan. The "controlling strings" of Johor's economy were in their hands, and probably always had been.

Emily Sadka, in discussing the relationship between revenue farming and mining ventures, has shown that there was, in fact, a general connection between economic development and revenue farming. While her remarks are relevant mainly for the Protected Malay States in the 1880s and early 1890s, they show a system similar to what was operating in Johor. "The economic significance of the farming system was that it provided, at least in theory, a means of attracting Chinese capital and labour to the states. The success of the farmer's speculation depended, of course, on the consumption of opium and spirits and the volume of business in the gambling houses, and he therefore had an incentive to increase consumption by investing in mines and other enterprises and introducing labour into the state." European administrators, according to Sadka, were well aware of this connection. "Estimates of the economic initiative to be expected from applicants for the farms played an important part in the calculations of government when farm tenders were being considered."

The combination between revenue farming in Johor and pepper and gambier planting was a natural one. Sadka shows this to have also been the pattern in other Malay states. "Capitalists who already had a large stake in the country were in a strong position when it came to tendering for the farms, for a number of reasons; they were in a position to expand their enterprises if their applications were successful, and restrict production and immigration in an attempt to break the farm if they were not; and since their prosperity was of some importance to the state, there was an incentive to support them financially by giving them the farms."[49]

In regard to their relationship with the government, Sadka concludes by showing that the farmers really took very little risk. Their ventures were so big that a collapse of the farms would wreck the entire economy. She quotes Swettenham's remarks on this eventuality: "... the failure of the signatories to the contract means almost invariably the ruin of a large number of people who are interested in the Farm or who depend upon the Farmer's assistance in their various industries, it means financial depression and the weakening of confidence, the stoppage of supplies and the closing of some avenues to capital; it means a fall in the value of real property, possible immediate loss to the Revenue and almost certain reduction at the next reletting of the Farms."[50]

Her comments on the farmer's economic position regarding the government show that the Chinese were well protected. "If the price of tin was high and immigration boomed, they made large profits; if trade was depressed and they were unable to meet their commitments, they were able to plead for relief, usually with some success, since the government could not afford to risk the financial collapse of large local interests."[51]

As a group, the Kongsi shareholders were differentiated from the group of *taukehs* who backed the planters by the treatment they received from the government. Since the Kangchu-Kongsi combination represented the basic unit of the state's revenue collecting apparatus, the government kept fairly close control over it by requiring that their activities be registered under *surat sungai* and other legal documents.

The Kanun Kangchu which describes the Kangchu's administrative responsibility on behalf of the government makes no mention of his revenue-collecting function. Stress is placed rather on his responsibility for assuring that planters observed their debts to the *taukeh*. It would appear that the failure of Kanun Kangchu to lay down conditions for the regulation of Kongsi and shareholders is a further indication that the Kongsi was treated as a separate body by the government. It is significant that no set of laws has been discovered which deals with the Kongsi in a systematic fashion. All our remarks on the topic must therefore be based on the apparent circumstances. The revenue farmers of the Kongsi were not regulated by a code of Johor laws but by the conditions laid down in their contracts with the government, in the *surat sungai*, *surat jual-beli*, *surat kongsi*, *surat pajak*, and other related documents.

In trying to fill out the picture of the Johor government at this time, one must bear in mind that the government shared responsibility with the Chinese. From the economic point of view, government consisted in the combination represented by the formal state administration, the Kongkek, and the Opium Syndicate. In fact, it appears that the Malay government was largely built up on the foundation of the Chinese side of the Kangchu system.

In Singapore, the Chinese had full control of the economic system of the pepper and gambier cultivation. There, the Kongkek (or its prototype in earlier years) and the Opium Syndicate were supreme. The pepper and gambier *taukehs* held the planters in economic thralldom. They monopolized both the production and consumption of the cultivators. The Opium Syndicate, operating through individuals who were also called Kangchu, was prepared to absorb the remainder of the planter's meagre earnings. Here too, in the 1840s and 1850s, one would imagine that the Kangchu was usually a secret society chieftain. He would have needed some sort of military force to police the

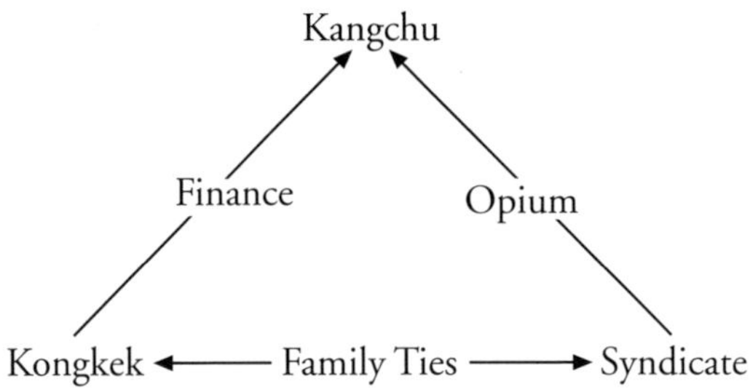

FIGURE 7
Kangchu Finance Structure

monopoly. There were thus two parallel hierarchies, each controlling different aspects of the economic system. To a certain extent they were competitive, in that each was trying to extract as much as possible from the planters. It was only natural that they eventually joined forces to a certain extent. However, it is impossible to say whether or not the relative separation of the hierarchies was ever eliminated. As we have seen, in Johor, they did remain separate despite the dual role of some of the more affluent *taukehs* such as Tan Hiok Nee and Seah Ling Chai.

In Johor the centralization of a large number of Kangchu concessions in the hands of one individual meant that the large economic interests of Singapore had to deal with the Johor Kangchus as a block. The system thus assumed a pyramid shape as suggested in Figure 7.

This was the foundation of the Johor government. The government, in fact, was superimposed over this structure (see Figure 8). The formal apparatus of control was the Kanun Kangchu which governed the Kangchu's activities so far as the cultivation was concerned. This, of course, affected relations with the Kongkek. A further control over the Kongkek was the Johor government's power to appoint the officers and committee members who controlled this body.

The Kangchu documents that we have examined and the Kongsi itself were the apparatus which gave the government control on the revenue-collecting side of the Kangchu system. Government influence was further expressed by the Malay shareholders in a number of Kongsi (all of them connected with the State Council) and by the Chinese officials in the Johor government. The latter included the Major, the Kapitans, and other individuals who succeeded them.

This was the shape of the Johor government as it appears in the materials that have been considered here. It was locked tightly into the Chinese economic system. The latter was characterized by the peculiar relationship

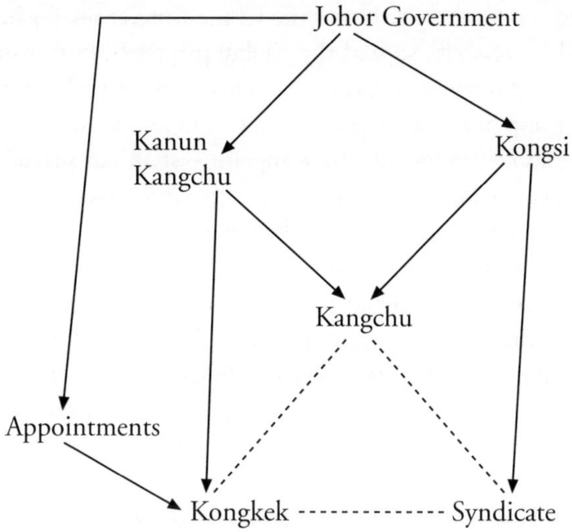

FIGURE 8
Governmental Controls on the Kangchu Systems

between the financiers and the opium farmers. As Sadka has shown, the same state of affairs prevailed in the tin industry as well. The arrangement which had evolved in Johor was not entirely unique. Neither the British nor any other Malay ruler, however, appears to have come to terms with the Chinese in quite the same fashion.[52] So far as the ruler and his council were concerned, it was a highly successful operation. There were, however, potential problems. Among these were the gradual deterioration of the agriculture in Johor, the decline of the opium business in Malaya and a change in the ruler's relationship with the English.

As shown here, the Johor government was in fact a business. While the state obviously possessed a certain measure of police power, it seems clear that by the 1880s this was on the decline. The economic aspects of the state had become of far greater importance to the ruler than the military/police aspects of government. This was one of the real changes which the colonial era had brought into Malaya. The Johor ruler had been systematically discouraged from maintaining and using a military force. The Pahang war had been his last venture of this kind, and its failure seems to have marked the change in orientation. After 1863, the power-holders in the state were not soldiers, generals, pirates, or other martially-inclined individuals but scribes, bureaucrats, and businessmen. The criteria for leadership had changed from the martial arts to the scribal and economic arts. Just as the Chinese secret society headmen had been replaced by *taukehs*, so had the Malay pirates been transformed into bureaucrats. The government was no longer held together by ties of personal loyalty and kinship but by written, contractual obligations.

While the above analysis of the Kangchu system has placed great stress on the content of the documents, a far more important factor is the very existence of the documents in themselves. The regular use of written contracts by a Malay ruler represents a clear break with the past. Even though the Johor state of 1885 can hardly be considered modern, the agency of change was already reshaping the nature of power relations within the polity. The Malay maritime format had been preserved in the riverine nature of settlement and the administrative divisions of the state. The locus of power within the state remained autocratic and traditional in its orientation and aspirations. The Malay masses, however, had been replaced by Chinese coolies. The *pengulu* had been turned into Kangchus. The ruler and his small group of followers ruled over a Chinese state. In the traditional state, the bonds between the ruler and the ruled were those of personal loyalty, kinship, and economic dependence. These had now been overridden by a system of written contracts which had been borrowed from the English. The traditional bonds did not cease to exist, nor do they appear to have decreased in importance at this time. The important change took place not in these relationships but in the government itself where the paperwork, by itself, created the need for bureaucrats, filing systems, and all the other personnel and apparatus that constitute a linear media system. In short, the state had been rationalized.

A final point is that Johor in 1885 could hardly have been considered autonomous or self-sufficient. It was an appendage of Singapore that had somehow been taken over by an independent-minded Malay chief. The ruler's authority was ultimately rooted in the colonial military establishment and not in his own forces. The Johor economy, likewise, was simply an extension of Singapore's economy. The Chinese had conquered the jungle and populated the land and the *taukehs* probably took most of the profits. The British sold opium to the Chinese and advised the Malays to protect their own interest in Johor. The Malays maintained the legitimacy of Malay rule and tried to survive between these two overwhelming forces.

NOTES

1. Parkinson, *British Intervention*, p. xiii.
2. Ibid., Ch. 3, pp. 41–72, for Parkinson's discussion of the general situation in these states in 1870.

3. W. Linehan, *A History of Pahang*, Ch. 8 (Kuala Lumpur. 1973), pp. 90–100. First published as *JMBRAS*, v. 14, pt. 2 (May 1936). All quotations are from the reprint edition.
4. *Singapore and Straits Directory 1874*, "Johore", p. 233.
5. Both Haji Mohamed, the father of Dato Ja'afar, and Panglima Perang, the grandfather of Mohamed Salleh, had been members of the Teluk Belanga community and chiefs under Temenggongs Ibrahim and Abdul Rahman.
6. Ibid., p. 3.
7. It has not been possible to locate all these places. The names may have been changed. Tanjong Bulas (one of the Residencies) should be on Johor's west coast somewhere near Pontian. Satengah Lahu (Laut?) should be in the same area. Sungai Seluang should be somewhere on the western bank of the Johor River.
8. Ibid., pp. 4–7.
9. Coope, "The Kangchu System", p. 252.
10. J. Elcum, *Johore in 1911*, Johor Annual Report (Johor Baharu, 1912), pp. 3–7.
11. F. Lees, "Chinese Settlement in the Kulai Sub-district of Johore, Malaysia", in *Geographers and the Tropics: Liverpool Essays*, ed. Robert W. Steel and R. M. Prothero (London, 1964), pp. 196–277.
12. In about 1874 an official letter of incorporation (*surat kongsi*) came into use. There are only a few examples of this type of document scattered through the collection of *surat jual-beli*. They do not appear to have been written each time a *surat sungai* or *surat jual-beli* was issued but only when the holders of the river decided to reorganize the Kongsi by bringing in new members. These documents contained a statement of the authority under which the river was originally held, the names of the new members, the share distribution, and statement of the total capital invested in the concession. Often there was a statement of why the reorganization was taking place.
13. *Register Surat Pajak Bahagian Sungai A. H. 1290–1300*, Johor Archives. See also Trocki, "The Johor Archives", pp. 4–5, 15–17.
14. Coope, "The Kangchu System", p. 248. Coope states that the size of a plantation was somewhere between 50 and 250 acres. Other reports from the period (e.g., *SFP*, 28 March 1839) indicate that a plantation required a labour force of five to six men. James Low, *The British Settlement of Penang* (Oxford, 1972), p. 63, gives a slightly different set of statistics, which are also relevant for the mid-1830s. Low states that the average plantation was about ten orlongs (13½ acres) and that the total cost for the first year amounted to $667. Unless there was large-scale inflation, these costs should have been roughly equivalent to those of the 1870s.
15. Tan Tek Soon, "Chinese Local Trade", pp. 90–93.
16. Ibid., pp. 91–92.
17. Ibid., p. 92.
18. *SSD* for 1883, pp. 128–29; for 1884, pp. 133–34; *SSD* for 1885, p. 175; and *SSD* for 1890, p. 306. Song Ong Siang is of little help in identifying the individuals named on *surat sungai*, etc., and one assumes that outside of rare cases

like Tan Hiok Nee most of the Kongsi shareholders and gambier dealers were not very important people in Singapore.

19. Trocki, "The Johor Archives", pp. 20–35.
20. Nong Yahya, according to the *SSD* 1874, "Johore", was both a member of the State Council and the Resident of Tanjong Surat, (pp. 1 and 3). In 1860, (*SKMK-I*, No. 26, 7 September 1860) he was listed as holding one share in a Kongsi which held Sungai Santi. A few weeks later, his name appeared again on a *surat sungai* for Temon (*SKMK-I*, No. 27, 25 September 1860). The latter document contains a rather puzzling injunction: "*Ini suroh ganti jangan masok Nong Yahya berkongsi sebab Ungku tiada beri Melayu berkongsi dengan China.*" (Translation: "This is an order to change; do not enter Nong Yahya in this company because Ungku [Temenggong] does not allow Malays to join companies with Chinese.") However, the next paragraph of the document lists him as holding one share. In the future, while Malays did not join Kongsi on a regular basis, it did happen quite often and Nong Yahya apparently continued to hold the shares he already had at the time, and later acquired even more. The only conclusion one can draw is that, after having initially disapproved the idea, the ruler later changed his mind. There is no statement reversing the policy stated in the above document; however the policy was clearly ignored, or, more correctly, Malay Kongsi membership was limited to Council Members and their families.
21. *SJB*, Nos. 75 and 16, 28 April 1873.
22. *SKMK-I*, No. 100, 5 December 1873.
23. *SKMK-I*, No. 101, ? October 1886.
24. Ibid.
25. *SKMK-I*, No. 66, 5 November 1865.
26. *SKMK-I*, No. 75, 21 May 1866.
27. *SKMK-I*, No. 96, 14 April 1874.
28. *SKMK-I*, No. 115, 27 August 1879.
29. *SJB*, No. 50, 9 May 1878.
30. *SKMK-I*, No. 94, 15 September 1872; *SJB*, No. 20, 10 August 1873; *SJB*, No. 74, 8 May 1883.
31. *SPBS*, No. 2, 25 August 1873.
32. *SJB*, No. 8, 26 March 1871; *SJB*, No. 77, 20 January 1884; *SKMK-II*, No. 8, 12 August 1882.
33. *SKMK-I*, No. 102, 7 January 1874.
34. *SSD*, 1887, p. 128; *SSD*, 1884, p. 133; *SSD*, 1885, p. 172.
35. *SKMK-I*, No. 114, 17 May 1878; *SKMK-I*, No. 129, 14 June 1881.
36. Song, *One Hundred Years' History*, p. 335.
37. Ibid., p. 132.
38. *KSSSU*, S–30, 30 March 1886, *Hutang Dato' Menteri Ja'afar kapada Keraja'an Johor*; S–31, 31 March 1886, *Hutang Seah Ling Chai kapada Keraja'an Johor*; S–32, 31 March 1886, *Hutang taukeh Seah Jim Quee kapada Keraja'an Johor*.

39. Seah Tee Heng held, *SKMK-I*, No. 99, 20 October 1873; and Seah Ling Chai held, *SKMK-II*, No. 15, 19 November 1882; *SKMK-II*, No. 18, 7 December 1882, and the *SSD*, 1874, also shows Seah Ling Chai as a Kangchu on Sekudai in that year. (See Appendix B.)
40. *SKMK-I*, No. 147, 6 August 1884.
41. Panti, *SJB*, No. 31, 8 August 1874; Kesang, *SKMK-II*, No. 9, 12 September 1882; Reling, *SKMK-II*, No. 11, 20 September 1882; Semberong, *SKMK-II*, No. 17, 6 December 1882; Rengit, *SKMK-II*, No. 19, 4 February 1883; Terap, *SKMK-II*, No. 25, 14 March 1884.
42. *SSD*, 1883, p. 128; 1884, p. 133; 1885, p. 172.
43. Song, *One Hundred Years' History*, p. 38. Tan Tek Soon, "Chinese Local Trade", p. 92, and Coope, "The Kangchu System", p. 259, are the only sources of information at the writer's disposal on the topic of the Kongkek. The names of the Committee members were listed in the *SSD* for the 1880s. Only one available document of the Johor Archives makes any reference to it. In 1896, on taking over the government after his father's death, Sultan Ibrahim appointed the Committee members of the Kongkek and recognized the *chap* of the members. Article 67 of the Kanun Kangchu (Coope, above) also indicates that the Kongkek sat in judgement to regulate disputes between planters and *taukeh*. Coope describes the organization as a "Chamber of Commerce".
44. Song, *One Hundred Years' History*, p. 38.
45. This is the writer's own term. At the time, this body was called the Opium and Spirit Farm. The farms were run by a syndicate, or Kongsi, made up of all the important revenue farmers of the region.
46. *SSD* for 1885, p. 171, lists Seah Leang Seah as the President of the Kongkek, Seah Ling Chai as the Johor Manager, Wee Yong Keng as the Singapore Manager, and Heng Seo Lew as the Singapore Manager and Secretary. There was also a Committee made up of twelve other pepper and gambier dealers. Of these fifteen individuals, only Seah Ling Chai and Buku Ah Tiam (one of the Committee members) were listed as holders of *surat sungai* in Johor.
47. Song, *One Hundred Years' History*, p. 131.
48. Ibid., p. 21.
49. Emily Sadka, *The Protected Malay States 1874–1895* (Kuala Lumpur, 1968), pp. 333–34.
50. Swettenham to CS, 28 September 1890, quoted in Sadka, *The Protected Malay States*, p. 335.
51. Ibid.
52. Some comparison might be made with the situation in Kedah where close relations with Penang Chinese and other Chinese in Kedah were important to economic development and governance in the state. Cf. Wu Xiao An, *Chinese Business in the Making of the Malay State, 1882–1941, Kedah and Penang* (London, RoutledgeCurzon, 2003).

7

Johor in 1885

Prospects

For the state of Johor and its ruler, the year 1885 represented the climax of the efforts of the past four decades. It was a high point of Johor's economic prosperity under the pepper and gambier regime. Politically, the ruler was at a peak of his power and popularity. In this year, he signed a treaty with Britain which stabilized Anglo-Johor relations and which recognized him as Sultan of Johor.[1] However, many changes had taken place in the world. For Southeast Asia, the most significant of these were the decided advances of European commerce and imperialism during the last twenty-five years of the nineteenth century.

Of particular importance in this period were the technological advances which served to bring Malaya much closer to Britain. These included the completion of the Suez Canal in 1869 and the establishment of telegraphic communication between Singapore and London in 1871. Parkinson has noted that the canal made steam communication between Europe and East Asia economically feasible: "... the best passage from London to Singapore in 1867 was made by the *Eileen Radford* in 116 days, whereas the *Shantung* steamed from Glasgow to Singapore in 1870 in forty-two days." He also notes that the telegraph brought an immediate revival of Singapore's sagging commerce in 1871–72.[2]

In the next fifteen years, these shifts were to wipe out many of Abu Bakar's gains. The first set-backs came in the area of the traditional political relationship between the Johor ruler and the British, particularly with regard to their policy towards the other states of the Peninsula. Between 1874 and 1885, Abu Bakar had been actively involved in the colonial advances in the Malay world. The disturbances in Perak and Selangor had led to British intervention and the eventual posting of Residents to those states. During these events the Maharaja had placed the resources of his state at the disposal of the English. This included allowing British agents to use one of his steamships on missions to the west coast states.[3] On some occasions, he also appears to have sent his own officials to assist them. Thus, Mohamed Ibrahim (later Johor's Dato Bentara Dalam) accompanied Birch and Irving on missions to Perak and Selangor in 1871 and 1872.[4] The Maharaja himself took a hand in some of the negotiating with dissident chiefs and gave asylum in Johor to such individuals as Raja Mahdi of Selangor.[5]

None of these services were without some ulterior motive — the advancement of the Maharaja's own ambitions. Governor Ord was happy to let Abu Bakar take charge of Mahdi since he thought it left the field in Selangor clear for his own candidate, the Viceroy Tungku Kudin. However, Parkinson points out:

> … it is far from clear that the Maharajah was well disposed towards the Viceroy, who was brother-in-law of Sultan Ali's daughter — Sultan Ali of Muar being the dispossessed claimant to the kingdom of Johore. In fact the Maharajah was rather friendly than otherwise towards Mahdie as a useful obstacle to Tunku dia Oodin's ambitions. The Maharajah was clearly on the side of Raja Musa, with whom the Viceroy had quarrelled. More than that, the Maharajah had friends in Singapore who were of his way of thinking … Mr. Thomas Braddell (whose advice Ord had followed) was in the Maharajah's pay.[6]

In 1876, Abu Bakar was recognized as the official intermediary between the chiefs of the various states of Negri Sembilan. Article Six of the agreement signed before the Governor of Singapore reads as follows: "And we agree that in case of any dispute or difficulty arising among our States which we are unable to settle, we will refer for advice to His Highness the Maharajah of Johore."[7]

In 1877, when Sultan Ali died, there was a succession dispute and so Colonel Anson, who was then administering the Straits government, asked Abu Bakar to take charge of the territory of Muar until such time as the controversy was settled. This was quickly decided by Abu Bakar himself, and by 1879 he had officially annexed the district, thus totally dispossessing the old line of the Sultans of Johor.[8]

In his study of the disturbances in Negri Sembilan, Gullick has drawn attention to Abu Bakar's ubiquitous involvement in the politics of the

Peninsula during this period. "It is a striking fact that the rebels in the three states Perak, Selangor and Negri Sembilan although not in communication with each other, were all in correspondence at some time or other with the Maharaja of Johore. The Maharaja owed his own position in Johore to a policy of identifying himself with the British regime in the Straits Settlements. He would hardly have planned a revolt against his own patrons. But he was seeking to restore the ancient position of the Johor Sultanate as overlord of all Malay states." He notes that Abu Bakar could gain no allies by supporting the pro-British parties in these states, thus he acted on behalf of the rebels. He presented their cause directly to the British, "describing the struggle in the Malay States as a Malay civil war in which the British had become identified with the wrong side … He hoped by this means to bring the British to terms with the 'rebels' who would thus become indebted to him for obtaining British recognition of their claims."[9]

Whether or not Gullick's conclusions are accurate, they reflect the thinking of British administrators who once again became very suspicious of the Maharaja. His take-over of Muar raised a great controversy in Singapore and appears to have used up a good deal of his influence.[10] Once Anson, who had been very favourably disposed towards Abu Bakar, left Singapore in 1878, the Maharaja faced a relatively hostile public and a succession of aggressively imperialist governors who saw no place in the empire for native chiefs.[11]

According to Eunice Thio, what opposition there was to further territorial expansion by the British was in the Colonial Office. The new Governor, Sir Fredrick Weld, had objected strongly to the traditional policy which he conceived to be: "… to let the British government remain as much as possible in the background, to throw all possible influence into the Maharaja's hands and extend his actual territory as occasion may serve … In accordance with this policy the Maharaja has received the GCMG and the KCSI — decorations which have a great effect upon Malays, which have not been conferred upon any Governor of the Straits Settlements, nor upon Malays of much higher rank than the Maharaja."[12]

The Colonial Office was inclined to let well enough alone and one official, "Herbert, the Permanent Under Secretary alleged that Weld was 'unconsciously rather jealous of "our good friend" the Maharaja of Johore and his decorations'."[13] However, they were swayed by Weld's arguments and from this time on the traditional policy was changed. No longer would the British continue the "experiment of relying on the Maharaja to further their interests in the Malay States". Weld was informed that he had the right to intervene in Negri Sembilan without reference to Abu Bakar "should necessity arise". Likewise, he was given the go-ahead to extend British influence in Pahang.[14]

This meant that the special relationship which the Straits government had maintained with the Temenggongs since 1836, when Ibrahim began his career as a private suppressor, was at an end. Weld, having destroyed this, was eager to move even further and appoint a Resident to Johor. This was how matters stood in 1885 when Abu Bakar and Weld both travelled to England to draw up a new treaty.

The resulting agreement, which superseded the original treaty of 1824 between Temenggong Abdul Rahman and the East India Company, was the result of six months of hard bargaining on both sides. Abu Bakar was recognized as Sultan, but so as to ensure that no one thought this meant a revival of the old Johor Sultanate, he was to be known as "Sultan of the State and Territory of Johore". Johor's sovereignty was recognized but was also qualified in that the Colonial Office was given charge of Johor's foreign relations and a provision was made for the appointment of a British agent.[15]

Weld, for his part, was satisfied that the new treaty would make the Sultan more amenable to control by the Governor of the Straits Settlements and envisioned appointing an agent to Johor and gradually bringing the state under formal direction. This, however, was not to be the case. Despite Weld's expectations, "the treaty did not either make Abu Bakar more amenable to the Governor's advice, or strengthen the latter's hold over Johore. On the contrary, after his recognition as Sultan, Abu Bakar tried even harder to make Johore 'the greatest Malay power, to keep her free and to make her rich' ... More important from the practical point of view was the formation of a Johore Advisory Board in London which enabled him to communicate directly with the Colonial Office."

Abu Bakar judiciously appointed high-ranking retirees of the Colonial Office to the Johor Advisory Board such as General William Fielding and Cecil Smith. They not only advised the Sultan, but took over the role of negotiating for him with the Colonial Office, thus short-circuiting the position of the Colonial Governor. "By this move Abu Bakar improved the machinery for obtaining British advice without adopting a position subordinate to the Colony or submitting to formal control."[16]

Abu Bakar saw that he would now need influential connections more than ever. The European presence was expanding at an alarming rate and somehow he had to swim with the tide. He had already begun to experiment and probe for new openings. He moved in a number of directions, both attempting to forestall a British take-over and seeking additional resources. First of all, he expanded the government. Secondly, he attempted to diversify the state's agriculture. Thirdly, he sought massive European investments through large-scale development schemes. Finally, and perhaps most successfully, he put on a flamboyant diplomatic offensive to make friends, influence people, and simply gain status in the world at large.

Let us look first at what was happening to Johor's government in 1885. The structure of the state's administration had grown considerably. Between 1883 and 1885, the Directories show a decided growth in the formal apparatus of the State. At the centre was the Council of State and a Secretariat. The latter was made up of the Dato Mentri's Office and the Office of the Dato Bentara Dalam. A Supreme Court had been added with a European magistrate in addition to the Hakim and Mufti who judged cases under Muslim law. The old Public Works and Land Department had been broken up and in its place was a Public Works Department, a Survey Department, and a Land Department. There was also an Education Department, six schools in the state, a Postal Department, and a Government Printing Office.[17]

The picture of local administration had changed somewhat. The police department had been expanded and the headquarters employed fifteen people. There were also twenty-one regional police stations. The old local Residencies seem to have been abolished. Instead there was a west coast Residency which administered Muar and Padang; and an east coast Residency at Endau. The west coast islands were under a Commissioner or *penggawa* and another had charge of the east coast islands.

The Malays named in the administration now numbered about 130, again most of these being clerks or policemen. Authority was still not spread very far. The most important officials — the Dato Mentri, Ja'afar bin Haji Muhamad; the Dato Bentara Luar, Mohamed Salleh bin Perang; the Dato Bentara Dalam, Mohamed Ibrahim bin Munshi Abdullah; and the Commissioner of Police, Abdullah bin Tahir — controlled the most important government departments. All but the Land Department and the Supreme Court were either under one of the above officials or were run by Europeans. The Survey Department seems to have been the most important. Both the Dato Bentaras and the Police Commissioner held posts within it.

What emerges from this picture is an administration controlled by Abu Bakar's few loyal and tested officials. All of them had served Johor since the 1860s or longer. Together with Ungku Abdul Majid, these were the people whom he took on trips to Europe, China, and Japan. Alternatively, when one or two did not go, they stayed home and ran Johor. All these officials were younger than Abu Bakar. After he died, they outlived him by about ten years. They became a kind of regency to look after the state while Sultan Ibrahim, who succeeded in 1895, became accustomed to government.

These changes represented mere expansion of already existing administrative bodies. There is no indication that the aims of Malay government had gone beyond the basic functions of servicing the state's agriculture (by means of roads and surveys), collecting revenue, and maintaining law and order. The Johor Archives documents show that there was a trend towards the formalization of the state's executive in the collections of *Surat² Titah Perentah* and the *Buku Peringatan Dato Mentri* which began to appear at this time.

There was also a group of European "advisers" and friends. These included Abu Bakar's secretary, William Hole, Howard Bentley, "Dato" James Meldrum, and of course Paterson & Simons, Rodyk & Davidson, the lawyers, and Metcalfe Larken. Most of these men appear to have had money invested in Johor. Larken represented one group of Europeans whom Abu Bakar was trying very hard to encourage; he was a planter.[18]

Abu Bakar was aware that the state had overspecialized in pepper and gambier. He was, no doubt, also conscious of his economic dependence on the Kongkek and the Opium Syndicate. The introduction of European planters in the 1880s was an attempt to diversify the state's agriculture. It was also a move designed to end the state's dependence on the Chinese-dominated economy of gambier and one which would introduce more capital into Johor.

In the 1870s, many European coffee planters left Ceylon after the failure of the agriculture there.[19] One of these planters, Thomas Heslop Hill, visited Johor in 1878. In 1879, he wrote a glowing report of the potentialities of Johor for the planting of tea and coffee.[20]

He climbed a number of hills in south Johor and pronounced them suitable for the cultivation of tea, coffee, and cocoa. Among the sites he observed were Gunong Pulai, Gunong Panti, Gunong Blumit, and Gunong Muntaha. He also noted the government's eagerness to encourage planting enterprises: "The Maharaja is so well known to be favourably disposed to those about to open up the Country that the natives would in no way be inimical, were they so disposed, which they do not appear to be." He went on to stress that the state was peaceful and there were relatively few Malays, but the government's orders were received everywhere with respect. Regarding communications in Johor, he noted that in addition to the many rivers there was a road from Johor Baharu to "Chukang" (probably Tan Chukang, or Tebrau) which was nine miles long.

His remarks on the population included rather detailed information on the labour force. Chinese could be hired for twenty cents per day, Javanese for eighteen cents and Tamils for sixteen to twenty cents. Malays could also be employed on contract for house-building and felling and clearing. The latter cost $8.00 per acre. He also announced a special land policy, especially for European planters. Applications for land leases were handled by Paterson & Simons in Singapore. Leases were available for blocks of 1,000 acres with separate contiguous blocks of at least 300 acres. Terms of these leases were for ninety-nine years. His report appears to have given positive encouragement to Ceylon planters and the *Straits Daily Times* reported, the week after Hill's report was published, that a number of planters from Ceylon had arrived in Singapore in May 1879 and had gone to Johor.[21]

The *SSD* for 1881 reports that ten plantations had been established. These were located in the places which Hill had described in his report — Panti, Pulai, Sekudai, and Batu Pahat.[22] By 1885, this nucleus of planters had grown considerably. "European pioneers have, in the last few years, made some experiments in planting, on a large scale, sago, tobacco, coffee, tea, and cocoa. These have grown in six different districts — Batu Pahat, Pulau Kokob, Pulei, Panti, Johor Bahru, and Pangerang; but none of them have yet been planted long enough to be considered established industries."[23]

The Directory for 1885 noted that European planters had opened eighty-five plantations and held leases on 44,052 acres. Most of this, however, was only on paper. Only 2,727 acres were reported as actually being under cultivation.[24]

This early move by European planters to begin estates in Johor was short-lived and soon failed. By 1890, these plantations were no longer listed in the Directory. Problems included a decline in coffee prices in the mid-1880s, disease, communications difficulties, and labour shortages. In other states of Malaya, coffee planting experienced a boom in the early 1890s, but this was too late to help Johor.[25] In 1895, the *Singapore Free Press* reported: "Some twenty years ago Sultan Abu Bakar took a vast deal of interest, and spent a good sum of money, in promoting European planting, and it was hoped that great things would come of coffee planting. The expenditure was futile, for the enterprise turned out to be unproductive."[26]

No definite statement beyond Jackson's general remarks can be made as to why the European plantations in Johor failed. It appears that labour was the most significant problem. Most of these planters were from Ceylon and thus preferred to employ Tamils. While there were obviously some Tamils in Johor at the time, they do not seem to have been very numerous. According to the census report of 1911, the first systematic survey of the state's population, there were only 5,600 Indians in Johor.[27] This shortage of Indians was probably why Metcalfe Larken, in opening his estate at Castlewood, near Tebrau, brought in Javanese and Hainanese labourers.[28]

The labour problem was one aspect of what was in fact, a deep-seated conflict between two very different economic systems. Johor was a pepper and gambier state. Despite anything the ruler could have done to encourage European planters, he still had to attend to the needs and requirements of the

Chinese. The organization of the gambier agriculture was the antithesis of everything that Europeans demanded.

The European system of estate management, then as now, placed heavy emphasis on long-term capital investment. The capitalist owned the property and labourers were hired on contract and given a fixed wage. The management of planting was centralized and directed from the top. Profits were derived from the difference between overhead and sales of the produce.

The contrast to the Chinese system was striking. The most significant difference was the fact that all the planters were independent. The capitalists did not own the estates. Here control was exercised through the debt structure. Planters were given a grub-stake and were treated as entrepreneurs. They were free to manage their estates as they saw fit, and were only directed by the Kangchu, who was neither the owner nor the manager but the revenue farmer. Real profits came not only from produce but also from the interest on loans and from the sale of taxable commodities such as opium and spirits. In theory, it was possible for every planter to become successful and independent, and this illusion was perhaps the real strength of the system. In practice, the pyramid of control brought large profits to the *taukehs* and the revenue farmers, and the planters were left with almost nothing.

The nature of the system also prevented the Chinese from trying other agricultural crops. Jackson noted that coffee planting was not taken up by the Chinese at this time: "A final point worthy of note is the very limited interest shown by the Chinese in coffee planting. Apart from nutmegs and cloves, this was the first type of plantation agriculture to appear in Malaya that did not owe much of its early development to Chinese enterprise. One reason for this situation is the fact that Chinese planters were already involved in the cultivation of several other remunerative crops."

In addition, coffee required a long-term investment. Capitalists could not expect returns until the fifth year. The whole style of Chinese business in nineteenth-century Malaya was strictly limited to short-term, quick-return investments. For the Chinese, interest rates were very high, thus they preferred to seek profits in fast-producing crops which could be easily replanted. These included tapioca, gambier, and sugar, which were "better suited to the requirements and methods of financing" practised by Chinese at this time.[29]

The basic economic and political systems of all the Malay states had not altered significantly by the 1880s. Indeed, there was to be no major alteration in this area until the 1890s and the introduction of large-scale European enterprise. Until that time, the exploitation of the resources of the Malay Peninsula was in the hands of Asians. It was only Asians who controlled the media necessary for organizing plantation agriculture and mining at that time.

The media through which power was exercised were inaccessible to Europeans except through Asian intermediaries. Thus, until the 1890s, all European enterprise was largely of a commercial or tertiary nature. Primary and secondary production was strictly controlled by Asians who monopolized the only lines of communication to the labour force. These included languages which the Europeans did not understand and systems of loyalty that Europeans could not penetrate. It was not until European technology had progressed to a point where traditional systems had become largely irrelevant that Europeans could themselves begin directly to exploit the resources of the Peninsula.

The incompatibility of the European and Chinese systems of commercial agriculture could have been overcome if it had been possible for the Europeans to bring in their own labour force, the Tamils. This would have freed them from the need to rely on Chinese workers and on the opium farmers and coolie brokers. However, the Straits government threw obstacles in the way here. Unlike the Chinese, the Tamils emigrated from a British territory; thus their entry to Malaya was more strictly controlled than that of the Chinese. In 1882, the Straits government demanded that Johor permit the Governor of the Straits Settlements to appoint a European official as the Protector of Indian Immigrants.[30] This move appears to have stopped Indian immigration to Johor. After this time, the only Malay state which was allowed to bring in Indians was Perak. It was not until 1890 that the Johor government appointed Howard Bentley, one of Abu Bakar's officials, to this post.[31] But, by this time, the planting had already begun to die out.

Abu Bakar's attempts to free himself of the constricting effects of the Chinese and, it appears, of Singapore as well were not restricted to new ventures in agriculture alone. In the years between 1878 and 1882, he also tried to organize large-scale investment projects which, although seriously compromising the independence of the state, would have placed control of the economy in Europe, rather than Singapore. Two of these so-called charter schemes have been described by Keith Sinclair.

The first was a concession which was granted to Johannes Mooyer of Great Winchester St., London. This charter amounted to a virtual monopoly over Johor's economy for ninety-nine years. It allowed Mooyer's company the right to act as sole agents for the state in terms of banking, mercantile activities, planting, mining, and to be the sole proprietors of railway, bridge, and ferry companies. The firm would have been exempt from taxes, have preferential rights on all public works contracts, and also have the right to issue notes and to hold the government bank account. It also had the sole right to loan money to the government at six per cent on temporary loans as well as the right to loan to planters. It also gave the company the rights to 100,000 acres for its own plantations. All other such charters were forbidden. The company was to be capitalized at £500,000, only ten per cent of which had to be paid up.[32]

This scheme not only caused concern in Singapore but also in the Colonial Office in London. Sinclair points out that the Colonial Office, fully expecting at some future date to take over Johor, could see no benefit in allowing a private firm to acquire such sweeping rights. These would only have to be bought out or otherwise compensated once full control was established. Thus, pressures were brought to bear on Abu Bakar and he was forced to disavow the scheme in the same year.

Not to be discouraged, however, he attempted the same thing again a few years later. This time he took the precaution of including powerful Singapore interests in the combination. The second charter scheme, launched in 1881, was called the Malay Peninsular Agency Ltd. and was promoted by Rodyk and Davidson, the Singapore legal firm which had advised Abu Bakar and Ibrahim for many years. This company was to have all of the rights initially given to the Mooyer company plus sole rights to all mineral leases and a total monopoly on the bank issue. It was initially advertised as being capitalized at £1,000,000, of which £300,000 had to be paid up. This was later reduced to a capital of only £300,000, with £50,000 paid up. The chairman was to be Charles Clifford, Governor Weld's cousin.[33]

The failure of these charter schemes and of the European plantations were not only set-backs for the ruler's attempts to diversify and expand the Johor economy but they further clouded relations between the ruler and the European community of Singapore. From the late 1880s on, there were continual complaints about the Sultan's personal extravagance and his lack of attention to the development of Johor.[34]

In response, the Sultan took to publicity. A regular column was published in the *Singapore Free Press* entitled "Johore" which carried a selection of chatty incidents and glowing descriptions of development in the state. One such column described the resettlement programme which had been launched in Kesang. The area had been depopulated in the 1870s while various factions fought over Muar.

> Now, however, that the country is under the prosperous rule of the Maharaja of Johore, the people are rapidly returning.
>
> Over one hundred families have now resumed their former occupations, and with the Maharaja's substantial assistance in the shape of money and buffaloes, this abandoned district is beginning to look quite prosperous and cheerful once again.
>
> As an encouragement to families to return to their former homes, I hear the Johore government have informed the people that there will be no taxes levied on their crops ...[35]

Another side of Abu Bakar's publicity campaign was his foreign travels and local entertainments. Following his trip to London in 1866, Abu Bakar began to make regular excursions abroad, where he began to associate with European royalty. Winstedt reports that he visited Calcutta in 1875 to meet the Prince of Wales. In 1878, he was in London again, making plans for a continental tour to Italy, Paris, and Vienna. In the early 1880s, he made the circuit of East and Southeast Asia, stopping at Java, Hongkong, China, and Japan. Winstedt writes, "For her Jubilee in 1887, he had presented Queen Victoria with a silver model of the Albert Memorial, which she treasured at Windsor."[36]

These activities were all very expensive. In 1889–90, he again travelled to Europe and was lavishly received in Cairo, Athens, Constantinople, and Vienna. "Flattered by all this attention, Abu Bakar was led to 'cut a great dash' involving heavy expenditure which Johore could not afford since the state had yet to pay off a debt of about $100,000 incurred by the Sultan on his previous trip. The governor therefore reported privately to the Secretary of State that the Sultan's personal extravagance 'seriously retarded' the development of Johore proper."[37]

The criticisms of Abu Bakar's ambitions, of his extravagance, and of his "neglect" of Johor's "progress" failed to bring any positive action by the Colonial Office at this time. The ruler had played his cards quite well. But, paradoxically, these three problems — ambition, extravagance, and neglect — were linked. He had taken his one resource, an empty piece of land, and allowed the Chinese to fill it up and produce revenue from it. His "administration" did little more than manage the revenue. This income provided him with the funds to go on jaunts around the world and "cut a great dash", but not much more. It would, however, be short-sighted to judge these expenditures as no more than personal gratification on Abu Bakar's part. Rather, they may also be seen as a well-managed publicity campaign to gain recognition and status beyond the limited world of Singapore. Abu Bakar, and his father before him, had depended on cordial personal relations with the power-holders who ultimately determined Johor's fate. Ibrahim had concentrated on the merchants and governors of the Straits Settlements. Abu Bakar pushed beyond this to England and Europe. He gained a congenial entry into the European aristocracy. It is true that his vast expenditures for trips to Europe, for the building and outfitting of lavishly appointed palaces at Johor Baharu, Tyresall in Singapore, and at Muar, and for his frequent and bountiful entertainments put a severe drain on the shrinking resources of the state. However, it was just this sort of thing that kept Johor independent during these years. The Governors of Singapore were perhaps right in calling attention to his extravagance. When he died, the state was some £200,000 in debt and even the members of the Johore Advisory Board in London felt that the state would soon be taken over.[38]

Abu Bakar must have been aware of this dilemma. With the failure of European development schemes in Johor and the gradual decline of gambier cultivation, he appears to have accepted that there was little he could do to bolster the state's economy. He did have an ample supply of cash and apparently very good credit, but he saw no way of investing it in the material resources of the state. Thus, the diplomatic effort. In addition to this, he also invested in the state's human resources and began training an elite to take over from him. The archetype of the new Malay elite was Enche Abdul Rahman bin Andak, the Sultan's personal secretary in his last years. He was also given the title of Dato Sri Amar di Raja, made Secretary to the Johor Government, and sat on the State Council. "Abdul Rahman, a nephew of the Sultan, was 'a very clever' English-educated Malay who became the Sultan's private secretary … Cecil Smith suspected that it was Abdul Rahman who drafted the Sultan of Johore's replies to communications from the Singapore authorities."[39]

While he was the most well known, perhaps most notorious, as far as the Straits government was concerned, there was a whole group of English-educated Malays now coming to maturity in Johor. When Florence Caddy visited Johor in 1889, she met two of the Sultan's nephews, both of whom were English-educated. One was a surveyor and the other an engineer. "The Sultan kept his nephews waiting at a distance in their launch till the Duke came on board the *Pantie*, when he called them alongside and on board and introduced them. Mr. Swan, who understands Malay, told us he said to them quite sharply, 'Now mind you talk to these English people; if you can't talk sense, talk nonsense, only talk plenty.' "[40]

Judging, however, from the training of his successor, Abu Bakar's aim was not so much producing English-educated Malays but Malays who were capable of conducting themselves like English gentlemen.

> Sultan Ibrahim, a young man of twenty-two, had little administrative experience when he ascended the throne. After a very brief period of schooling, he joined the Johore Military Forces and on being commissioned as Second Lieutenant, became his father's aide-de-camp. He paid the first of many subsequent visits to Europe before he was seventeen because his father wanted to introduce him to European royalty. Proclaimed Crown Prince in 1891, he was given only routine duties. He worked off his energies on the sports field apparently, rather than in preparation for the throne.[41]

Given that Abu Bakar was well aware that Johor would be taken over by the British soon after his death, one wonders whether Ibrahim did not have everything he needed to know when his father died. The state already possessed a corps of loyal and capable officials. With the British take-over seen as inevitable, a ruler who was also a capable administrator would have been quickly put out of a job. What was needed, in Abu Bakar's estimation, was not an administrator but a respectable figurehead who could uphold the dignity of the office of Sultan and who knew the kind of people a sovereign ought to know.

The resurgence of the state's economy could not come until the British took over in Johor. Writing in 1937, Rupert Emerson could say that Johor had been bypassed by large-scale development until relatively late. He noted that although gambier and pepper cultivation had "achieved some proportions", planting in Johor was relatively unsuccessful until the twentieth century.

European planters did not take an interest in Johor until after 1909. This waited on a number of developments. Among these were the appointment of a British Advisor to Johor in 1910 and the completion of the railroad crossing the state from the Federation to Singapore. The major crop of this period was of course rubber, which did not get underway until the late 1890s. At that time, European attention turned first towards the Malayan states which were already under British protection. Johor had to wait until available land in the Federated States was appropriated before rubber planters began to look elsewhere.[42]

The slippage which had taken place in Johor's economic position was an inevitable product of the gambier and opium economy of the Kangchu system. Another factor was the rapid development now taking place in the Malay states which had recently been brought under British protection. By 1890, large numbers of gambier planters were settling in Selangor, Negri Sembilan, and Malacca. The decline of the tax-farming system in the British settlements, which also occurred in the 1890s, had serious repercussions for the individuals who had financed the Johor economy. The opium and gambier regime was dying. The road to prosperity in Johor lay in new directions and, at the time, no one was certain what these were. The fact that the state's entire administrative system had been structured around the Kangchu system appears to have limited the options of Johor's rulers. In addition, the blocks which the Colonial Office placed in the way of Abu Bakar's grandiose development companies also prevented European investments.

The state was going through a traumatic change whose magnitude was only matched by the one which had taken place in the period 1825–50. During the earlier period, Temenggong Ibrahim had ended his dependence on the *orang laut* and had shifted his base of power to the Chinese. Had Abu Bakar been twenty years younger in 1885, perhaps he would have expended more energy and creativity in making this second transition, from the Chinese to Europeans. Thus lacking viable alternatives for the development of the state, he chose to employ his resources in the work of building up his personal prestige at the cost of everything else.

It is important to remember that the Temenggongs were not accorded very high status by the other ruling families of the Peninsula. Even though the Johor rulers were wealthier and more influential during this period, other Malays regularly called attention to their supposedly meaner origins. The *Hikayat Johor Serta Pahang* has preserved a Kampong Gelam *pantun* commenting on Abu Bakar's elevation to the rank of Sultan:

> The gaudy lantern is bound in rattan
> Humble *kemuning* wood holds the kris.
> The Temenggong has become a Sultan
> Through his royal forebears the Bugis.[43]

In the face of this disdain, Abu Bakar's ambitions exceeded the Sultanate which he gained. There is undoubtedly some truth in Gullick's conclusion that he sought to make himself the Sultan of most of Malaya. The British, of course, had never seen the need for such a ruler; so in 1885 they acknowledged the sentiments of the other chiefs and served their own interests by qualifying Abu Bakar's title and made him only Sultan of the "State and Territory" of Johor. Denied the worlds he had meant to conquer in Malaya, Abu Bakar sought status among European royalty, built palaces, bought steamboats and other "baubles", and "laid a fine table".

In 1885, personal independence meant a great deal more to him than it did to the rulers of the other states. In Perak, Selangor, and Negri Sembilan, British intervention increased the power of the rulers and acted to downgrade the regional chiefs. In Johor, the situation had been quite different. There were no regional chiefs whose power challenged that of the ruler. The Temenggongs had been autocrats from the beginning and the Malay side of the state's administration was, by contemporary standards, highly centralized. The acceptance of a British Resident in Johor at that time would have meant the loss of the very things on which the ruler based his somewhat questionable prestige — his personal wealth, his freedom of movement, and his ability to accumulate what he considered to be the appurtenances of kingly power. This pursuit of prestige, independence, and the forms of power came to characterize the policies of the state's rulers for the next twenty-five years.

From a humanitarian point of view and from a practical economic standpoint, this policy did very little to benefit the state or its subjects. The economy deteriorated, the investors lost money, and the state went into debt while the ruler used Johor's wealth and whatever he could borrow to buy friends in London and in Europe. Abu Bakar's activity perhaps best reflects the mentality of the maritime chiefs who were his ancestors. As port and sea chiefs, they saw the land as a place from which one gained wealth, not as a place in which one invested resources. The business of governing a piece of land was not the proper occupation of a true maritime ruler. Abu Bakar, and to a large extent his son after him, continued to see Singapore and the world beyond it as their appropriate sphere of activity.

This attitude is best shown by the fact that the aims of the Malay administration in Johor were highly limited. Revenue management appeared to be the major preoccupation. The day-to-day administration of the population and of the state's economic life was in the hands of the Chinese. According to the sociological study done by F. Lees, the result of the Kangchu system was that "Chinese colonies had been established in an area where previously only a few aborigines had lived. They were completely Chinese in nature, the culture of the inhabitants being modified only to suit the needs of colonization of a tropical climate. Hardly any of the settlers learned to speak Malay and the sole contact with the Malay Government of Johore was through the *Kang Chue*."[44]

Thus the Malay administration did nothing to integrate this alien population. If we are to assign responsibility for the communal split in modern Malayan society, it seems logical to conclude that it was created by traditional rulers operating according to the priorities of the ancient maritime political system. It has been common for Malays and some British historians to fix the blame for the Chinese presence with the colonial power. If we can learn one thing from the history of Johor, it is that the Malay rulers themselves, in their pursuit of power were largely responsible for this situation.

The British contribution here was that they left the Malay rulers no alternative. They had displaced the traditional rulers by taking over the entrepot. Their elimination of the *orang laut* and the maritime peoples who had once formed the military and administrative infrastructure of the traditional state left the Malay chiefs without a subject class. This situation was most acute for Johor's rulers, the Temenggongs, whose entire "state" had once been maritime. The Malay rulers were driven from the seas and driven from the port and left only with the hostile and unfamiliar environment of the land. Thus, the Malay rulers turned to the Chinese whose inexhaustible numbers and adaptable technology made them the first human beings to conquer the Malayan rainforest. It was only by using these resources and by making the compromises required by the situation that the Johor Malays managed to survive the radical changes that had overtaken them.

NOTES

1. Maxwell and Gibson, *Treaties*, p. 125.
2. Parkinson, *British Intervention*, p. 35.
3. Parkinson, in *British Intervention*, notes the use of several Johor steamships during the period 1874–76 by the Straits authorities, e.g., the S.S. *Johore*, pp. 123 and 127; S.S. *Pulai*, p. 187; and the S.S. *Pantai*, p. 301.
4. Mohamad Ibrahim, *Kesah*, pp. 19, 25–34, 35–69. Ibrahim gives his account of these voyages.
5. Parkinson, *British Intervention*, pp. 62–66; and Eunice Thio, *British Policy in the Malay Peninsula 1880–1910*, v. 1 (Singapore, 1969), pp. 20–21.
6. Parkinson, *British Intervention*, p. 64.
7. Ibid., p. 326.
8. Winstedt, "A History of Johor", pp. 112–16.
9. J. M. Gullick, "The War with Yamtuan Antah", *JMBRAS*, v. 27, pt. 1 (May 1954), p. 5.
10. Thio, *British Policy*, pp. xxx–xxxiii. Thio discusses the opposition raised against Maharaja Abu Bakar in Singapore as a result of his annexation of Muar. One of the most vocal of his opponents was Frank Swettenham. His version of the history of relations between the Straits government and the two native chiefs of Singapore, given in his *British Malaya* (London, 1920), pp. 84–103, was largely coloured by the take-over.
11. Thio, *British Policy*, pp. xv–xvi.
12. Ibid., p. 24.
13. Ibid., p. 26.
14. Ibid., p. 27.
15. Maxwell and Gibson, *Treaties*, p. 125.
16. Thio, *British Policy*, pp. 108–9.
17. *SSD*, 1885, pp. 168–71.
18. Metcalfe Larken was a prominent figure in Johor in the 1880s. He owned the Castlewood Estate located near Tebrau and also built the road in Johor Baharu which today bears his name.
19. Jackson, *Planters and Speculators*, p. 177. "In 1869 the fungus *Hemileia vastatrix* appeared on the coffee estates of Ceylon; it spread rapidly, causing considerable devastation, and within a matter of twenty years had destroyed the Ceylon coffee industry."
20. Thomas Heslop Hill, "Report on Johore", Pamphlet (Singapore, 1879), p. 22. This was also published in the *Straits Daily Times* in serial form; *SDT*, 6, 9, 23, and 24 May 1879.
21. *SDT*, 13 May 1879.
22. *SSD*, 1881, p. 101.
23. *SSD*, 1885, p. 166.
24. Ibid., pp. 176–77.

25. Jackson, *Planters and Speculators*, pp. 188–89. "Slavery was abolished in Brazil in 1888, temporarily dislocating the coffee industry in the world's major producing centre. Prices began to rise and reached a peak of over $40 per *pikul* in 1894 and 1895."
26. *SFP*, 11 June 1895.
27. Elcum, *Johore in 1911*, p. 1.
28. Interview with Mr. Wee Chee Ming, Local Commissioner of Tebrau, 7 February 1971.
29. Jackson, *Planters and Speculators*, p. 186.
30. British Parliamentary Papers, C-3458, No. 6, Kimberley to Weld, 31 August 1881, p. 40.
31. *SSTP*, Nos. 12, 15, and 16, all dated 27 February 1890.
32. Keith Sinclair, "Hobson and Lenin in Johore: Colonial Office Policy towards British Concessionaires and Investors 1878–1907", *Modern Asian Studies*, v. 1, pt. 4 (1967), p. 339.
33. Ibid., pp. 339–40.
34. Thio, *British Policy*, p. 223.
35. *SFP*, 11 April 1885.
36. Winstedt, "A History of Johore", p. 119.
37. Thio, *British Policy*, p. 233.
38. Ibid., p. 228.
39. Ibid., p. 225.
40. Mrs. Florence Caddy, *To Siam and Malaya in the Duke of Sutherland's Yacht, "San Peur"*, Chs. 10 and 11 (London, 1889), pp. 231–60, 261–79. These two chapters are devoted to the ten days, 4–14 March 1888, which the ducal party spent as the guests of Sultan Abu Bakar.
41. Thio, *British Policy*, p. 227.
42. Emerson, *Malaysia*, pp. 213–14.
43. *Hikayat Johor Serta Pahang*, p. 10. *Tanglong simpai rotan/Kemuning sampir kris/ Temenggong menjadi Sultan/Asal-nya dari Raja Bugis.*
44. F. Lees, "Chinese Settlement", pp. 282–83.

8

The Transformation of the Maritime Polity

The aim of this study has been to identify and explore the dimensions of change in the traditional Malay state system during the nineteenth century. Until 1800 or so, the Malay political system had been characterized by the division between land and sea peoples, by the dependence on sea-borne communications, and by the strategic location of the port and the power of the Johor ruler. It is a fundamental conclusion of this study that this political structure had not been destroyed by the century of British occupation before 1885. It had actually been taken over by the colonial power.

The British take-over in the Malay world was in fact a process of substitution, at least in its initial stages. When Raffles founded Singapore, he restored the maritime empire, but this time it was under the auspices of the British East India Company. By taking over the entrepot and at the same time by assisting in the elimination of the Sultanate, the British themselves became the focal point of the Malayan political system. When the British forces collided with the fabric of the ongoing Malayan state system, their power tended to flow through previously established channels and to express itself in traditionalistic patterns. In 1885, the power structure of British Malaya bore a striking resemblance to old Johor. Territorially, the size of the state had shrunk because Singapore had no political authority in the Dutch possessions, but the port's economic network, regardless of the boundaries of its political authority, came very close to duplicating the traditional one. The major differences were that the Malays had been completely ousted from the port and driven from the seas, and that a vast number of Chinese had moved into the area.

On this point the writer parts company with the prevailing trend in Malaysian historiography. It is generally accepted, at least implicitly that the British built a new state on the long-dead ruins of old Johor. While a full-scale critique of this school of thought is out of place here, this study has dealt extensively with two of the relevant problems — piracy and slavery. The historians of British Malaya since Frank Swettenham have filled their books with the intentions and policies of a small group of men who rarely left Singapore. They exhibit a tendency to ignore, or at least inadequately explain, the vast gap that generally existed between stated policies and ultimate results. On the other hand, they tend to treat the Malay political system as an obstacle in the way of progress rather than what it appears here to have been: a communications system which in fact made most of their progress possible.

The anti-piracy campaign was launched in the name of free trade and peaceful commerce. Ultimately these aims were in fact achieved. When the archipelago trade came to be carried only in square-rigged ships owned by British, Chinese, and Arab merchants, there was free trade. When British men-of-war and steam gunboats had swept the seas clean of pirates and razed their bases, there was peaceful commerce. For the Malays it was the peace of oblivion, as the English solution was to wipe out native commerce altogether. Control of the seas was one of the first steps in the traditional state-building cycle. Of course, the Malay empires had achieved this by unifying the sea peoples; the British did it by eliminating them and substituting their own naval and merchant forces.

An integral part of the anti-piracy campaign was the elimination of slavery. The pirates had been the major slave traders and generally sold the victims of their raids. Raffles had objected to this and slavery and slave-trading were forbidden at Singapore. It is probable that most Malay empires in the past had been built on an enslaved population. Singapore likewise needed a population which could be similarly exploited. Singapore's economy was supported by the production and consumption of several hundred-thousand Chinese coolies who were locked in a perpetual cycle of indebtedness and opium addiction. Many of these resided in Singapore but the vast majority lived and worked in Johor, Riau, Sumatra, and other nearby settlements. Personal slavery had ended only to be replaced by a system of servitude which was probably far more destructive than old-style slavery had ever been. In the past, people were felt to be responsible for the welfare of their slaves, but no one cared for the coolies. The elimination of piracy brought an additional benefit to Singapore since it meant that the coolie ships from China could reach the port unmolested. Thus, the labour supply was protected and monopolized by Singapore, which then became the major coolie market of the region.

In the final analysis, the British followed the traditional scenario for conquering the area, and by 1885 appear to have controlled it very much on the same basis as had former Johor rulers. In 1819, Raffles seized the most strategic location in the region. His successors built up the port and grew wealthy. Next they took over the seas and enslaved, or perhaps dominated, an agricultural population. Then they followed the trade routes and reestablished the traditional economic dependence of the riverine principalities. Finally, they recreated the traditional power configuration of the old maritime state. They took on the legitimizing and arbitrating functions of the former Sultan. In 1885, British Malaya was a maritime state ruled largely from the market-place and the deck of a ship. This had often been the case before, but this time the difference was in the size of the market, the kind of ship, and in the ultimate loyalties of the men who controlled them.

The proof offered for this viewpoint is the history of the Temenggongs. Their story tells us what it was like to be colonized — to see one's institutions seized by another more powerful agency and then turned against oneself. The Temenggongs' unique relationship with the Singapore government was one of the primary mechanisms by which the British were assimilated into the Malayan state system. These chiefs must be treated as the partners of the British. It was the Temenggongs who led the Europeans to the wellsprings of power in the Malayan state system and acted as their guides through the tangled web of Malay politics. While the Temenggongs were, in every event, seeking power for themselves, they did not at first conceive of a significant distinction between their own interests and those of the port. As port officials from the very start, they acted consistently as agents of the port in regard to the surrounding territories. The ultimate effect of their activities was to spread the power of Singapore and conversely to weaken the autonomy of the riverine states. The paradox was that, as the Temenggongs led the British from prize to prize, they found themselves successively dispossessed by the Europeans.

The dispossession began with Raffles' occupation of Singapore, the most strategic base, which Temenggong Abdul Rahman already controlled with his own navy. The establishment of the Company's factory was the first appropriation. When it became clear that the entrepot possessed manifold economic resources, the Temenggong claimed the most lucrative of these for himself. This state of affairs was found to be highly "inconvenient and embarrassing". So the British took over the tax farms themselves and forbade the Temenggong from taxing the native and the Chinese traders. Full control of the entire island was claimed in 1824. They felt forced to do this because the Temenggong would have laid and was in fact laying claim to whatever privileges and economic monopolies that the Europeans did not specifically claim for themselves or otherwise forbid to him. Theoretically, Crawfurd's move then made it possible for the British to govern the port and its trade without reference to the native authorities. This was a serious mistake in the short run, and perhaps in the very long run too. It caused immediate trouble because this legal take-over was not backed up by adequate material resources. They had bitten off more than they could chew. The British suddenly found themselves alone in a sea of very angry Malays. For the next decade, the unhappy ghost of Temenggong Abdul Rahman lurked in the swamps and shoals and took vengeance on Singapore.

Between 1825 and 1836, the Straits authorities faced a sporadic and fitful guerrilla-style war waged by small men in small boats — mostly against each other. A Malay civil war was actually taking place — or so it would seem. More research needs to be done on this period. This conclusion is suggested by Tarling's evidence, which shows that after a decade of "piracy", Bonham decided that the British could not handle the situation on their own. His solution was to accept Daing Ibrahim's offer to assist in ameliorating the "pirates". This constituted intervention because it automatically gave the Temenggong tacit recognition as the "policeman" of Singapore. This was the first in a remarkable series of diplomatic coups which mark the career of Temenggong Ibrahim.

It was he who led the British on their next steps towards involvement in Malay politics. After 1836–37, he appears to have brought about some lessening of "piracy". He negotiated with Pahang on the Company's behalf and formed alliances with Riau and perhaps Selangor. These moves paved the way for economic penetration by the agents of the port — Chinese and British merchants. The Temenggong also dragged the Europeans into his long, desultory campaign against the successors of Sultan Hussain. But if the Temenggongs sought to replace the Sultan, they were doomed to disappointment. It was the English themselves who fell heir to the authority once exercised by the Sultanate. The Temenggongs had to be content with the title to Johor — the jungle and swamp at Singapore's back door.

The foundation of Johor was, in the first instance, a purely Chinese undertaking. The state's agriculture was established by pepper and gambier planters who had been crowded out of Singapore. It is one of the paradoxes of Malayan history that, as the British built their government on the foundation of the Malay maritime state, the ousted Malay rulers of Johor built their state on the foundation of a Chinese economic system. The transition from the sea to the land, and from the port to the hinterland, was not an easy one for the

Temenggongs. Unlike many other Malay chiefs, they really had no government on the land before the 1840s. The Temenggongs had always been port officials or sea chiefs. The true innovators in the Malay world at this time were the Chinese.

With very little reference to either Malays or Europeans, the Chinese had set up their own economy based on planting, tin mining, and opium taxing. The foundations of this economic establishment can be traced back to the mid-eighteenth century. The beginnings of an indigenous yet purely Chinese economy date from the fall of Riau. By the mid-nineteenth century, the gambier *taukehs* and the opium farmers of Singapore had come to control a vast system of plantation agriculture held together by a combination of debt slavery, secret society terror, and opium addiction. These men financed the Temenggong's state in Johor from the very outset.

The Temenggong's government in Johor came to be a blend of three elements. At the foundation was the Chinese-dominated system of agricultural settlements under the Kangchu. Built on these was the system of *surat sungai* which, while it was derived from a traditional-style *kuasa*, or letter of authority to a *pengulu*, also owed much to the Temenggong's British lawyers. By the 1870s, the Malay in which these documents were written was full of direct borrowings from English legalese. Despite the webbing of paper being woven around them, the Temenggongs followed traditional institutional models for the control of foreign communities and appointed a Kapitan to govern the Kangchu. This individual in the first instance was the secret society chieftain, Tan Kye Soon.

The cap-stone of the Johor government was the following of the ruler. The small group of kin and associates from Teluk Belanga became the managers of the Chinese agricultural and tax-farming system. This group developed into the State Council and eventually grew into the Malay administration. Individuals such as Ungku Abdul Rahman and Ungku Abdul Majid, Dato Mohamed Salleh bin Perang, Dato Mohamed Ibrahim bin Munshi Abdullah, and Dato Mentri Ja'afar bin Haji Mohamed managed day-to-day relations with the Chinese. Their primary function seems to have been the issuing of revenue farms and, beyond that, laying down the ground rules within which the Chinese were to operate. In establishing relations with the Chinese on a systematic basis, they laid the foundation for the patterns of political and economic domination which continue to characterize the present-day Federation of Malaysia.

The key to understanding the nature of the Temenggong's control of Johor is to be found in the position which he held as an unofficial policeman of the Singapore government. As the chief pirate suppressor, his authority was first established in Singapore's off-shore waters. From here it was a natural step to begin policing the coast of neighbouring Johor, where he profited from the gutta-percha boom of the 1840s. The spread of the gambier cultivation from Singapore to Johor is seen as a mere extension of the port. As the policeman of Singapore's frontier zone, the Temenggong came to control this agriculture. The statements in the earliest *surat sungai*, that the Kangchu was subject to the same laws as those laid down by the Company in Singapore, add weight to this argument. It was not until Temenggong Ibrahim died that any attempt was made to resolve the ambiguities and anomalies in the status of the Temenggong and of Johor.

The early 1860s were another watershed period. The treaty of 1855 had given the Temenggong full control of Johor. However, no move was made to establish an effective government there, let alone attempt to separate the state from Singapore, until Abu Bakar succeeded his father. Abu Bakar appears to have taken the initiative here and decided that the time for ambiguities had ended. Taking the offensive in the Pahang civil war, he sought to translate Ibrahim's intermediary role into one of outright hegemony. His failure here appears to have resolved the question of Johor's military domination of the Peninsula once and for all. From this time until 1885, he retained the intermediary status and continued to make his influence felt on the Peninsula as an agent of the entrepot, but his dreams of empire were checked.

Whether or not the Temenggong's policies regarding the gambier traffic can be construed as an aggressive act, or as a reaction to the current economic crisis, may remain a matter of dispute. The Tanjong Putri controversy demonstrated a few more realities of the Temenggong's position. The first was that the Johor/Singapore economy was indivisible. The second was that the Temenggong would be allowed no economic preserves inside the port. Abu Bakar could only claim Johor revenues and not a portion of Singapore revenues as both his father and grandfather had done. The Temenggong had retreated another step and the British had taken over what he left behind.

If these were set-backs for Abu Bakar's grand design, he certainly found ways of compensating for them. He became the first internationally recognized Malay ruler. In his day, he was the only Malay to hold such status. His connections with British and European royalty opened a channel of communications which did have an impact on British policy. He was the only Malay who, despite years of "cooperation", could face the colonial rulers on their own ground. It may have had only symbolic significance, but in the years after 1885 the best any Malay could offer the imperial advance was token resistance. Sultan Abu Bakar reversed his relationship with Singapore when he was forced out of his port official status by Weld. He had been transformed, at long last, from an agent of the port to one of the hinterland. He then assumed an adversary stance towards the port and the colonial government.

Singapore has generally been treated by historians only in its function as an entrepot. The fact that it possessed a rather broad and sound agricultural base in the nineteenth century has been virtually ignored. Naturally the gambier agriculture did not feed the urban populace of the port — it simply provided one of its exports, and a relatively minor one at that. However, its status as an export provides no accurate measure of the crop's significance. Its real importance was in the number of people for which it provided a living. This vast population of Chinese planters and coolies, living not only on Singapore Island but also in Johor and the islands of the Riau Archipelago and, by the 1890s, in Malacca, Negri Sembilan, and Perak, by their consumption of cheap European manufactures and Indian opium, provided an important market for English merchants and the East India Company. They likewise provided the economic base for the newly emerging native states and their ancient dynasties — particularly that of Johor. It is also important to recognize that the revenues of the opium monopoly provided the greatest share of Singapore's tax base, thus making it possible to have a free port and still pay for the government. There were few years during the nineteenth century when the return from the opium monopoly constituted less than forty per cent of Singapore's total revenue.

Even these factors, however, pale to insignificance when one considers the social, political, and economic structures which grew up around the gambier agriculture. Starting in 1836, gambier became one of the first major tropical crops cultivated commercially to service the European industrial revolution. In these days of rubber and plastic, it is easy to forget the role which leather (the tanning of which gambier was destined to aid) once played in the industrial mechanisms and the horse-drawn transportation system of the period. Malaya's role as a producer of primary crops to fuel the industrial west — its role as a dependent commodity producer — was well established long before the advent of rubber and the expansion of tin production, both of which occurred in the 1890s. Needless to say, this condition continued to characterize the Malaysian economy into the 1980s.

Viewing the vastly more important role which crops like rubber and oil palm have come to play in the international economy today, these remarks on gambier may seem to inflate its importance. However, it should be understood that gambier, in almost every respect, was the pioneer of the rubber economy. Not only did rubber replace much of the leather, both in industry and in transportation, but it also replaced the gambier crop. It took over the land, the labour force, and the capital which had been accumulated as a result of the gambier agriculture.

Locally, the gambier/opium economy provided the means whereby a few Chinese in and around Singapore became very wealthy. This not only gave them great social and political influence, but it established concentrations of capital which made future Chinese economic ventures feasible. Thus, the foundation of the Chinese-dominated Malaysian economic system was laid. The vast population of coolies provided the constituency which the *taukehs* dominated, first economically, then, as Lee Poh Ping has shown, socially through the clan and other organizations, and finally, after independence, politically.

The Temenggongs' contribution to twentieth-century Malaya is still not clearly understood. This study has attempted to demonstrate that a number of currently significant aspects of modern Malaysia resulted from the historical experience of the Temenggongs. Johor was the first new model Malay state to emerge in the colonial situation. The Temenggongs and Johor were the first testing-ground for traditional institutions and the birth-place of new ones. The British policy of indirect rule, which characterized the colonial government in Malaya, seems to have been born out of the relationship with the Temenggongs. The same is true of the bureaucratic nature of the new Malayan polity and such hallmarks of modern Malaya as the Chinese problem, the ethnic division of labour, and the Singapore/Malaysia split.

With the Temenggongs' help, the British had recreated a state shaped very much like the traditional maritime empire in 1885. After this date, the Europeans introduced some important innovations. Their technology now allowed them permanently to alter the Malayan environment. This threw the traditional ecosystem out of balance. They were thus able to move very quickly from the coasts onto the land after 1885. This move brought the forces of the port into direct command of the land — something which had never happened before. This penetration was effected by the introduction of railroads, rubber trees, Indian labourers, bicycles, motor-cars, good roads, and finally electricity. The entire traditional aristocracy, which had always been military by profession, was transformed into a bureaucracy. The Malayan naval and military elite was gone by the turn of the century. It had been swept away with the pirates, the Johor Sultanate, the native maritime population and their culture — the old maritime world had disappeared.

In its place stood the rather diverse collection of colonial dependencies known as British Malaya. This, with minor modifications, would ultimately gain independence as the Federation of Malaysia. The two mainstays of the economy, rubber and tin, and the emphasis on primary production were already well established. Likewise fixed were the social and economic patterns which characterized the state in the 1970s. The changes of the post-war era had simply permitted the indigenous economic elites which were established in the nineteenth century to assume full political power.

Appendix A

Reports on Piracy

There are four more or less contemporary (1825–50) reports on the "pirates" of the Riau-Lingga Archipelago. Most important are the *Tufhat* (especially p. 296); Presgrave, "Report on Piracy"; and the report of the Dutch Resident of Riau, Angelbeek, dated 14 August 1825, quoted in J. R. Logan, "The Piracy and Slave Trade of the Indian Archipelago", *JIA*, v. 3 (1849), pp. 584–85, 634. There is also a detailed list of the maritime peoples of the Riau-Lingga Archipelago in Begbie, *The Malayan Peninsula*, pp. 270–72, which lists almost every "tribe" or *suku* of *orang laut* and gives population figures.

Table 1 is the composite picture they give. *Tufhat* claims that the islands of Buru and Karimon had been under the Temenggong and also names Galang, Moro, Sugi and Pekaka as piratical (p. 296). Begbie's list indicates that Pekaka is the same as Bulang. Presgrave reports that Galang, Moro, Sugi, and Trong were under the Temenggong. Trong is not listed by Begbie, but the map in Moor, *Notices*, pp. 268–69, shows a "S. Trang" on Batam Island as well as a village. Perhaps this was the base of *suku Trong* which Presgrave mentions. In addition to being pirates, he claims that they collected *agar-agar* and sold it to the Temenggong for a fixed price. Angelbeek, as quoted by Logan, (p. 634) claimed that the Temenggong ruled a fleet "consisting of 48 vessels and about 1,200 men, which had seven places of rendezvous, Galang, Timian, Pulo Bocaya, Salat Singapura, Sughi, Pakako and Bollang". Angelbeek reported that the chief of these islands was "the Raja Lang in the island of Bulang, under whom are all the *Rayats* of Gallang, of Bulang and some other islands situated at or near the entrance of the straits of Malacca".

Appendix B

Comparative List of Kangchu and Surat Sungai

The list on pp. 217–21 is intended to show that by 1874 a real separation had come into being between the holder of the *surat sungai* (or related authority, e.g. *surat jual-beli* and *surat pajak*) and the office of Kangchu.

The left-hand columns contain the names of the Kangchu and his river or district as given in the *Singapore and Straits Directory* (*SSD*) for 1874, "Johore", pp. 5–6. They are given in the same order as presented in the *SSD*. I have not altered the spelling given in the *SSD*. The rivers are listed in geographical order from east to west following the Johor coastline.

The right-hand columns contain the information given for what I take to be the same river or district as based on the documents of the Johor Archives. In most cases, the source is a *surat sungai* from the collection, *SKMK–I*. However, the most recent (before 1874) authority may also be a *surat jual-beli* (SJB) or *surat pajak* (SPBS). The source and date are given at the far right-hand side.

The name of the river is based on spelling given in the map "Johore", Survey Dept., Federation of Malaya, No. 178–1958. The name of the river or district is given twice because of discrepancies in spelling and the occasional use of different names for the same place.

The centre column on the right gives the names of the members of the river-holding Kongsi as listed in the *surat sungai* or other authority. The (k) beside a name in the Kongsi indicates that he was named Kangchu at the time the document was issued. He may or may not be the Kangchu named in the *SSD* list.

In cases where one of the members of the Kongsi appears to be identical with the name given in the *SSD* as Kangchu, the name of that Kongsi member is in italics. It appears that out of the seventy-three Kangchu named in the *SSD* only thirty or about forty-one per cent are also named in a *surat sungai* or related authority. In the cases where they are not, it is assumed that the Kangchu was not the "owner" of the river, but was a deputy or manager hired by the Kongsi.

Directory 1874 (SSD)		***Johor Archives Records (JAR)***		
Kangchu	*River*	*River*	*Kongsi*	*Source*
Eue Lye Tchue	Sedeli Besar	Sedili Besar	*Ngiu Lee Chew* (k) Ngiu Chang Poh Ngiu Chang Hee Ngiu Chang Meng Ungku Abdul Rahman	SKMK – I No. 100 5 Dec. 1873
Ting Atong	Tingar	Tengar	Ngiu Tee Soon *Teng Ah Teng*	SKMK – I No. 85 16 Dec. 1863
Tchew Ah Tcheya	Tanjong Balow	Tanjong Balau (Tengar)	Chua Ah Long (k)	SKMK – I No. 97 21 July 1873
Tchew Ah Heog Lee	Pungai	Punggai	Soon Poo Yang Chua Nam Seng Chua Ah Kui Chua Ah Kau Chua Ng Moo *Chua Ah Yong*? Ban Yang Seng	SKMK – I No. 43 31 July 1863
Tchew Ah Tylee	Ringat	Renggit	*Chua Tee Lee*	SPBS No. 1 5 July 1873
Tchew Ah Esing	Cussam	Kesam Kechil and Besar	*Chua Seng Huat*?	SKMK – I No. 35 14 Sept. 1863
Tan Ah Thak	Palawan	Palawan	*Tan Ah Ngok*?	SJB No. 14 1 Nov. 1872
Ang Ah Hee	Joolootong	Jelutong	none	
Goh Ah Piek	Santee	Santi	Goo Loon Hee	SKMK – I No. 38 8 July 1863
Goh Hak	Rayah	Raya (& Sening)	Koo Leng Kee Koo Seng Oon	SKMK – I No. 37 5 June 1863
Goh Ah Sing	Seening	Sening (& Raya)	Koo Leng Kee *Koo Seng Oon*?	SKMK – I No. 37 5 June 1863
Eng Kik Kang	Labuan	Lebam	*Ng Gek Kang*	SKMK – I No. 104 21 March 1875
Eng Amang	Chimarang	Chemarang	*Ng Ah Mang* (k)	SKMK – I No. 104 21 March 1875
Eng Kek Kum	Pe'chi Perok	Pecha Periok (& Tembaga)	Tiong Sit Tiong Luat Tiong Yau Hoon	SKMK – I No. 11 16 Oct. 1852
Eoa Kim Cha	Papan	Papan (Mengchoh & Layu)	Ngiu Chee Kor Ngiu Tiang Teck	SKMK – I No. 55 3 March 1864
Eng Yim Kwang	Garue	?		
Eoa Chee Kor	Meng Choo	Mengchoh (Papan & Layu)	*Ngiu Chee Kor* Ngiu Tiang Teck	SKMK – I No. 55 3 March 1864
Eu Ah Mee	Lyo	Layu (Papan & Mengchoh)	Ngiu Chee Kor Ngiu Tiang Teck	SKMK – I No. 55 3 March 1864
Eu Ah Kubah	Johore			

SSD		*JAR*		
Kangchu	*River*	*River*	*Kongsi*	*Source*
Eu Layang Sayang	Timoan	Temon	Ng Yang Lek Ng Ah Lee Ng Ah Kun Ng Yok Seng Ng Ton Ng Yong Wan (k)	SKMK – I No. 27 25 Sept. 1860 & SJB No. 3, 4 Sept. 1868 SJB No. 12, 3 Oct. 1871 SJB No. 18, 15 July 1873
Tan Chew Wan	Nipah	Nipah	*Tan Chiu Kuan*	SKMK – I No. 25 9 March 1862
Tan Tean Nahak	Silooyat	Seluyut	*Tan Tin Mok*?	SKMK – I No. 25 9 March I862
Tan Teck Sing	Tanjong Pootus	Tanjong Putus (Panti)	*Tan Teck Seng*	SKMK – I No. 105 3 August 1874
Ang Ack Sing	Perseesei	Persisek (Panti)	*Ng Hock Seng* Ng Ah San (k) Ng See Tong Ng Ah Swee Ng Seng Heng	SKMK – I No. 73 22 May 1866
Tan Twaet Tow	Libah	?		
Kee Ah Yang	Samangah	Semanggar	*Kee Ah Yang* (k) Kee Ah Koi Kee Heng Huat Nong Yahya	SKMK – I No. 82 20 Sept. 1866
Seah Yew Sah	Ching Kedang	Telar	*Seah Yau Sah* Seah Tee Seng alias Seah Chiu Hong Seah Chee Yang	SJB No. 8 26 March 1871 also SJB No. 77 20 Jan. 1884
Tan Yok Tye	Pankalong Putai	?		
Tan Bwoan Tye	Brengan	Bukit Berangan	*Tan Ban Tee*	SKMK – I No. 79 22 August 1866
Tan Tean Ee	Serayah	?		
Tan Ang Tye	Raidan	Redan	Yang Ah Yang *Tan Ah Tim*?	SKMK – I No. 34 17 March 1862
Lim Tchyong	Teerum Tingah	Tiram Ulu	Lim Ban Soon (k) Lim Ah Sui Lim Gee Sok *Lim Chai Wong*? Lim Ak Sui Lim But	SKMK – I No. 51 4 Jan. 1864 SJB No. 26 28 April 1874
Lim Keep Soon	Teerum Elier	Tiram Hilir	*Lim Kiok Soon* Lim Seng Lee	SKMK – I No. 64 16 Jan. 1865
Seah Ling Wat	Kong Kong	Kong Kong, (Kering- Kim & Tukang)	Tan Hiok Nee	SKMK – I No. 45 5 Sept. 1863
Woo Kwong Tye	Kong Kim	Keringkim (Kong Kong & Tukang)?	Tan Hiok Nee	SKMK – I No. 45 5 Sept. 1863

SSD		JAR		
Kangchu	*River*	*River*	*Kongsi*	*Source*
Tan Chin Peow	Booloo	Buloh Besar	Tan Ah Ji Tan Ann (k)	SKMK – I No. 9 29 Nov. 1845
Lee Kik Soon	Massai	Masai	*Lee Kek Soon* (k) Lee Kek Lee Lee Kiok Lee Lee Kiok Loi Goh Joon Hue	SKMK – I No. 76 18 June 1866
Gok Soon	Long Ko	Longkor	*Lee Gek Soon* Lee Cheo Guan	SKMK – I No. 39 24 July 1863 also SJB No. 33 27 May 1875
Ting Meah Pees	Long Chew	Lunchu? (& Paksi)	Chin Ah Lin Kee Nga Ah Tin Ah Yoo Ah Ji	SKMK – I No. 6 27 Oct. 1845
Ang Yeong Tuen	Railway	Sekudai? (right bank, down-stream)	*Tan Hiok Nee?	SJB No. 9 22 April 1871 & SJB No. 15 28 April 1873
Tan Ah Tong	Railway	Sekudai, ulu	*Tan Ah Tong*	SKMK – I No. 138 23 Oct. 1873
Ang Ah Ah	Secoodai	Sekudai	*Seah Tee Heng?	SKMK – I No. 99 19 Oct. 1873
Ang Eye Yew	Ding Uloo	Danga?	Ng Ah Koo Ng Chai Chang	SKMK – I No. 61 13 July 1864
Ang Ting Kak	Ding Elier	Danga?	Ng Ah Koo Ng Chai Chang	SKMK – I No. 61 13 July 1864
Bu Koh Kian Wan	Malayu Elier	Melayu	Ah Meng	SKMK – I No .28 26 Sept. 1860
Chia Apoo Tik	Malayu Uloo	Melayu	?	
Chia Tchew Chee	Pandas	Pendas	Baa Li Baa Ning	SKMK – I No. 7 26 April 1846
Ting Song Lie	Plantong	Pelentong (Tiram & Pandan)	Lim Ah Soi	SKMK – I No. 93 1 July 1871
Chew Keng	Pandan	Pandan (Tiram & Pelentong)	Lim Ah Soi	SKMK – I No. 93 1 July 1871
Tan My Ah Cha	Tubrow	Tebrau	Shaik Abdul Rahman bin Mohd. Al-Khatib Shaik Mobd. bin Ali Al-Tawi (Seah Yau Sah) *pajak*	SJB No. 20 10 August 1873 & SPBS No. 2 25 August 1873
Tan Chong What	Singquan	Sengkuang	Tio Nguan Lee	SKMK – I No. 52 29 April 1864

SSD		JAR		
Kangchu	*River*	*River*	*Kongsi*	*Source*
Lue Bon Hen	Nibong	Nibong	*Lau Boo Nian* Lau Boo Tong (k)	SKMK – I No. 92 15 May 1871
Tan Wee Chen	Railway	Sekudai? (left bank, downstream)	*Tan Hiok Nee?	SJB No. 1 11 March 1867 & SJB No. 15 28 April 1873
Seah Ling Tchi	Railway	Sekudai	*Seah Ling Chai*	(ref) SKMK – I No. 138 23 Oct 1873
Teow Ah Him	Poah	Tiram Duku (Po' Besar & Po' Kechil)	Teo Ah Hock *Teo Ah Hin* Tan Soon Heng	SKMK – I No. 13 13 July 1845? SJB No. 10 5 July 1871
Tan Ah Kim	Teerum Dookoo	Tiram Duku (Po' Besar & Po' Kechil)	Teo Ah Hock Teo Ah Hin Tan Soon Heng	SKMK – I No. 13 13 July 1845? SJB No. 10 5 July 1871
Bu Koh Leoman	Glam Pata	Tajun Galang Patah	Bu Koh Ah Kow Bu Koh Ah Noi Bu Koh Boo Hin	SKMK – I No. 12 11 April 1853
Ang Yong Nooa	Pulai	Pulai *ulu*	Ng Too Beng (k)	SKMK – I No. 19 21 Oct. 1853
Tchew Ming Key	Tcho	Choh	Teng Heng Kee	SKMK – I No. 14 18 April 1853
Tan Nootee	Pontean Kechil	Pontian Kechil	Tan Moo Kiang *Tan Too Nee*?	SKMK – I No. 75 21 May 1866
Teow Low Say	Ayer Etam	Pontian Besar (Ayer Hitam)	Chin Ah Chit Tan Koi Soon	SKMK – I No. 81 22 August 1866
Tching Tchan What	Pontean Besar	Pontian Besar	Tan Yong Sek Chan Kong Chu Tiong Kan Chang Chau Ah Hock Lau Koo Tung	SKMK – I No. 88 25 August 1866
Tan Noong Keai	Bunoot	Benut	*Tan Nong Kia*	SKMK – I No. 96 15 April 1873
Low Keah Tyng Wat	Kerim Chop	Kerichap	Lau Kang Foo (k) Lau Ah Teng	SKMK – I No. 71 29 April 1864
Low Assat	Ayam	Ayam (Buloh)	*Lau Ah Sad* (k) Lau Ah Kee Lau Tan Mui	SKMK – I No. 72 29 April 1864
Law Ah Team	Sooloo	Suloh	*Lau Ah Tiam* (k) Lau Ah Wee Lau Ah Ji Lau Ah Koo	SKMK – I No. 70 29 April 1864

*This association of these three holdings may be mixed up. Tan Hiok Nee had two holdings on Sekudai; Seah Tee Heng had one. From the available information there is no way of telling which of the three Railway *kangkar* they held.

SSD		*JAR*		
Kangchu	*River*	*River*	*Kongsi*	*Source*
Low Eye Ow	Koris	Kuris	*Lau Kit Ngo* (k)? Lau Ah Teng Lau Ah Kun Lau Lee Poh Ali bin Abdul Majid	SKMK – I No. 67 6 Nov. 1865
Bu Koh Tchew Kang	Batu Pahat	Rengit (Batu Pahat)	Bu Koh Ki Ki (k) Bu Koh Ah Tiam Lim Ah Sin	SKMK – I No. 102 7 Jan. 1874
Teu Ah Lim	Batu Pahat	Batu Pahat (Simpang-kiri)	*Tio Ah Lui* (k)? Tio Ah Sud Tio Ah Liok Tio Ah Heng Tio Ah Goo Tio Ah Cheng Ungku Abdul Rahman	SKMK – I No. 65 29 March 1865
Tan Ah Bit	Railway	?		
Yeo Kik Keo	Tubrow Rd.	?		
Lim Ah Sway	Teerum Rd.	Tiram *ulu*	*Lim Ah Swee* Lim Chai Wong	SJB Nos. 24 & 25 23 April 1874 SJB No. 26 28 April 1874

Glossary

Unless otherwise stated, all words defined below are Malay. Chinese terms are designated by "Ch.". Where possible the Chinese characters have also been given. All Chinese terms are romanized according to their pronunciation in the Teochew dialect.

amok	To attack fiercely in battle; to run "amuck", a culturally conditioned form of insanity common among Malays whereby the disturbed individual arms himself and then goes out and kills, indiscriminately, every person that he meets until he himself is killed.
atap	Roofing, thatch, usually made from the fronds of the nipa palm.
arak	Whisky, any distilled alcoholic drink.
bahagian	A division, a share.
bangsal	Lit. shed, booth, coolie lines; also a plantation.
batin	A pagan proto-Malay headman.
beli	Buy, Purchase. (*surat jual-beli* — bill of sale)
bendahara	Chief minister, commander-in-chief.
bentara	Court herald, Johor government minister.
benua	Continent, land. (*orang benua* — land people)
besar	Big, great. (*orang besar* — "big man" magnate, notable)
chandu	Opium paste, prepared for smoking.

chap	Trade mark, seal.
chukang	Ch. 厝港 — the name of a *kangkar*, or river-mouth settlement, usually prefixed by a surname, such as 陈厝港, Tan Chukang — peculiar to the pepper and gambier agriculture of Singapore, Johor, and Riau.
daing	Bugis title of nobility. (also *daeng*)
dalam	Inside, in, interior.
dato'	Grandfather, grandsire; Malay title of distinction.
gadai	Mortgage, pawn. (*pajak gadai* — pawnshop)
getah	Sap, latex, rubber. (*getah taban* — gutta-percha or *Blanco palaquim*)
gunong	Mountain.
hikayat	History, story.
hilir	Down-river
hui	Ch. 会 — any kind of social organization or assembly. Also spelt "hue", "hooee", etc. Often used to refer to branches of the Chinese Triad, or secret societies, e.g. 义兴会 Ngee Heng Hui, or 天地会 Tiandihui, Heaven and Earth Society.
hulu	Upriver. Var. of *ulu.*
hutang	Debt, owing, due.
jawi	Arabic script; Malay written in Arabic script.
jati	Pure, native-born.
jennang	Assistant to a *batin*, proto-Malay headman.
jual	Sell. (*surat jual-beli* — bill of sale)
judi	Gambling, *pajak judi*, gambling concession.
kampong	Village, Malay settlement.
kang	Ch. 港 — port or river mouth.
Kangchu	Ch. 港主 — Chinese river headman. Peculiar to the pepper and gambier agriculture of Singapore, Johor, and Riau in the nineteenth century.
kangkar	Ch. 港脚 — Lit. "river foot", the settlement of the Kangchu, usually located at the foot of the river e.g. Kangkar Tebrau. See *chukang.*
kanun	Law code.
kaya	Rich, wealthy. (*orang kaya* — magnate, notable, minor official)
keraja'an	The government.
Kongkek	Ch. 公局 — title of the Chinese Pepper and Gambier Society of Singapore in the nineteenth century. It was said to function as a kind of Chamber of Commerce. It was an organization of

	pepper and gambier traders which fixed weights and measures, settled disputes, fixed prices, and governed economic relations within the agricultural system.
Kongsi	Ch. 公司 — here the term generally means a business partnership or company, organized to capitalize the revenue farms of the Kangchu. In the nineteenth century the word was used to describe a wide range of communal efforts (usually economic, but not always) such as Chinese secret societies, groups of miners, the long row-houses inhabited by any kind of labourers, etc. Today the word means any kind of small business.
kuala	River mouth, confluence, swamp.
laksamana	Admiral, eighteenth-century Malay court official.
laut	The sea. (*orang laut*, sea nomads, sea gypsies, sea peoples)
luar	Outside, exterior.
menaban	(*v*) To gather *getah taban* or gutta-percha.
muda	Young, minor. (*raja muda*, heir apparent)
negeri	Country, state, nation.
orang	Man, people, human being.
padang	Open field used for a public meeting-place, markets, fairs, and sports.
pajak	Monopoly. (*surat pajak*, monopoly lease)
pegangan	Holding, feudal territory.
penggawa	Government official, clerk.
pengulu	Headman of a small district or of a river.
perahu	Malay canoe, usually about twenty feet long and capable of carrying seven or eight men. There were also larger versions of this vessel used for warfare and raiding. These had a burden of about a thousand pounds, and were capable of carrying twenty men and two or three small cannons.
peranakan	A person who has been locally born. Here, this generally refers to Bugis who had been born at Riau and distinguishes them from the native Bugis, or *jati*, and from the Malays. Now generally used to refer to locally-born Chinese and their hybrid culture.
perompak	Pirate, sea rover, raider.
pulau	Island.
pukat	Chinese junk or coasting vessel, *sampan pukat*.
ra'ayat	The people, the common people, the masses. (*orang ra'ayat* — the subject class; *ra'ayat laut* — sea peoples)

sejarah	History, story.
selat	Strait.
shahbandar	Harbour master.
suku	Clan or tribe of proto-Malay people.
sungai	River.
surat	Letter or official document. (*surat sungai* — "river document", the document given by the ruler of Johor to the Chinese Kangchu which authorized him to open pepper and gambier plantations within a given watershed)
taban	A tree whose sap yields gutta-percha.
tanah	Land, earth, country. (*tanah Melayu* — land of the Malays)
tanjong	A peninsula or any piece of land surrounded by water on three sides. It is also applied to the land enclosed by a bend in a river or an outcropping of a hill.
taukeh	Ch. 头家 — Chinese merchant, trader financier, capitalist, boss.
tawarikh	History.
temenggong	Police chief, port official, Malay minister in charge of defence and markets.
tope	Siamese or Vietnamese junk or trading vessel.
tuah	Old, aged — of people. (*orang tuah* — old man)
tuan	Gentleman, lord; polite form of address to a superior.
tun	Malay prince.
tungku	Malay prince of royal blood. Also *ungku.*
ulu	Up-river or up-country. Also *hulu.*
ungku	Malay prince of royal blood. Var. of *tungku.*
wan	Malay princely title.
yamtuan	Var. of *yang di-pertuan.*
yang di-pertuan	Lit. "he who is made lord", official title of a ruler or Sultan (*yang di-pertuan besar — Sultan; yang di-pertuan muda —* heir-apparent). In eighteenth-century Riau, this title was held by the Bugis prime minister.

Bibliography

Abdullah bin Abdul Kadir. *The Hikayat Abdullah.* Translated by A. H. Hill, Oxford, 1970.

Abdullah bin Ayub. "The Johore Succession Controversy 1850–1878". Academic Exercise, University of Malaya, Singapore, 1953.

Ali Haji ibn Ahmad, R. *The Precious Gift (Tuhfat al-Nafis).* Kuala Lumpur, Oxford University Press, 1982.

Andaya, B. W. *To Live as Brothers: Southeast Sumatra in the Seventeenth and Eighteenth Centuries.* Honolulu, HI, University of Hawaii Press, 1993.

Andaya, Leonard Y. *The Kingdom of Johor 1641–1728.* Oxford, Kuala Lumpur, 1975.

______. "Raja Kechil and the Minangkabau Conquest of Johor in 1718". *JMBRAS*, v. 45, pt. 2 (1972), pp. 51–75.

Anderson, John. *Mission to the East Coast of Sumatra in 1823.* Oxford, 1971. First published, London, 1826.

______. *Political and Commercial Considerations Relative to the Malayan Peninsula and the British Settlements in the Straits of Malacca.* Reprinted as *JMBRAS*, v. 35, pt. 4 (December 1962), pp. 1–224. First published, Prince of Wales Island, 1824.

Balestier, J. "A View of the State of Agriculture in the British Possessions in the Straits of Malacca". *JIA*, v. 2, no. 3 (March 1848), pp. 139–50.

Barnard, T. *Multiple Centers of Authority: Society and Environment in Siak and Eastern Sumatra, 1674-1827.* Lieden, KITVL Press, 2003.

Bartley, W. "Population of Singapore in 1819". *JMBRAS*, v. 11, pt. 2 (1933), pp. 177–79.

Bassett, D. K. "British Commercial and Strategic Interest in the Malay Peninsula During the Late Eighteenth Century." In *Malayan and Indonesian Studies: Essays Presented to Sir Richard Winstedt on His Eight-fifth Birthday*, ed. John Bastin and R. Roolvink. Oxford, 1964, pp. 122–40.

Bastin, John. "Raffles and British Policy in the Indian Archipelago". *JMBRAS*, v. 27, pt. 1 (May 1954), pp. 84–119.

———. *Essays on Indonesian and Malayan History*. Singapore, 1965.

———, and Robin W. Winks, eds. *Malaysia: Selected Historical Sources*. Kuala Lumpur, 1966.

Begbie, P. J. *The Malayan Peninsula*. Kuala Lumpur, Oxford University Press, 1967.

Blussé, L. *Strange Company: Chinese Settlers, Mestizo Women and the Dutch in VOC Batavia*. Dordrecht, Holland; Providence, RI, Floris Publications, 1988.

Blythe, Wilfred L. "Historical Sketch of Chinese Labour in Malaya". *JMBRAS*, v. 20, pt. 1 (1947), pp. 64–113.

———. *The Impact of Chinese Secret Societies on Malaya: A Historical Study*. Oxford, 1969.

Boden-Kloss, C. "Notes on a Cruise in the South China Sea". *JSBRAS*, no. 41 (January 1904), pp. 53–80.

Bonney, Rollins. *Kedah 1771–1821: The Search for Security and Independence*. Kuala Lumpur, 1971.

Braddell, Roland St. J.; Brooke, Gilbert E.; and Makepeace, Walter. *One Hundred Years of Singapore*, Two volumes. London, 1921.

Braddell, T. "Notes of a Trip to the Interior from Malacca". *JIA*, v. 7 (1853), pp. 73–104.

Brown, C. C., trans. *Sejarah Melayu*. [Malay Annals] Kuala Lumpur, 1970. First published as *JMBRAS*, v. 25, pts. 2 and 3 (October 1952), pp. 1–276.

Bruijn-Kops, G. F. de. "Schets van den Riouw Archipel". *Natuurkindig Tijdschrif voor Nederlandisch Indie*, v. 4. New Series, v. 1 (1853), pp. 41–90.

———. "Sketch of the Rhio-Lingga Archipelago". Translated. *JIA*, v. 8 (1854), pp. 386–402; v. 9 (1855), pp. 96–108.

Buckley, Charles B. *An Anecdotal History of Old Times in Singapore*. Reprinted, Singapore, 1969. First published, Singapore, 1902.

Burkhill, I. H. A *Dictionary of the Economic Products of the Malay Peninsula*, Two volumes. London, 1935.

Butcher, J. G. and H. Dick. *The Rise and Fall of Revenue Farming: Business Elites and the Emergence of the Modern State in Southeast Asia*. New York, N.Y., St. Martin's Press, 1993.

Buyong bin Adil, Haji. *Sejarah Johor*. Kuala Lumpur, 1971.

Caddy, Florence. *To Siam and Malaya in the Duke of Sutherland's Yacht*, "*Sans Peur*". London, 1889.

Cameron, John. *Our Tropical Possessions in Malayan India*. Kuala Lumpur, 1965. First published, London, 1865.

Campbell, P. C. *Chinese Coolie Emigration to Countries within the British Empire*. London, 1923.

Cavenagh, Orfeur. *Reminiscences of an Indian Official.* London, 1884.

Cheeseman, H. R., comp. *Bibliography of Malaya Being A Classified List of Books Wholly or Partly in English Relating to the Federation of Malaya and Singapore.* London, 1959.

Chiang Hai-ding. "Sino-British Mercantile Relations". In *Studies in The Social History of China and Southeast Asia: Essays in Memory of Victor Purcell.* Cambridge, 1970, pp. 247–66.

Ch'in Ting Ta Ch'ing Hui Tien Shih Li (钦定大清会典事例). 1898 Edition, Taiwan, 1963. *Chuan* 503 and 504.

Comber, Leon F. *Chinese Secret Societies in Malaya.* New York, 1959.

Coope, A. E. "The Kangchu System in Johore". *JMBRAS*, v. 14, pt. 3 (1936), pp. 247–63.

Cortesao, A. *The Suma Oriental of Tome Pires.* London, 1944.

Cowan, C. D., ed. "Early Penang and the Rise of Singapore, 1805–32: A Series of Documents from the Manuscript Records of the East India Company". *JMBRAS*, v. 23, pt. 2 (March 1950), pp. 1–210.

_______. *Nineteenth Century Malaya: The Origins of British Political Control.* London, 1961.

Cowgill, J. V. "Chinese Place Names in Johore". *JMBRAS*, v. 2, pt. 3 (1924), pp. 221–51.

Crawfurd, John. "The Agriculture of Singapore". *JIA*, v. 3 (1849), pp. 508–11.

Cushman, Jennifer Wayne. "Fields from the Sea: Chinese Junk Trade with Siam during the Late Eighteenth and Early Nineteenth Centuries". Ph.D. Thesis, Cornell University, Ithaca, N.Y., 1975.

_______. *Family and State: The Formation of a Sino-Thai Tin-mining Dynasty, 1797–1932.* Singapore, Oxford University Press, 1991.

Dalton, H. G. "A Visit to Some Islands off the East Coast of Johore and Pahang". *JMBRAS*, v. 6 (August 1928), pp. 78–96.

Darby, H. C. "The Medieval Sea-State". *Scottish Geographical Magazine*, v. 48 (1932), pp. 136–49.

Descours-Gatin, C. *Quand L'Opium Financait La Colonisation en Indochine: L'elaboration de la regie generale de l'opium (1860–1914).* Paris, Editions L'Hartmann (Ouvrage publie avec le concours du Centre National des Lettres), 1992.

Earl, George Windsor. *The Eastern Seas.* Oxford, 1971. First published, London. 1837.

Elcum, J. *Johore in 1911*, Johor Annual Report. Johor Baharu, 1912.

Emerson, Rupert. *Malaysia: A Study in Direct and Indirect Rule.* New York, 1937. Reprinted, Kuala Lumpur, 1964.

Evans, Ivor H. N. *Papers on the Ethnology and Archaeology of the Malay Peninsula.* Cambridge, 1927.

Feldwick W., ed. *Present Day Impressions of the Far East Prominent and Progressive Chinese at Home and Abroad.* London, 1917.

_______, ed. and W. H. Morton, comp. *Ports and Cities of the World: New Zealand, Australia, Nederlands East Indies, Malaya, Siam, Burma.* London, 1924.

Firmstone, H. W. "Chinese Names of Streets and Places in Singapore and the Malay Peninsula". *JSBRAS*, no. 42 (February 1905), pp. 54–208.

Fitzgerald, C. P. *The Southern Expansion of the Chinese People. "Southern Fields and Southern Ocean"*. London, 1927.

Forrest, T. *Voyage to New Guinea.* London, 1792.

Freedman, Maurice. "Immigrants and Associations in Nineteenth Century Singapore". *Comparative Studies in Society and History*, v. 3, no. 1 (1960), pp. 24–48.

———. "Overseas Chinese Associations: A Comment". *Comparative Studies in Society and History*, v. 3, no. 1 (1960), pp. 478–80.

Furber, H. *John Company at Work.* Cambridge, Massachusetts, 1948.

Gage, A. T., ed. and Burkhill, I. H. "William Jack's Letters to Nathaniel Wallich 1819–1821". *JSBRAS*, no. 72 (May 1916), pp. 147–268.

Gerini, G. E. "Historical Retrospect on Junkceylon Island". *JSS*, v. 2, pt. 2 (December 1905), pp. 1–148.

Gibson-Hill, C. A. "The Orang Laut of the Singapore River and the Sampan Panjang". *JMBRAS*, v. 25, no. 1 (August 1952), pp. 161–74.

———. "Singapore: Notes on the History of the Old Strait, 1580–1850". *JMBRAS*, v. 27, pt. 1 (May 1954), pp. 163–214.

———. "Singapore Old Strait and New Harbour". *Memoirs of the Raffles Museum*, no. 3 (December 1956), pp. 10–115.

Goh Keat Seng. "Piracy in the Straits of Malacca 1867–1877". Academic Exercise, University of Malaya, Singapore, 1959–1960.

Gray, C. S. "Johore, 1910–1941, Studies in the Colonial Process". New Haven, Department of History, Yale University, 1978.

Gullick, J. M. "The Negri Sembilan Economy of the 1890's." *JMBRAS*, v. 24, pt. 1 (February 1951), pp. 38–55.

———. "The War with Yamtuan Antah". *JMBRAS*, v. 27, pt. 1 (May 1954), pp. 1–23.

———. *Malaya.* Second Edition, London, 1964.

———. *Indigenous Political Systems of Western Malaya.* London, 1958. Reprinted in London School of Economics Monographs on Social Anthropology, no. 17, 1965.

———. *Malay Society in the Late Nineteenth Century: The Beginnings of Change.* Singapore and New York, Oxford University Press, 1989.

Harrison, Brian, trans. "Trade in the Straits of Malacca in 1785, Memorandum by P. G. De Bruijn, Governor of Malacca". *JMBRAS*, v. 26, pt. 1 (July 1953), pp. 56–62.

Heidhues, M. S. "Company Island: A Note on the History of Belitung". *Indonesia*, v. 51 (April 1991), pp. 1–20.

———. "The First Two Sultans of Pontianak". *Archipel,* 56 (1998), pp. 273–94.

"Hikayat Johor Serta Pahang", undated typescript, Johor Archives.

Hill, Ron D. "Materials for Historical Geography and the Economic History of Southeast Asia in Nineteenth Century Malayan Newspapers". Unpublished Manuscript, University of Singapore, 1969.

Hill, Thomas Heslop. *Report on Johore.* Pamphlet Singapore, 1879.

———. "Report on Johore". Extracts published in *SDT*, 6, 9, 23, and 24 May 1879.

Hooi, Christopher Liang-yin. "Piracy and Its Suppression in Malayan Waters, 1800–1867". Academic Exercise, University of Malaya, Singapore, 1955.

H., H. T. "Landing of Raffles in Singapore by an Eye-Witness". *JSBRAS*, no. 10 (1882), pp. 285–86.

Horsfield, Thomas. "Report on the Island of Bangka". *JIA,* 1 and 2 (1848), pp. 229–336, 373–427, 705–25, 779–824.

Irwin, Graham W. "Nineteenth Century Borneo". *Verhandelingen van het Koninklijk Institut voor Taal- Land-en Volkenkunde*, v. 15 (1955), pp. 24–29.

———. "The Dutch and the Tin Trade of Malaya in the Seventeenth Century". In *Studies in the Social History of China and South East Asia*, ed. Jerome Ch'en and Nicholas Tarling. Cambridge, 1970, pp. 267–88.

Ismail Hussein. "Hikayat Negri Johor, Satu Penyeleggaraan Teks". M.A. Thesis, University of Malaya, 1962.

Jackson, James C. "Chinese Agricultural Pioneering in Singapore and Johore, 1800–1917". *JMBRAS*, v. 88, pt. 1 (1965), pp. 77–105.

———. *Planters and Speculators: Chinese and European Agricultural Enterprise in Malaya 1786–1921*. Kuala Lumpur, 1968.

———. "Mining in 18th Century Bangka: The Pre-European Exploitation of a 'Tin Island'." *Pacific Viewpoint*, 10, no. 2 (1969), pp. 28–54.

———. *Chinese in the West Borneo Goldfields: A Study in Cultural Geography.* Hull, University of Hull, 1970.

The State of Johore Malaya, an Illustrated Outline of Johore's History, Government, Industries and People. Singapore, 1939.

Johore Baharu Sa-ratus Tahun. Johor Baharu, 1955.

Johore, *Undang² Tubohan Kerajaʼan Johor.* Constitution of Johor, Johor Baharu, 1895.

———. "Supplement to the Constitution of the State of Johore and Standing Rules and Regulations of the Council of the State of Johore". Johor Baharu, 1912.

Kanayson, A. "The Newspapers of Singapore 1824–1914". *JSSS*, v. 18, pts. 1 and 2 (1962–63), pp. 31–95.

Kathirithamby-Wells, J. and J. Villiers, eds. *The Southeast Asian Port and Polity: Rise and Demise.* Singapore, Singapore University Press, 1990.

Kirby, S. W. "Johore in 1926". *Geographical Journal*, v. 71 (March 1928), pp. 240–60.

Koh Teck Chong. "The Emergency in Johore 1948–1959". B.A. Thesis, University of Malaya, Singapore, 1960.

Kirby, J. A. "The Straits Settlements and the Malay Peninsula". *JSBRAS,* no. 28 (1895), pp. 19–51.

Lake, H. W. and Kelsall, H. J. "A Journey on the Sembrong River". *JSBRAS*, no. 26 (January 1894), pp. 1–25.

———. "Johore". *Geographic Journal*, v. 3 (1894), pp. 281–302.

Le Failler, P. "Le mouvement international anti-opium et l'Indochine, 1906–1940." *History.* Provence, Université de Provence, 1993.

Lee, K. Y. *The Singapore Story: Memoirs of Lee Kuan Yew*. Singapore and New York, Prentice Hall, 1998.
Lee Poh Ping. "Chinese Society in Nineteenth and Early Twentieth Century Singapore: A Socioeonomic Analysis". Ph.D. Thesis, Cornell University, Ithaca, N.Y., 1974.
Lees, F. "Chinese Settlement in the Kulai Sub-district of Johore, Malaysia". In *Geographers and the Tropics: Liverpool Essays*, ed. Robert W. Steed and R. Mansell Prothero. London, 1964, pp. 277–96.
Lewis, D. "The Dutch East India Company and the Straits of Malacca 1700–1784: Trade and Politics in the Eighteenth Century". Ph.D. Thesis, Australian National University, Canberra, 1970.
———. "The Growth of the Country Trade to the Straits of Malacca 1760–1777". *JMBRAS*, v. 43, pt. 2 (1970), pp. 114–30.
———. "The Last Malay Raja Muda of Johor". *JSEAS*, XIII, pt. 2 (September 1982), pp. 221–35.
———. *Jan Compagnie in the Straits of Malacca, 1641–1795*. Athens, Ohio, Ohio University Center for International Studies, 1995.
Lim, Lena U-wen (Cheng). "British Opium Policy in the Straits Settlements 1867–1910". Academic Exercise, University of Malaya, Singapore, 1960.
Linehan, W. *A History of Pahang*. Kuala Lumpur, 1973. First published as *JMBRAS*, v. 14, pt. 2 (May 1936).
Little, R. "On the Habitual Use of Opium in Singapore". *JIA*, v. 2 (1848), pp. 1–79.
Logan, J. R. "Ethnology of the Johore Archipelago". *JIA*, v. 1 (1847), pp. 336–40.
———. "The Orang Binua of Johore". *JIA*, v. 1 (1847), pp. 242–93.
———. "The Orang Sletar of the Rivers and Creeks of the Old Strait and Estuary of the Johore". *JIA*, v. 1 (1848), pp. 302–4.
———. "Range of the Gutta Taban Collectors, and Present Amount of Imports into Singapore". *JIA*, v. 2 (1848), pp. 529–33.
———. "Notices of European Intercourse with Borneo Prior to the Establishment of Singapore in 1819". *JIA*, v. 2 (1848), pp. 498–512.
———. "Notices of Chinese Intercourse with Borneo Proper Prior to the Establishment of Singapore 1819". *JIA*, v. 2 (1848), pp. 611–16.
———. "Borneo". *JIA*, v. 2 (1848), pp. 495–97.
———. "*Memoirs of Malays: Che Saliman's Narration*". *JIA*, v. 2 (1848), pp. 353–63.
———. "Agriculture in Singapore". *JIA*, v. 3 (1849).
———. "The Piracy and Slave Trade of the Indian Archipelago". *JIA*, v. 3 (1849), pp. 582–88, 629, 634; v. 4 (1850), pp. 45–52, 144, 162, 400–10: v. 5 (1851), pp. 374–82.
———. "The Sultan of Johore". *JIA*, v. 2, New Series (1857), pp. 46–67.
———. "Journal of an Excursion from Singapore to Malacca and Pinang". *Miscellaneous Papers, Relating to Indo-China and the Indian Archipelago*, Second Series, v. 1 (1887), pp. 1–20.
Low, James. *The British Settlement of Penang*. Oxford, 1972. First published, Penang, 1836.

Low Siew Chek. "Gambier-and-Pepper Planting in Singapore 1819–1860". B.A. Thesis, University of Malaya, Singapore, 1955.

MacGowan, D. J. "Note on Maritime Malays". *JIA*, v. 4, (1850), pp. 687–91.

MacMillan, Allister, comp. and ed. *Seaports of the Far East: Historical and Descriptive, Commercial and Industrial Facts, Figures, and Resources.* London, 1923.

Makepeace, Walter; Braddell, R. St. J.; and Brooke, G. E. *One Hundred Years of Singapore,* Two volumes. London, 1921.

Marriot, H. trans. and ed. "A Fragment of the History of Trengganu and Kelantan". *JSBRAS*, no. 72 (May 1916), pp. 3–23.

Matheson, Virginia. "Mahmud, Sultan of Riau and Lingga (1823–1864)". *Indonesia*, no. 13 (April 1972), pp. 119–46.

______. "The Tufhat Al-Nafis: Structure and Sources". *Bijd*, 127, 3 (1971), pp. 375–92.

Maxwell, W. E. "Raja Haji". *JSBRAS*, no. 22 (December 1890), pp. 173–224.

______. and Gibson, W. S. *Treaties and Engagements Affecting the Malay States and Borneo*. London, 1924.

Meilink-Roelofsz, M. A. P. *Asian Trade and European Influence in the Indoneisan Archipelago Between 1500 and About 1630.* The Hague, 1962.

Meldrum, James. "The Johore Forests, Some Cursory Notes on Them". *SFP*, 25 April 1885, pp. 227–29.

Middlebrook, S. M. "Pulai: An Early Chinese Settlement in Kelantan". *JMBRAS*, v. 11 (1933), pp. 151–56.

Milburne, William. *Oriental Commerce; Containing a geographical description of the principal places in the East Indies, China and Japan, with their produce, manufactures, and trade, including the coasting or country trade from port to port, also the rise and progress of the various European nations with the Eastern world, particularly that of the English East India Company from the discovery of the passage round the Cape of Good Hope to the present period with an account of the Company's Establishments, Revenues, Debts. Assets, etc. at home and abroad,* Two volumes. London, 1813.

Miller, H. Eric. "Extracts from the Letters of Col. Nahuijs". *JMBRAS*, v. 19, pt. 2 (October 1941), pp. 169–209.

Mills, L. A. *British Malaya 1824–1867*. Kuala Lumpur, 1966. First published as *JMBRAS*, v. 3, pt. 2 (1925).

Milner, A. C. *Kerajaan: Malay Political Culture on the Eve of Colonial Rule.* Tuscon, University of Arizona Press, 1982.

______. *The Invention of Politics in Colonial Malaya: Contesting Nationalism and the Expansion of the Public Sphere.* Cambridge, Cambridge University Press, 1995.

Mohamad Ibrahim, Munshi. *The Voyages of Mohamed Ibrahim Munshi.* Trans. with an Introduction by Amin Sweeney and Nigel Phillips. Kuala Lumpur and New York, Oxford University Press, 1975.

Mohamad Said bin Haji Sulaiman, Major Dato Haji. *Hikayat Johor dan Tawarikh Al-Marhum Sultan Abu Bakar Johor.* Johor Baharu, 1950.

———. *Hikayat Johor, Yang Kedua, Tawarikh Yang Maha Mulia Ibrahim, Sultan Johor, dari Pemulahan hingga Kedatangan Jepun, 1941*. Johor Baharu, 1951.

Mohamad bin Haji Ilyas, comp. *Tawarikh Dato Bentara Luar Johor, Mohamad Salleh bin Perang*. Johor Baharu, 1928.

Moor, J. H. *Notices of the Indian Archipelago and Adjacent Countries*. Singapore, 1837.

Morse, Hosea Ballou. *The Chronicles of the East India Company Trading to China 1635–1834*, Four volumes. London, 1966.

Muhammad bin Anas. "Geographic Notes to the Tufhat Al-Nafis or Malay History of Riau and Johor". B.A. Thesis, University of Malaya, Singapore, 1958.

Munir bin Ali, ed. *Tufhat Al-Nafis, Al-Marhum Raja Ali-Haji Riau*. Singapore, 1965.

"Dato Meldrum". *The Straits Chinese Magazine*, v. 8 (1904), pp. 54–58.

Netscher, E. "Beschrijving van een Gedeelte der Residentie Riau". *Tijdschrift voor Indische Taal-, Land- en Volkenkunde*, v. 2 (1854), pp. 108–270.

Newbold, T. J. *Political and Statistical Account of the British Settlements in the Straits of Malacca*, Two volumes. Oxford in Asia Historical Reprints, Oxford 1971. First published, London, 1839.

Ng Soo Ching, P. "The Character and Career of Mr. William H. M. Read". B.A. Thesis, University of Malaya, Singapore, 1958.

Onn bin Ja'afar. *Selamat Johor*. Singapore, 1935.

Overbeck, H. "Silsilah Melayu dan Bugis dan Sakalian Raja^2-nya". *JMBRAS*, v. 4, pt. 3 (1926), pp. 339–81.

Oxley, Thomas. "Gutta Percha". *JIA*, v. 1 (1847), pp. 22–29.

Pan, Hsing Nung. *The Teochews in Malaya* (潘百星晨，马来亚潮侨通金监). Singapore, 1950.

Papendrecht, P. C. Hoyck Van. "Some Old Private Letters from the Cape, Batavia and Malaya". *JMBRAS*, v. 2, pt. 1 (1924), pp. 9–24.

Parkinson, C. Northcote. *British Intervention in Malaya, 1867–1877*. Singapore, 1960.

Pickering, W. A. "Chinese Secret Societies". *JSBRAS*, no. 1 (July 1879), pp. 63–84.

Purcell, Victor. *The Chinese in Malaya*. London, 1948.

———. *The Chinese in South-East Asia*. London, 1951.

———. *The Chinese in Modern Malaya*. Background to Malaya Series, no. 9. Singapore, 1960.

Raffles, Sophia. *Memoirs of the Life and Public Services of Sir Thomas Stamford Raffles*. London, 1830.

Raffles, Thomas Stamford. *History of Java*, Three volumes. London, 1817, 1830.

Read, W. H. *Play and Politics: Reminiscences of Malaya by an Old Resident*. London, 1901.

———. "The Landing of Raffles at Singapore". *JSBRAS*, no. 12 (1883), pp. 282–83.

Ridley, H. N. "The Orang Laut of Singapore". *JSBRAS*, no. 41 (January 1904), pp. 129–30.

Rush, J. R. *Opium to Java: Revenue Farming and Chinese Enterprise in Colonial Indonesia, 1800–1910*. Ithaca, New York, Cornell University Press, 1990.

Rutter, Owen. *The Pirate Wind: Tales of the Sea Robbers*. London, 1930.

St. John, Horace. *The Indian Archipelago*, Two volumes. London, 1853. Reprinted by Heppenheim/Bergstrasse, Western Germany, 1969.

Sadka, Emily. *The Protected Malay States 1874–1895*. Kuala Lumpur, 1968.

Seah Eu Chin. "The Chinese of Singapore". *JIA*, v. 2 (1848), pp. 283–90.

______. "Notes on the Chinese in the Straits". *JIA*, v. 9 (1855), pp. 120–4.

Shaharil Talib. *After Its Own Image: The Trengganu Experience, 1881–1941*. Singapore, Oxford & New York, Oxford University Press, 1984.

Sharom Ahmat. "The Structure of the Economy of Kedah 1879–1905". *JMBRAS*, v. 43, pt. 2 (1970), pp. 1–24.

Sinclair, Keith. "Hobson and Lenin in Johore: Colonial Office Policy towards British Concessionaires and Investors 1878–1907". *Modern Asian Studies*, v. 1. no. 4 (1967), pp. 335–52.

Singapore and Straits Directory (various titles), *SSD* for 1870; 1874, "Johore", pp. 1–8; 1883, "Johore Directory", pp. 123–31; 1884, "Johore Directory", pp. 127–36; 1885, "Johore Directory", pp. 165–77; 1890, "Johore Directory", pp. 293–308; 1895, "Johore", pp. 243–55.

Skeat, Walter William and Blagden, Charles Otto. *Pagan Races of the Malay Peninsula*. London, 1906.

Skinner, G. William. *Chinese Society in Thailand: An Analytical History*. Ithaca, 1957.

Smyth, H. Warington. *Mast and Sail in Europe and Asia*. London, 1906.

Song Ong Siang. *One hundred Years' History of the Chinese in Singapore*. Singapore, 1967. First printed, Singapore, 1923.

Sopher, David E. *The Sea Nomads: A Study Based on the Literature of the Maritime Boat People of Southeast Asia*. Memoirs of the National Museum, no. 5. Singapore, 1964.

Sundram, P. Shanmuga. "The Economic Development of Johore (1862–1895)". B.A. Thesis, University of Malaya, Singapore, 1958.

Swettenham, Frank A. *British Malaya: An Account of the Origin and Progress of British Influence in Malaya*. London, 1920.

Tan, Rosie Kim Neo. "The Straits Chinese in Singapore; A Study of the Straits Chinese Way of Life". B.A. Thesis. University of Malaya, Singapore, 1958.

Tan Soo Chye. "British Relations with Johore, 1855–1869". Academic Exercise, University of Malaya, Singapore, 1951.

Tan Tek Soon. "Chinese Local Trade". *The Straits Chinese Magazine*, v. 6, no. 23 (September 1902), pp. 89–97.

______. "Local Chinese Social Organizations by a Straits Chinese". *The Straits Chinese Magazine*, v. 3, no. 9 (1893), pp. 43–47.

Tarling, Nicholas. *Anglo-Dutch Rivalry in the Malay World 1780–1824*. Singapore, 1962.

______. "Intervention and Non-intervention in Malaya". *JAS*, v. 21, no. 4 (1962), pp. 523–27.

______. *Piracy and Politics in the Malay World: A Study of British Imperialism in Nineteenth-Century South-East Asia*. Singapore, Donald Moore Gallery, 1963.

———. *British Policy in the Malay Peninsula and Archipelago, 1824–1871*. Kuala Lumpur, 1969. First published as *JMBRAS*, v. 30, pt. 3 (October 1957), pp. 1–228.

T'e Teng-o, comp. *Ch'in Ting Li Pu Tse-li* (特登客页钦定礼部则例). 1844 Edition. Peking.

Thio, Eunice. *British Policy in the Malay Peninsula 1880–1910*, vol. 1: *The Southern Malay States*. Singapore, 1969.

Thomson, J. T. "A Glance at Rhio". *JIA*, v. 1 (1847), pp. 64–74.

———. "Remarks on the Sletar and Sabimba Tribes", *JIA*, v. 1 (1847), pp. 341–52.

———. "Description of the Eastern Coast of Johore and Pahang with Adjacent Islands". *JIA*, v. 5 (1851), pp. 83–92, 135–54.

Tiwary, R. A. "Raffles at Singapore". Academic Exercise, University of Malaya, Singapore, 1958.

Tregonning, K. G., ed. *Papers on Malayan History*. Published by the *Journal of Southeast Asian History*, Singapore, 1962.

———, ed. *Malaysian Historical Sources*. Singapore, 1965.

Trocki, C. A. (1975). "The Johor Archives and the Kangchu System, 1884–1910". *JMBRAS*, 48, pt. 1, pp.1–46.

———. *Opium and Empire: Chinese Society in Colonial Singapore 1800–1910*. Ithaca, New York, Cornell University Press, 1990.

———. *Opium, Empire and the Global Political Economy: A Study of the Asian Opium Trade*. New York and London, Routledge, 1999.

Turnbull, C. M. "The Johore Gambier and Pepper Trade in the Mid-Nineteenth Century". *JSSS*, v. 15, pt. 1 (June 1959), pp. 43–55.

———. "Origins of British Control in the Malay States before Colonial Rule". In *Malayan and Indonesian Studies*, ed. John Bastin and R. Roolvink. Oxford, 1964, pp. 166–83.

———. *The Straits Settlements, 1826–67: Indian Presidency to Crown Colony*. London, 1972.

———. *A History of Singapore 1819–1988*. Kuala Lumpur, Oxford University Press, 1989.

Vos, R. *Gentle Janus, Merchant Prince: The VOC and the Tightrope of Diplomacy in the Malay World, 1740–1800*. Leiden, KITLV Press, 1993.

Wake, C. H. "Nineteenth Century Johore: Ruler and Realm in Transition". Ph.D. Thesis, History, Canberra, Australian National University, 1966.

———. "Raffles and the Rajas: The Founding of Singapore in Malaya and British Colonial History". *JMBRAS*, v. 48, pt. 1 (1975), pp. 47–73.

Wang, T. P. *The Origins of Chinese Kongsi*. Selangor Darul Ehsan, Malaysia, Pelanduk Publications, 1995.

Wheatley, Paul. "Land Use in the Vicinity of Singapore in the Eighteen-Thirties". *MJTG*, v. 2 (1954), pp. 63–66.

———. *The Golden Khersonese: Studies in the Historical Geography of the Malay Peninsula before 1500 A.D.* Kuala Lumpur, 1961.

———. *Impressions of the Malay Peninsula in Ancient Times*. Singapore, 1964.

Wildman, Rounsville. *Tales of the Malayan Coast from Penang to the Philippines.* Boston, 1899.

Wilkinson, R. J., ed. *Papers on Malay Subjects.* Kuala Lumpur, 1971.

Winstedt, R. O. "The Bendaharas and Temenggongs". *JMBRAS,* v. 10, pt. 1 (January 1932), pp. 55–65.

______. "A History of Johore (1673–*c.* 1800 A.D.)". (Introduction in English: text in *jawi.*) *JMBRAS,* v. 10, p. 1 (January 1932), pp. 164–70 and 1–31.

______. "A History of Johor 1365–1895 A.D.". *JMBRAS,* v. 10, pt. 3 (December 1932), pp. 1–167.

______. " 'Abdu'l-Jalil Sultan of Johore (1699–1719). 'Abdu'l-Jamal, Temenggong (*c.* 1750) and Raffles' Founding of Singapore". *JMBRAS,* v. 11, pt. 2 (December 1933), pp. 161–65.

______. "Outline of a Malay History of Riau". *JMBRAS,* v. 11, pt. 2 (December 1933), pp. 157–60.

______. "A Malay History of Riau and Johore (*Tufhat Al-Nafis*) by Raja Haji Ali bin Raja Haji Ahmad". *JMBRAS,* v. 10, pt. 2 (August 1932), pp. 1–320.

______. "A History of Malaya". *JMBRAS,* v. 13, pt. 1 (March 1935), pp. 1–270.

______. *A History of Malaya.* Revised edition. Singapore, 1962.

______. "Romance of Modern Johore". *Asiatic Review,* N.S. 33 (1937), pp. 539–44.

______. *A History of Classical Malay Literature.* Oxford, 1969. First published as *JMBRAS,* v. 17, pt. 3 (January 1940), pp. 1–259.

______. "The Temenggongs of Muar", *JMBRAS,* v. 10, pt. 1 (1932), pp. 30–31.

______. *The Malays: A Cultural History.* Sixth Edition. London, 1961.

Wolters, O. W. *The Fall of Srivijaya in Malay History.* London, 1970.

Wong Lin Ken. "The Revenue Farms of Prince of Wales Island 1805–1830". Academic Exercise, University of Malaya, Singapore, 1954.

______. "The Trade of Singapore, 1819–1869". *JMBRAS,* v. 33, pt. 4 (December 1960), pp. 1–315.

______. *The Malayan Tin Industry to 1914.* Tucson, 1965.

Wu, X. A. *Chinese Business in the Making of a Malay State, 1882–1941: Kedah and Penang.* London & New York, RoutledgeCurzon, 2003.

Wurtzburg, C. E. "Early Reference to the Suitability of Singapore". *JMBRAS,* v. 3, pt. 3 (December 1925), p. 105.

Wynne, Mervyn Llewelyn. *Trial and Tabut: A Survey of the Origin and Diffusion of Chinese and Mohamedan Secret Societies in the Malay Peninsula A.D. 1800–1935.* Singapore, 1941.

Documentary Sources

Straits Government Records (volumes quoted)

Straits Factory Records (University of Singapore, Library)

Vols. 181, 182, 182a.

Straits Settlements Records (National Library, Singapore)

Vols. N 5, O 1, R 3, R 4, S 4, V 41, V 42, W 56.

Colonial Office Records
CO 273/16
Johore Government Records (volumes quoted). Unless otherwise stated all volumes are in *jawi.*
Kumpulan Surat[2] di-Simpan Oleh Setia Usaha Keraja'an Johor, 1843–1927.
Buku Daftar Surat[2] Keterangan Berkebun, 1844–1903.
Buku Daftar Surat[2] Keterangan Membuka Kebun Gambir dan Lada Hitam Johor, 1880–1907.
Letterbook of His Highness the Maharaja of Johor, 1885–1868 (English).
Correspondence between His Honour the Governor of the Straits Settlements and His Highness the Raja of Johor on the Subject of the Jurisdiction of the Port of Tanjong Putri in the Old Strait of Singapore, Singapore, Mission Press, 1865. (English)
Buku Daftar Surat[2] Jual dan Beli, Pajak dan Gedai dan Hutang, 1868–1884.
Buku Daftar Surat[2] Jual dan Beli, Pajak dan Gadai dan Hatang, 1888–1895.
Undang[2] Gambir-Lada, Johor Government Publication, Johor Baharu, 2 February 1872.
Kanon Ya-itu Undang Yang di-Pakai Bagai Segala Kangchu[2] di dalam Da'erah Johor, 1873.
Undang[2] Kangchu, 1873. (*rumi* typescript)
Letterbook of His Highness the Sultan of Johor, 1885–1888 (English).
Salinan Surat[2] Titah Perentah, 1888–1910 (*rumi* transcription).
Salinan Surat[2] Titah Perentah, 1911–1920.
Buku Peringatan Dato Mentri Johor, 1888–1894.

Index